THE TECHNIQUES OF
INNER LEADERSHIP

THE TECHNIQUES OF INNER LEADERSHIP

Making Inner Leadership Work

Gilbert W. Fairholm

Foreword by Natalie K. Houghtby-Haddon

Westport, Connecticut
London

Library of Congress Cataloging-in-Publication Data

Fairholm, Gilbert W.
  The techniques of inner leadership : making inner leadership work / Gilbert W. Fairholm ;
  foreword by Natalie K. Houghtby-Haddon.
      p.   cm.
  Includes bibliographical references and index.
  ISBN 0–275–98034–0 (alk. paper)
      1. Leadership.   2. Leadership—Moral and ethical aspects.   3. Corporate culture.   I. Title.
  HD57.7.F3525   2003
  658.4′092—dc21   2003048830

British Library Cataloguing in Publication Data is available.

Library of Congress Catalog Card Number: 2003048830
ISBN: 0–275–98034–0

First published in 2003

Praeger Publishers, 88 Post Road West, Westport, CT 06881
An imprint of Greenwood Publishing Group, Inc.
www.praeger.com

Printed in the United States of America

The paper used in this book complies with the
Permanent Paper Standard issued by the National
Information Standards Organization (Z39.48–1984).

10   9   8   7   6   5   4   3   2   1

Contents

Foreword

Natalie K. Houghtby-Haddon

The longing for leadership is a longing as old as human community. From Mesopotamia to Egypt, to the peoples along the Silk Road to China, to the city-states of Greece and the vast expanse of the Roman Empire, to the empires of the Americas, much of the history of humanity is the history of leadership. In our time, leadership has become the subject of much debate: What is good leadership? Is a leader born or made? Is one a leader by virtue of one's position, or can one exercise leadership regardless of where one fits in an organizational hierarchy?

Gil Fairholm has taken on the challenge of proposing leadership that makes sense for the twenty-first century. Rejecting the past century's equating of leadership with management, Dr. Fairholm suggests that leadership is a practice in its own right, with its own set of skills, techniques, and theoretical foundations. Much of his previous work has been dedicated to exploring these theoretical foundations, including the identification of distinct leadership perspectives that shape how persons approach the responsibilities of being a leader. Among his important contributions to the field of leadership studies is his exploration of leadership in the inner reaches or organizations, *Mastering Inner Leadership*. The present work builds on that exploration by identifying practical, hands-on techniques for leading from the middle of an organization—techniques that are extremely useful for the majority of us who spend our lives as "inner leaders"—whether or not we have claimed the name of "leader" for ourselves.

Dr. Fairholm grounds his understanding of leadership in the notion that one's values are embodied in the way one leads. His vision of inner leadership—that it releases the potential of those who follow (and who lead) to do and to be more than they had thought they could—is empowering leadership that respects and inspires, trusts and engenders trust in those who are led, and acknowledges that the relationship between leader and led is a voluntary relationship that works best when it is seen as a partnership to which all parties bring their best.

In our work with hundreds of mid-level and senior managers in local, regional, and federal governments, The George Washington University Center for Excellence in Municipal Management has found that Dr. Fairholm's work provides a solid theoretical foundation for building the capacity of these public administrators to meet the challenges of today's complex, ever-changing organizational environments. We have found that his work speaks to those who are in the middle of organizations, giving them a framework for understanding what they have been doing intuitively all along. We have also found that his work speaks to those who work with volunteers, for inner leadership is needed in all organizations, whether in the public, private, or nonprofit sector.

We are looking forward to incorporating the techniques he explores in *Making Inner Leadership Work: The Techniques of Inner Leadership* in our executive education programs, to further enrich and strengthen the ability of persons in the middle of organizations to work with—and to lead effectively—those both above and below them. Our practice suggests that the techniques explored by Gil Fairholm are critical to organizations undergoing significant change, while experiencing pressure to "do more with less." They are also critical for those persons who are simply seeking to be the best they can be—because working together effectively is always the way that leads to excellence. I can't wait to try out Dr. Fairholm's techniques myself, so that I can be the best leader I can be!

Natalie K. Houghtby-Haddon is former Executive Director (Acting) of the Center for Excellence in Municipal Management at The George Washington University.

Preface

Leadership—its theory, patterns, and practice—is, perhaps, the paramount idea in corporate—indeed, in all social—life today. While many still cling to traditional models of leadership that equate it with management, headship, or merely preeminence in any field of endeavor, some are focusing on leadership as a separate and unique body of presumptions and conventions. After a hundred years of trying to force leadership activities and relationships into a management model of action have failed, researchers are coming to see leadership as fundamentally different from management. In sum, new leadership theory is just now beginning to catch up with leadership practice.

Of course, leadership—that is, its practice—is not new. Some individuals have always stood out in their group as guides, facilitators, boosters, examples—in short, as leaders. The problem is that, while the practice of leadership is of ancient origin, past theories of leadership have been confused with or actually promulgated as relevant to the practice of management. The result is that we have not developed a "language of leadership" commensurate with its practice. Consequently, many would-be leaders have been seduced into behaving like managers. Others have opted to act like leaders but have been left to fend for themselves as they struggle to make their leader behavior correspond with an inadequate system of so-called leader-cum-manager techniques summed up in ideas like POSDCORB—a mnemonic coined by Luther Guilic and Lynwood Urwick in 1935 to summarize what, for them, were the essential tasks of management: Planning, Organizing, Staffing, Directing, Coordination, Reporting, and Budgeting.

Leaders are not managers, and both researchers and practitioners need to re-order their conceptions of this work and the necessary preparation for success (Antonioni, 2000). The recent explosion of research redefining leadership (or, more accurately, defining it as a discrete professional specialty for the first time) necessitates a revolution in both traditional leadership theory and the methods used in training and developing leaders. These new ideas have made many traditional leadership skills obsolete. Instead new leadership techniques or methods are needed to operationalize new theoretical ideas.

Many of these leadership techniques are not yet included in the familiar literature. Neither have they entered into contemporary leadership development training programs and seminars. The purpose of this book is to summarize the essential nature of leadership and delineate the techniques leaders must master to be successful in the twenty-first century. The book constitutes a primer on leadership techniques specifically geared to the new techniques and the new theory describing and explaining leader actions. No attempt is made to be comprehensive. The intent is to highlight some of those leadership techniques that seem to lend themselves to the application of values leadership skills, knowledge, and abilities to work communities sited in the middle of the corporation.

Instead of being guided by a sterile efficiency measure, leadership is now seen as embracing a wide variety of values particular to a given leader that are sometimes distinct from advertised corporate values. For a growing number of people, leadership is now seen not merely as a task assigned to the person occupying the top box in the organization chart but as a function of multiple members of any work community, each sharing leadership at some times, and followership at others (Carson, 2001). And, critically, the leadership exercised by these non–chief executives is often seen as more important to corporate success than the work done by the CEO (Fairholm, 2001). Thus, leadership has evolved to the point where now it is seen as a shared activity, triggered by common values, and practiced mostly—most importantly to corporate success—by persons with personal values they want to realize within the vast middle regions of the corporation, not just—or even—at the top.

The focus here is not on leaders generally but specifically on inner leaders, not because they are better than other human beings—they are not—but because the human condition depends so profoundly on how well these leaders perform their roles and responsibilities. Obviously, it is important for the reader to understand leadership, both its theory and its practice, for indeed leadership is a routine part of life. All interpersonal interactions are characterized in part by leadership of one person in relationship with others in the group—whether that group is a corporation or merely a subunit of it.

The key characteristics of leaders are in the values they promulgate to their group and in their actions to get others to do, think, value, or be something that they may not have wanted to do or think or become before the leader's intervention. The leader's goal is to induce followers—transform them—to come to accept the leader's values—his or her standards of what are acceptable goals, behavior, and overall conduct—as their own. It is an intimate, personal life-transforming task.

LEADERSHIP TECHNIQUES

While it may have been true in the past that managers were the key actors in social groups—a perception I personally would challenge—it is certainly no longer the case. While managers and management processes have been hugely instrumental in building our social, economic, political, and security institutions, the nature of the world has changed so that these skills and these functional tasks are no longer as critical, indeed, may no longer suffice to protect and prosper society.

Management deals with the tangible things of the world, with manpower, structure, and organization; with raw materials, equipment, and tools; and with formal systems and standard practices. Success in today's world demands people who can cope with intangibles—with attitudes, values, creativity, commitment, innovation, loyalty, and happiness in a world defined now as global, diverse, and (while large in physical size) small and intimate in associations—a world where information about whatever one feels important is available to anyone, not just those formally "in charge." In a word, the world needs now (as I believe it has always needed) leaders who can work effectively in an ambiguous, complex, ever-changing environment and with people who are often more informed, educated, and wanting than ever before. The age of an almost reverent awe of management is ending. The world is coming to recognize the unique qualifications and qualities of leadership and is heralding its value in our global, complex, rapidly evolving world.

The task of leadership generally and of inner leaders specifically resolves itself into a set of discrete techniques—a unique set of attitudes, actions, and intentions—that distinguish leaders from managers, technicians, functional specialists, or other corporate workers. Of course some of the tasks and techniques leaders use are shared with other professionals. Leaders communicate with others, issue orders, establish routinized systems of interaction and behavior, and otherwise interact in the real world of social intercourse. Much is written about each of these common tasks of human dynamics so they are not included here.

The special focus here is on those unique techniques of social interaction that characterize leadership action in the middle of the corporation. While great effort has been made to identify critical leadership techniques, no representation is made that all leadership techniques are discussed herein. Those techniques shown here and elaborated in ensuing chapters represent a substantial enough body of inner leadership practice to set it apart from all other group roles and functions.

The word *technique* is defined here to refer to the complex of theory elements, attitudes, skills, knowledge and abilities, leader attributes, and work processes and systems encompassing the work of practitioners of any discrete discipline—in this instance leadership action and behavior. The notion of technique also includes ideas of common patterns of action (Slywotzky and Morrison, 2000), procedures and processes, and systems of action and interaction that define and characterize the regimen of any systematic discipline. Thus, *leadership techniques* refers to the special activities, customary behaviors, man–machine interactions, and thought processes characteristically performed by leaders that set these tasks apart from management or any other organizational activity. The leadership techniques discussed in this book are divided into five categories and include twenty-one leadership techniques:

The Techniques of Inner Leader Preparation

Technique 1: Authentically Respecting Stakeholders

Technique 2: Maintaining a Relationship Focus

Technique 3: Learning to Help Followers

Technique 4: Fostering Follower Change and Transformation

Technique 5: Learning Followership

Technique 6: Taking a Horizon Perspective

The Techniques of Values Leadership

Technique 7: Orchestrating Meaning in the Work Community

Technique 8: Emphasizing Values

Technique 9: Leaders Create a Higher Moral Standard

Technique 10: Servant Leadership

Technique 11: Celebrating Success

The Techniques of Inspiring Inner Leadership

Technique 12: Being Inspiring

Technique 13: Persuading Others

Technique 14: Using Humor

The Techniques of Inner Leadership Power Use

Technique 15: Using Power

Technique 16: Empowerment

Technique 17: Teaching and Coaching Stakeholders

Technique 18: Follower Self-Governance

The Techniques of Trust Leadership

Technique 19: Learning to Trust Others

Technique 20: Creating Community

Technique 21: Developing Stewardship Structures

LEADERSHIP DEVELOPMENT AND TRAINING

Mastering inner leadership skills, knowledge, techniques, methods, and abilities asks leaders to intervene in the life and actions of all stakeholders with whom they work. Practicing this kind of leadership involves both leader and led in experiences that change their attitudes and behavior and the values that support such change. Leadership of others is, essentially, a teaching activity resembling coaching as much as anything else (Lombardi, 2000). In their coaching role, leaders go beyond normal pedagogy, or the mere imparting knowledge, and a context (Klenke, 1996) within which that knowledge can be integrated into the learner's cumulative wisdom. Leaders in the middle of the corporation impart knowledge and context, of course, but they also do more. They engage participants in activities that let them work with, manipulate, and experience that knowledge in actual—insofar as is possible—or simulated situations and with problems and issues reminiscent of real life.

Inner leaders not only inform but also excite workers. They deal with their followers individually according to the followers' specific needs and capacities. These leaders coach them as they grow, develop, and change. They encourage and create situations within which individual followers can practice taking independent action in successfully accomplishing group goals. Obviously, then, leadership (and by extension, leader training and development) is best understood in its practice in situational contexts that are as real as possible. The activities and other learning tools included at the end of each chapter have been selected to describe and to simulate the attitudes and actual situations in which leaders function. Dealing successfully with the values, ideas, problems, and situations embedded in these activities asks the reader to exercise skills and to use values and knowledge that real-world leaders typically use to resolve them.

Implicit in each activity—and explicit in some—are values commonly held by practicing leaders and their core of followers. Thus, the information and activities presented are designed to illustrate both the real world of leadership, the values and attitudes leaders adopt, and the problems and issues they encounter on the job (Badaracco and Ellsworth, 1989). The specific leadership techniques presented in subsequent chapters define and elaborate both the mindset and the expertise leaders employ in successfully leading their followers.

THE CONTENT AND CONTEXT OF THIS BOOK

Most of this book identifies, discusses, and explains a variety of leadership techniques that are unique to leadership—especially inner leadership. The first three chapters set the stage for the discussion of the leadership techniques as they isolate key elements of leadership theory as it has evolved in a century of modern leadership thought. The argument made is that inner leadership is an applied complex of specialized knowledge, theory, skills, attitudes, and attributes that some members of any work community possess and use to get their desires made real for them and in the lives and behavior of other community members. They do this to satisfy their own motives and the values that support and activate their deeply held values, desires, and needs.

Acknowledgments

I am indebted to a great many leaders for both ideas and inspiration. I owe each one thanks. Their example is so deeply immanent in my life—in my thinking and experience with leadership—that it is reflected in whatever the reader may find significant here. I am indebted to them for their wisdom and recognize their leadership in my life, even though I cannot identify all of them individually.

Not the least of these leaders that merit recognition and a part in anything others find commendable in this book are the members of my family: For me, the best examples of leadership in the middle is in the lives of Barbara, Ann, Paul, Corey, Dan, Laurie, Scott, Marcy, Matthew, and Shannon and in the promise of Jason, Craig, Michael, Kaitlyn, Sarah, Chad, Emily, Abegail, Rachael, Thomas, Jacob, Connor, Carl, Jillian, Benjamin, Blake, and Don. They are and have always been models of the best of leadership and of all else good.

Thank you all.

PART I

INTRODUCTION: THE
THEORY OF LEADERSHIP

Leaders do not arise from a grant by others of the powers of command claimed and exercised by them. Rather, leaders are selected by followers who willingly accept their lead. Leaders attract followers by stimulating their emotions (Plas, 1996) and offering suggestions to their instincts. This definition runs counter to the authority basis some claim for it. Authority is a management idea and focuses the analyst on concepts of system, structure, and procedure. Instead, leaders use follower values, aspirations, emotions, and intrinsic needs to insure commitment to group purposes and to inspire behavior to make those purposes real. Thought of in these terms, leadership is distinct from traditional management theory. It bases its utility on different theory, different action techniques, and different outcomes.

Of course, management skills can enhance leadership. Both are necessary to success. Effective executives have to be both leaders and managers. The capacity to lead is within each person and needs only to be tapped. Leadership is a set of special techniques that executives at any level in the organization—especially the middle regions—can use to add a substantively new element to their behavior. Leadership adds new values also, like integrity, accountability, and vision. Discussion and analysis of the elements of inner leadership, the values component of the leader's tasks, and the unique techniques leaders use is a necessary first step in bringing leadership alive. This introductory section includes material helpful to emergent and practicing leaders about the special skills, knowledge, and techniques they need as they prepare to lead.

The three chapters in Part I provide a definitional basis for leadership generally and values leadership in particular. An evolving and key part of values leadership is the notion that workers come to work armed with their full range of talents, skills, knowledge, and desires—including a desire for personal spiritual growth and maturation. They expect that their work—the place where they spend most of their productive time—will satisfy their spiritual values, as well as their economic and social needs. Part I also identifies the special nature and character of inner leadership, the kind of leadership practiced in the middle ranges of the corporation. This definitional discussion serves as a foundation for the detailed treatment of specific leadership techniques that follow in the succeeding parts of this book.

CHAPTER 1

An Overview

Leadership is, perhaps, the distinguishing social idea of our time. It is seen in individual actions taken by a many people in every organization and group within which people daily interact. It is only when we try to pin the idea of leadership down in a specific, concrete definition that it becomes confusing and illusive. This is not to say that leadership is a figment of organizational imaginings, that there is no such thing as leadership. On the contrary, we see leadership practiced every day as literally millions of group members act in leaderlike ways. Of course, they may also act in other ways during that same day—as technicians, managers, experts, clerks, or laborers. Understanding of leadership need only be placed in the context of careful observation and experience to be understood.

The widespread interest in leadership today is merely the latest iteration of a sustained interest in leadership theory and practice throughout recorded history. Unfortunately, this interest had failed in capturing its essential essence. There remain about as many definitions of this dynamic as there are people who write and talk about and teach leadership. The full nature of leadership continues to elude us. For example, some people see leadership as any head person, as the nominal chief executive, whatever the title given. Others see it as a function of charisma or personality, an attribute of the personality of a few extraordinary people. Still others define it in terms of skills, knowledge, or abilities by some people and not others, and so on. In sum, after a hundred years of discussion, leadership remains an idea in flux.

DEFINING LEADERSHIP

While intellectually it may be hard to define, operationally leadership is part of all organizations, at least occasionally, often continuously. The careful observer of leadership must conclude that the leader's role is different from that of other group members. Leaders are set apart from their fellows by their personal appeal or the allure of their programs, ideas, and ideals. A few character traits frequently cited in the literature include integrity, concern for results, and desire for responsibility. Less frequently cited are desire for conformity, formal business training, likability, and appearance. As we begin a new century, coalescence around a few, more comprehensive dimensions of leadership is also forming. The following discussion delimits much of the essence of leadership as it has evolved over the past hundred years. Thus, leadership includes a few contextual factors, some common values, some specific tasks, and a few personal characteristics.

Leaders are sensitive to their own intimate personal needs, as well as those of their followers. Their task is to honor the innate uniqueness of each stakeholder and at the same time develop skill in integrating all followers into work communitys to make a difference. Theirs is a task of helping individual stakeholders develop their full selves, of energizing their innermost—spiritual—cores along with their current job skills. They understand that to ignore the whole person—the spiritual dimension—of each follower is to waste valuable talent and to deny workers of some valuable job benefits and the corporation of valuable contributions. Leadership, of necessity, deals with the core, spiritual values that define the whole person (Pinchot and Pinchot, 1994).

Competent leaders have learned to deal comfortably with ambiguity in both people and program. They are integrated themselves and in their approach to leading others. Their task is to attain stated goals while finding ways to let followers develop their full talents, drives, and desires. Today's world is one of interdependence, not dependence; of uncertainty, not order; of negotiation, not edicts; of persuasion, not command (Gareau, 1999). The need is for leaders who will use their power to empower others and help them become leaders and practice spiritual leadership themselves (Fairholm, 2000a).

Leaders are self-confident risk takers willing to make hard, risky decisions of the kind not routinely required of most managers. These leaders operate on the margin as they move the organization forward, into the unknown. The payoff is commitment to the common cause, increased energy applied to the task at hand, and satisfaction in knowing that followers accept the leader's goals and expend effort in their attainment.

Finally, leaders understand and respond to their followers. Today's workers are demanding more personal attention and concern for their special needs and capacities. Today's workers are blurring the connection between work and nonwork activities. Increasingly their private activities are impinging on their professional work lives and vice versa. Today's worker is generally better educated, and educated workers want to use their knowledge in ways that benefit them and their community(s) of interest. Leaders accept their role as encompassing all stakeholders and the need to share their leadership with them.

The Social Context of Leadership

Three factors define the social context (Klenke, 1996) of leadership: the work community led, the followers, and the situation. Each factor is critical because leadership happens in a matrix of interaction and interdependency between a leader and a follower reiterated for each work community member. Leaders assemble around them people who see the potential for satisfying their personal needs in following the leader and adhering to his or her values, programs, methods, and goals. Indeed, leadership is inseparable from followers' needs and goals. Given this situation, the leader's success—even leadership per se—is best gauged by the willingness of followers to follow.

The leader's task is to create cooperative, action-oriented work communities that provide the environment—culture—within which both leader and led can operate out of a sense of spiritual wholeness and personal authenticity. The task is one of correlation of a variety of experts, each knowing more about his or her specialty than does the leader, and wanting about what the leader wants. In this cultural context, leaders construct work community visions that will tie leader, coworkers, customers, and their larger communities of interest together into an integrated whole while retaining the integrity of each individual, including themselves.

The Attitudes That Define Leadership

Leadership can be circumscribed by a few attitudes, and behaviors that support them, permeate all that the leader does (Crosby, 1996). Leaders use their personal professional values to focus the group and get their support. They love—care for—their followers, respect their individuality, and are interested in and concerned for them (Bilchik, 2001). They also trust their followers (Bedell, 2001) by behaving predictably (Bennis and Nanus, 1985). Greenleaf (1977) adds an attitude of service to this definition. He says followers will follow only leaders who are proven servants. McClelland (1976) relates leadership to confidence. He says people must have confidence in their leader before they will follow.

The Tasks That Define Leadership

Leadership is also defined by certain behaviors or tasks that focus leader behavior and describe its distinctiveness. Obviously, leaders execute some tasks common also to managers. They also perform some fundamentally different tasks. Leaders hold some values managers—or other organizational actors—

do not; they behave in unique ways and seek some similar, but other quite dissimilar, goals that differentiate the leaders from other work-community members. For example, leaders are influential in the work community and with its members in ways that use positional authority power but go beyond this typically managerial tool. They use personal types of power that lets them influence others and secure their willing compliance when they do not have command (managerial) authority over their followers.

Leaders are horizon thinkers ("Forecasting techniques for managers," 2001). They create a future for the work community in the form of a vision that articulates a compelling description about what life, the work community, and the individuals involved can or should be like. Leaders communicate that vision and focus member attention and energies on attaining this "good" future state of being. They spend less time on day-to-day problem solving and more on simulation of a future no one has experienced yet. They are symbol users who communicate their meaning to all stakeholders and engage their minds in ways that imply equality, caring, and respect for the ideas and logic of the other persons (Bennis and Nanus, 1986).

The essence of leadership—and all of this discussion—casts the leader in the role of change agent, but a different kind of change agent (Gareau, 1999), the object of which is to transform both the client and the client system. Leaders inspire and preside over a broad-scoped change process that impacts each leader personally and each individual stakeholder. Many of the results sought take many years to attain.

Nonroutine approaches to routine problems are becoming the norm. The impact of the move to creative, encompassing leadership will place new pressures on the leaders to both be creative and teach stakeholders to follow suit. Successful leaders influence change in the values, attitudes, abilities, and behaviors of followers (Bass, 1987). In this sense, it is transformational of the people and their organization (Caill, 2000).

Given these observations, it follows that our past models of leadership are faulty. They focus on skills, structure, and system. These concepts are firmly within the scope of management, not leadership. Leadership is more than technical skill in analysis, control, and structure formation (Covey, 1991). It doesn't deal primarily with programs or structure. Rather, it deals with people, their development, growth, and a commitment to work community values and results. To the degree the past theories focus on management ideas, they divert our thinking from real leadership issues.

Leadership in the twentieth century was essentially an iteration of Scientific Management, a "hard sciences" technique of management masquerading as leadership. The effect has been to try to make leadership, like management, a science, controlled, precise, predictable. The fact is leadership is not management. Management systems cannot be substituted for leadership. Leadership is fundamentally simple, not scientific. It is a series of dynamic relationships between people at their core—spirit—level.

The times call for results-oriented, spirit-focused leaders with an uncompromising commitment to their stakeholders, for leaders who urge others to share their vision for the work community and get involved. This kind of leader is out front with a vision of what the organization is and can become. It asks the leader to move the organization's people from *believing* to *doing* to *being* to *becoming*. This task is vastly different from directing, planning, and controlling. It is enlarging work community member's perceptions of themselves and their role. It is getting them to explore the possibilities in themselves and in the situation. It is drawing out the individual, raising his or her capacity and ability to perform.

Differentiating Leadership from Management

The idea of leadership is often confused with that of management. Yet understanding of neither the theory of this discipline nor its practice can be successful until the special elements of the leader's task are clearly articulated and integrated into the mind-set of stakeholders—whether leaders or followers. Both traditional and contemporaneous definitions of leadership deal at least in part with common traits. Leaders are those persons who demonstrate traits of character in common with all other leaders (Deal and Kennedy, 1988). That is, unless a person is defined in terms of the following definitional characteristics, one can assume that that person is not a leader or only partially meets the necessary definitional criteria. Experience with work groups suggests that at least the following definitional characteristics describe leadership:

- Leaders are different from others—they may be described as charismatic, magnetic, powerful people, set apart from the average (Cashman and Burzynski, 2000).
- They are self-confident (Bass, 1981).
- They are enthusiastic (Braham, 1999).
- They are risk takers (Cashman and Burzynski, 2000).
- They have a future focus (Bjerke, 1999).
- They are characterized by a participative style (Bennis, 1999).
- They have an integrating perspective (Tesolin, 2000).
- They are committed to help others become leaders and then practice leadership themselves (Plas, 1996).
- They have a sensitivity about leader–follower relationships (Santovec, 2001).
- They demonstrate a respect for the changing situation (Gareau, 1999).

Leadership defined as it is above is not management. Management deals with such issues as performance, productivity, system, control, and measurement (Antonioni, 2000). The burden of management is to make every system, activity, program, and policy countable, measurable, predictable, and therefore controllable. Leadership, on the other hand, partakes of a different value-set. Leaders think differently; value people, programs, and policy differently; relate to others differently. They have different expectations for followers and seek different results from the work community or individual members.

Loosely, one can consider leadership to be the art of influencing people to accomplish the leader's aims. On the other hand, management is the ancillary and subordinate science of specifying and implementing means to accomplish the ends others—leaders—set. Managers maintain the balance of operations, leaders create new approaches and imagine new areas to explore (Zaleznick, 1977). Managers are transactional; leaders are transforming (Burns, 1978). The leader integrates the goal of the individual with the goal of the organization (Plas, 1996; Hersey and Blanchard, 1978). Leaders define the goals of the organization and then design an enterprise distinctively adapted to these ends (Selznick, 1957).

Given these essential differences between leadership and management, past theories that combine the two systems of behavior and ideology must necessarily be faulty. They ignore essential features of each or else overemphasize features of one to the detriment of the other. What is needed is a new conception, a new theory, that focuses fully on leadership as a discrete set of values, attitudes, and techniques, a discrete systems of behaviors, skills, and methods. Such a theory is found in the new leadership model described in the following chapters.

The special characteristics of leadership versus management is summarized in the following kinds of statements taken from the conventional wisdom of the past few years. These statements are illustrative only. No claim is made to delimit the range and scope of this difference so fully documented in the literature. This list serves only to point to the essential differences in these two concepts.

- Leadership is doing right things, not just doing things right (Bennis and Nanus, 1985).
- Leadership involves horizon thinking, thinking in the longer term, and thinking in more global terms ("Forecasting techniques for managers," 2001).
- Leadership emphasizes the intangibles as well as the specifics working with others (Kalafut, 2001).
- Leaders are cheerleaders, not cops, enthusiasts, not referees, coaches, not detractors (Lombardi, 2000).
- Leaders look beyond the unit to all stakeholders impacted by the organization (Plas, 1996).
- Leaders reach and influence constituents beyond their immediate jurisdiction (Badaracco and Ellsworth, 1989).
- Leaders put heavy emphasis on the intangibles of vision, values, and motivation (inspiration) (Spreitzer, De Janasz, and Quinn, 1999).
- Leaders understand the nonrational element in leader–constituent interaction (Spreitzer, De Janasz, and Quinn, 1999).
- Leaders have political skill to cope with conflicting requirements and multiple constituencies (Fairholm, 1993).
- Leaders think in terms of renewal (Caill, 2000).

Leadership Mind-Sets

Leadership is a multidifferentiated idea. Understanding it is, like all important aspects of life, a thing of the mind. An individual's idea of leadership is not so much the objective reality of leadership as it is his or her perception of it. Defining any dynamic concept like leadership is therefore difficult. In spite of this difficulty, for current purposes we can describe leadership in terms of several paradigms, or mind-sets currently in vogue in the discipline. The specific mind-set individuals adopt to understand leadership is personal; it is selected as they experience, read, and think about leadership.

Everyone has a mind-set that tells him or her what his or her truth is. These mental (not necessarily objectively real) perceptions are often so strong that no other perspective seems reasonable or even true—even when that mind-set is contradicted by observable reality. Each person thinks leadership is what his or her current mind-set tells him or her it is. Viewpoints other than the individual's current reality are seen as wrong, incorrect (it may be that alternative conceptions are simply inconceivable).

Five mental models of leadership can be identified in the 100-year history of the intellectual movement to full understanding of leadership. Each is true in the sense that it helps describe some part of the leadership task. But it is only together that they define the full picture. They rank along a continuum from control to spiritual holism and include the following ideas:

- Leadership is the same as management.
- Leadership is synonymous with good management.
- Leadership is a function of the values held by leader and led.
- Leadership is a task of creating a culture high in mutual trust.
- Leadership flows out of the core spiritual values held by both leader and led—it is ultimately these core values that determine individual and group action, success, and satisfaction.

The sense of leadership today revolves around these descriptive ideas. Which, if any, are the real leadership perspective—or if none are, or if only together can we sense the real idea of leadership—remains in the mind of the beholder.

Defining leadership this way fundamentally changes the nature of leadership practice and of leader development and training.

METHODS OF PRACTICING LEADERSHIP

In one sense, leadership can be thought about in terms of several activities or mind-sets centering around three elements of the leader's job: (1) leading others, (2) helping followers grow and develop, and (3) fostering compatible organizational culture creation and maintenance. As leaders of work communities, leaders inspire, and widely broadcast a community vision by focusing on what they, as leaders, think is important and communicate authentic caring for each coworker. In their relationships with followers, leaders concentrate on power tactics like influencing followers to vision-directed action and empowering them to work toward that vision independently (Spreitzer, De Janasz, and Quinn, 1999).

Leadership of Others

Leaders set values, establish norms and standards, and set expectations about follower performance. Each of these activities describe elements of the techniques leaders use in working with others. Each is described briefly here (They are elaborated in later parts of this book). These activities describe the leadership process generally, constitute guidelines for its practice and evaluation, and are content benchmarks for leadership training programs.

Inspiration. Leaders go beyond motivation to inspiration. They tap something deep within the stakeholder team that strikes a responsive chord. Leaders are inspiring because they are inspired (Cashman and Burzynski, 2000).

Visioning. Leadership involves horizon thinking—thinking beyond the problems of the day toward the possibilities of what the organization and its members can become (Yearout, Miles, and Koonce, 2001).

Focusing. Leadership is paying attention to what is important (Antonioni, 2000). It is spending time and resources on one thing (or a few things) as opposed to other things—programs approaches, methods, tasks, and the like—that the leader could focus on.

Caring. Leaders place priority on authentic caring about things—employees, services, clients, all people with whom they work (Bender, 1997).

Sharing Power with Employees. Leaders lead with and by example. They share power, encourage personal initiative, invite ideas and feedback, and motivate via values (Bender, 1997).

Influence. Leadership involves the leader in intense interpersonal relationship with followers, the central nature of which is influencing followers to do what they want done (Gareau, 1999).

Empowerment. Leaders simultaneously follow two purposes: to attain the mutually desirable end-state both leader and follower desire and importantly empower followers to develop into mature personalities capable of being the best they can be (Kulwiec, 2001).

Shaping Organization Culture

Values. Leaders lead through shared values. They articulate values that followers also hold, or they help followers shape their own values in ways that prioritize the leaders' values that followers come to desire (Bjerke, 1999).

Expectations. Leaders set high expectations for performance for the group, expectations that focus and direct vision, values, and standards (Gareau, 1999).

Standard Setting. Leaders set group standards, teach them, live them, and inspire others to live them (Serven, 2002).

Using Symbols. Leaders use symbols—ideas, words, tangible objects representing aspects of its culture to define the work community (Denison, 1990), and give it its character.

DISCUSSION ISSUES AND QUESTIONS

Issues

1. Leadership is, like all important aspects of life, a thing of the mind.
2. The essence of leadership is helping others to develop in their work and their lives.
3. Shared values form the foundation of community, the essential context of leadership.
4. Values determine leader judgments about what is good, right, appropriate.
5. Leaders create values that community members believe foster their development.
6. Leaders personify the values of the group.
7. Leaders convey the shared values and culture of the group.
8. Leaders use values to focus the work community and get member support.
9. Leaders respect, value, and trust their coworkers.
10. Leaders model work-community values and ideals.
11. Leaders communicate to their followers their respect, interest, and concern for them.
12. Leaders are uncompromisingly committed to their stakeholders.
13. Leaders move the organization and its people from *believing* to *doing* to *becoming*.

Questions

1. What are some of the essential components of a definition of leadership?
2. Based on your experience with leaders and managers, what are some of the most clear and persuasive differences between these two functions of work communities.
3. In your personal experience, what are the most effective leader skills (techniques) in getting other people to do what the leader wants them to do? How does you experience compare with the ideas presented in this chapter? Explain. Which are the most effective—yours or the textbook-advocated skills?
4. What is your mind-set about leadership (which of the five presented above do you believe is most true)? From that perspective, evaluate the other

four. What are their strengths and weaknesses? Why did you select your mind-set and not another one?

LEADERSHIP LEARNING ACTIVITIES

Activity 1: Self-Assessment—
Type A Leader Behavior Pattern

Instructions. Leaders are confident, self-assured, and posess what some would call a Type A personality. The following questions might help you if you share these leadership personality characteristics. Indicate whether each of the following items is true (T) or false (F) for you.

_____ 1. I am always in a hurry.

_____ 2. I have list of things I have to achieve on a daily or weekly basis.

_____ 3. I tend to take one problem or task on at a time, finish, then move to the next one.

_____ 4. I tend to take a break or quit when I get tired.

_____ 5. I am always doing several thing at once both at work and in my personal life.

_____ 6. People who know me would describe my temper as hot and fiery.

_____ 7. I enjoy competitive activities.

_____ 8. I tend to be relaxed and easy going.

_____ 9. Many things are more important to me than my job.

_____ 10. I really enjoy winning both at work and at play.

_____ 11. I tend to rush people along or finish their sentences for them when they are taking too long.

_____ 12. I enjoy "doing nothing" and just hanging out.

Scoring key: Type A individuals tend to indicate that questions 1, 2, 5, 6, 7, 10, and 11 are true and that questions 3, 4, 8, 9, and 12 are false. Type B individuals tend to answer in the reverse (1, 2, 5, 6, 7, 10, and 11 as false and 3, 4, 8, 9, and 12 as true).

Activity 2: What Is Your Strategic Leadership Type?

Instructions. For each of the following items, rate yourself using the following scale (you can also use the items to rate a leader in your organization):

My Ranking _____ Ranking for my organization _____

1	2	3	4
Always	Never	Occasionally	Often

_____ 1. I enjoy working on routine tasks.

_____ 2. I am looking for new ways of doing things.

_____ 3. I have trouble delegating tasks to my subordinates.

_____ 4. I like my subordinates to share the same values and beliefs.

_____ 5. Change makes me uncomfortable.

_____ 6. I encourage my subordinates to participate in decision making.

_____ 7. It is hard for me to get things done when there are many contrasting opinions.

_____ 8. I enjoy working on new tasks.

_____ 9. I feel comfortable giving power away to my subordinates.

_____ 10. I consider myself to be a risk taker.

Scoring key: Reverse scores for items 1, 5, 6, 7, and 9 (0 = 3, 1 = 2, 2 = 1, 3 = 0).

Challenge-Seeking Score: Add items 1, 2, 5, 8, and 10. Your score will be between 0 and 15. Total: _____

Need for Control Score: Add items 3, 4, 6, and 9. Your score will be between 0 and 15. Total: _____

The larger the number the stronger the tendency is toward that leader characteristic.

Activity 3: Leadership and Gender

Instructions. The leadership literature includes broad discussion about differences between gender roles and leadership This activity is designed to explore the relationship between gender roles and leadership.

1. Develop a list of *your* leadership characteristics. You may use specific personality traits or a behavioral description. Set that list aside.

2. Select another leader of the opposite gender. Develop a list of the personality traits or behaviors of that other leader.

3. Compare and contrast the two lists. Determine what, if any differences are apparent. Discuss these differences and the reasons why men and women differ in their approach to leadership.

4. Write a brief report highlighting your findings and their implications for your future leadership actions.

CHAPTER 2

Values Leadership

Work has become the core activity of life and the corporation the most significant community. As a result, workplace values now frame people's actions and their motivations more than any other social institution. Work values often are more dominant in the life of most Americans than values shaped by politics, family, or even religion. Whether they recognize it or not, work has become a prime source of most people's values-sets and the locale of their most worthwhile social contributions. Work is fast becoming the place where most people find their sense of full meaning as human beings. While they are critical to economic well-being, a growing litany of concerns suggest that work experiences are not meeting their full obligations to feed workers spirits as they feed their intellectual, social, and physical needs (Bolman and Deal, 1995).

In the 100-year history of modern leadership theory, two ideas have dominated theory-building. The first is a focus on task, the second a focus on people. The task focus was first illustrated in the Scientific Management movement of the early twentieth century. It has seen several iterations over the past century. The people focus is captured in the several versions of the human relations model begun in the 1920s and 1930s and continuing today. Until recently, leadership model-building has ignored important evidence that values are and have always been part of the job of leadership and that values permeate, if only implicitly, the discussions of both task and people orientations.

DEFINING VALUES-BASED LEADERSHIP

There is a shift in theorizing about leadership today as theorist and practitioner alike begin to see that their personal inner life of personal values is the single most powerful force guiding their work action (Fairholm, 2001). The professional literature is just beginning to reflect that personal values about what is right or wrong, helpful or hurtful, useful or not are more important then organizational form, function, system, or procedure in determining the behavior of both leader and led. This inner-looking has confirmed that it is one's intimate, inner values that trigger action more consistently and more powerfully than one's context.

Today, values dominate both leadership discussion and theory-building and inform the techniques leaders practice in their groups and with individual followers. Nevertheless, most textbooks still reflect a century-old leadership mindset that places management—that is, science, order, predictability, and control—at the core of many definitions of leadership. So powerful is this mind-set that many still think that leadership and management are the same thing or, at minimum, inextricably interrelated. Based on this definition, many people assume a leader is any head person—president, CEO, director, or other.

The fact is that headship per se does not make anyone a leader. Given the complex, global, diverse, and information-rich nature of modern society, management control will no longer work, if it ever did, in getting people to commit to the organization's work. And, even if one clings to outmoded theory, the modern workplace has drastically changed. No longer is work characterized by routine, repeated production of large quantities of the same thing. Increasingly, it is characterized by an exploding information base, global markets, fast-changing, short-shelf-lived products, a labor pool made up mostly of knowledge workers, and an increasingly diverse workforce that mirrors its client population in being educated and in demanding that its special needs be met.

Modern writers are beginning to define leadership in terms that deal directly with the task of gaining other's acceptance of and commitment to a common corporate vision. They now see that corporate vision is not a mere summary of its main tasks but an integrated synopsis of its core values. They are beginning to recognize the leader's values as the key to work community accomplishment. The leader's values establish what is good, true, and beautiful for them and for their group's members. Values also measure movement toward realization of what the leader thinks of as "good." This modern leadership model is philosophical, proposing a kind of leadership rooted in the reality of human nature and conduct: that everyone has values and values trigger our behavior.

Having given priority to their work, workers are asking that that work also meet their deepest intimate—spiritual—needs. Explicitly for some and implicitly for most others, they are seeking and finding emotional fulfillment on the job. For after all, life is about spirit, and humans have only one spirit that manifests itself in both life and livelihood. A growing literature is confirming a felt need for work communities, leadership, and work processes that celebrate the whole individual's needs, desires, values, and their spirit self (see, for example, Jacobson, 1995; Fairholm, 2000a). This research suggests that values leaders find the vocabulary and values of spiritual leadership to be significant in their understanding of their role as leaders (or as members of a work community). They see leadership as including a spiritual component (Vaill, 1998). In addition to whatever else can be said about it, values leadership is concerned with bringing out the best in people. And an individual's best is tied intimately to his or her deepest sense of self, to his or her spiritual core (Moxley, 2000). While definitive conclusions cannot be drawn from this early research, it suggests a new and potentially powerful spiritual focus for the practice of values leadership in the new millennium.

Shortcomings of Traditional Leadership Models

This emerging leadership theory describes a special action dynamic that focuses on ideas like innovation, concern for customers, quality, and simple structure (Samuelson, 1984). Values leadership is a new orientation governing the leader's role around principles that include service to others, individual development and growth, and self-determination and that prioritize excellent performance (Deal and Kennedy, 1988) and a stewardship orientation (Block,1993) toward their followers.

The values leadership model sees leadership not so much in structure or system terms but as a way to think about leader–follower relationships. Past models contain parts of the central, guiding principles of values leadership and behaviors but not its essential whole. The new values leader model sees leadership as a new mind-set better described in philosophical terms than as a theory or technique of management. Instead, values leadership techniques operationalize a people-oriented philosophy of growth toward self-leadership within the community (Crosby, 1996).

Past theories confused leadership with management, focused narrowly on the group's task or the personality of the individual leader or isolated factors in the situation. These are management concepts, not factors descriptive of leadership. Older models also focus on leadership as a function of one individual. The reality is that many people in the work community are leaders (in specific circumstances, or for given tasks, activities, or groups). Past leadership theories also defined the leader–follower relationship as a leader task of increasing follower performance and a follower task of protecting job security.

Values Leadership

Given the ubiquity of leadership practice, it is difficult to believe that leadership theory is so amorphous. Fortunately, a century of leadership study is beginning to come together as contemporary writers narrow the focus of definition to the central leadership task of joining group actions together via a common set of values. This model suggests that leadership is a part of the routine actions of many people in the organization, not just the preserve of the few in headship positions. The key discriminator is: If the individual creates a purposeful relationship with others based on shared values and mutual development, that person is a leader (Bjerke, 1999).

Current values leadership models involve the whole person—they activate the motivating values, the intellect, and the emotions (Stogdill, 1957) of both leader and led. They rely on a motivational foundation of individual growth and development of the leader him or herself and the maturation of all stakeholders. That is, values leadership deals with the whole self of the leader and led, with the spiritual as well as the physical, emotional, and economic dimensions of the individual person's life. The values leadership focus is a new approach to thinking and behaving in organizational relationships.

Values leadership describes a way to think about leadership and a values basis for action (Crosby, 1996). The leader's personal, intimate values are and have always been a part of leadership. These underlying values are implicit in planning, structural design, application of technique, and organization and management theories (Badaracco, 1989). Their primary role is in ordering work-community action, defining how people will live and work together, and measuring successful behavior or results. The leader's job is to set shared work values, arbitrate disagreements, and validate changes in the guiding value-set the work community adopts.

The Spiritual Character of Leadership

The values leadership model says that those leaders succeed who model their leadership on a comprehensive picture of humankind that respects all the dimensions of followers' beings. This perspective subordinates the materialistic values to internal spiritual ones. That is, an individual's core—spiritual—values are the essential force in shaping leader behavior (Plas, 1996). Operationally values leaders respond to their spiritual core as they build community, foster a higher moral standard, and function in their community from a stewardship perspective. These three techniques of leadership are elaborated in separate chapters. They are summarized here as a way to help leaders use the strength of followers' spirits to induce them to do the leaders' work.

METHODS OF PRACTICING VALUES LEADERSHIP

Three ideas undergird the practice of values leadership. The first is the power of values in shaping human behavior singly and in groups. The second relates to the need for work communities of mutual interactive trust as the environment within which leadership takes place. And finally, the focus on the spiritual center of the individual—leader and follower—as the locus of individual control and the arena of leadership action (Bolman and Deal, 1995). Each of these three elements of definition are techniques values leadership employs in working with its followers. Together, they describe the essential mechanism through which values leaders lead—and its techniques.

The Power of Personal Values

Values leadership theory revolves around the unique mind-set and the action sequence individuals adopt, guided by their own set of values. Individuals—leaders and followers—create value systems for themselves and promulgate these values in the groups in which they have membership. The individual's belief system—that defines and measures his or her definition of truth and of success—is at its core a system of ranked values that proscribe and delimit his or her perception of the world. That is, persons' sets of values delimit their belief system and define the acceptable way they and, by extension, all other people should behave. Values also define the goals work-community members seek and what they desire to become by virtue of living their values. Values connote desirability—they are statements of the "oughts" in life. They are conclusive beliefs individuals evolve about what is true or beautiful or good about the world.

A person's values are not merely rules of conduct (Braham, 1999). They determine rules and rank rule systems. They are the criteria for selecting actions, goals, and methods. Values are learned. Some values are explicit, others are not. They nonetheless trigger some specific behavior and constrain behavior that contravenes the values. Institutions also have values which often are codified in mission or vision statements. They provide frameworks for transmitting and implementing specific desired work community's and member's behavior toward specific goals and results. They are powerful in shaping a worker's behavior and in validating institutional policy and mission. They determine acceptable action, resolve conflicts, determine sanctions systems employed, and are integral to reward systems. They define the desirable and acceptable for the individual and the organization.

The essence of values theory is that values dictate individual and work-community action (Bjerke, 1999). Whether they emanate from the individual member or from the collective membership (the work community), they dominate organizational action, dictate reward systems, and measure individual and work community success. Because individual and institutional values systems are so powerful in shaping behavior, leaders continually act to shape stakeholder values—via propaganda, training, policy, advertising, conversation, procedures, sanction systems, friendships, and so on. Leaders have always done this. It is only now that we are talking about it as legitimate leader behavior and modeling its practice in theory. Leaders have always inculcated values in the same ways that teachers, parents, and religionists do.

Several writers have tried to identify the central values governing corporate life and dictating member behavior. For Scott and Hart (1979) the dominant modern organization value is that what is good for the organization is "good." Such a value orientation skews leader behavior away from human concerns and toward corporate health. Hodgkinson (1978) identifies four "metavalues"—efficiency, effectiveness, values, and growth. He sees values as operationally akin to objectives, goals, ends, purposes, and policies and express desirable future states that become "facts" in the sense they are generally accepted and acted upon. Bjerke (1999) says shared values control how people behave by expressing what is expected of individuals associated with the organization.

Shared values are strong determinants of work-community action. The leadership challenge is to examine organization values and bring consensus among stakeholders on value as well as productivity issues. For Burns (1978) values are crucial to leadership. In a sense they are motives, or at least they have a strong motivational content (see also Rokeach, 1979). Burns says the leaders' key tasks are as values clarifiers and values communicators throughout the work community. Burns also suggests that values can be a source of vital change in people and organizations. As leaders reach into this level of follower needs and values structures, they can induce them to change. These values express fundamental and enduring needs. Burns goes on to suggest that leadership is bound up in a concern for these higher-order values but, more precisely, with these values in conflict within the group. The central task is to manage values conflict by moving to a shared value system. Leaders appeal to these widely held ends values.

Building a Trust Culture

The kind of leadership that grows out of shared values flourishes only in a work culture within which individuals can accept the individuality of others without sanctioning all their words or deeds. Such a culture is one that prioritizes high interpersonal trust. In a climate of trust, individuals can give open, candid reactions to what they see as right or wrong. A key leader task, therefore, is building a work community characterized by high level of interpersonal trust. In trust communities, there is little manipulation, there are few hidden agendas, and no unreasonable controls, nor is there the cloying sweetness that discounts real problems. Instead, there is a congruency in concepts, conduct, and concern—a unity appropriate to work community membership that does not risk individuality. Without trust, work-community values can become strictures, impeding individual progress.

It does very little good, for instance, to develop elaborate corporate work flow charts if the people who inhabit the real world symbolized by these charts do not trust each other or really communicate with each other. Nor does it do good to strive to achieve goals if leaders allow themselves to be too much at the mercy of their moods so followers see them as ambivalent administrators whom they find unpredictable or capricious about the goals mutually embraced.

Trust becomes both an expectation and a personal obligation to be authentic, trustworthy, reliable, which is provable by ensuing experience. Seen in this light, trust is one of the values supporting a given culture that helps define how and in what degree members value others. Trust places obligation on both the truster and the person in whom we place our trust. It is the foundation of success in any interpersonal relationship. While organizational theory assumes, but largely ignores, the idea of trust, it is nevertheless integral to that set of interpersonal relationships.

Shaping a work community based on trust is a critical leadership task. It creates the context within which leaders can lead, followers can find reason for full commitment, the organization can attain its goals, and all can achieve to their full potential (Klenke, 1996). Unfortunately, there is little research advice available to aspiring leaders to guide them in developing a trust culture. Nevertheless, trust is central to leadership in work communities because followers are people who *choose* to follow leaders. They are not forced to do so. High trust by followers allows leaders to lead (Bedell, 2001) just as low trust cultures force leaders to manage.

Some current literature suggests that a given work community culture implies a level of trust (Fairholm, 1994), that the work community culture defines and delimits the nature and extent of member trust. The cultures we create allow us to behave with varying levels of assurance that certain actions or events will produce known results—that is to trust people, systems, and process. The work communities leaders create must produce a trust situation where members can trust that certain actions will produce certain results. Culture also prescribes our willingness to trust. The work-community culture may allow members to trust some colleagues more or less than others. But without the constraints imposed by cultural features we would not, maybe could not, exercise trust at all.

Trust is transforming. It is a process of change. Having trust in a person or in something we believe to be true impels (empowers) personal change. It lets people act out of that trust. Properly placed trust is empowering, misplaced trust spells defeat. For example, among the potential problems leaders face in creating and maintaining a trust culture are those dealing with the emotions of followers. Feelings of apathy and alienation present in the larger society sometimes bleed over into the organization's culture and cause similar emotions among the workers there. Personal self-interest may hamper development of a fully trusting culture. And, too, the personal and institutional risk of loss, or failure to meet necessary goals may constrain full trust.

Trust is the prime mechanism for work-community cohesion. Indeed, organization per se cannot take place without at least some level of interpersonal trust. And leaders cannot ignore the powerful element of trust as they go about creating and leading their work community's culture that induces stakeholders to behave in needed ways. Of course, the risk is always present in trusting others or in relying on given systems or policies or procedures or specific structural forms that they will not behave as expected (Cashman and Burzynski, 2000). In essence trust is a unifying and coalescing idea. Without it the idea of joint cooperative action would be unthinkable, let alone practical.

Focusing on the Individual's Spiritual Center

Some leaders and some work communities enhance members' lives, while others seem to make them more difficult. Looking for answers as to why this is the case has led leaders to their own inner lives and to the inner lives of their followers—to the values and experiences that define them and from which extend their operating assumptions and principles. It is increasingly clear that all people want to be accepted as whole persons at work, and that corporations continue to concentrate on the small portion of worker talent, knowledge, and experience they pay for. The resulting tension has led to feelings of alienation, anomie, and frustration (Brumback, 1999).

This situation coupled with a general loss of potency of the traditional value-creating and maintaining institutions in the larger communities of interest—family, friends, church, government—has led to the movement to pursue whole-self (spiritual) development on the job (see Greenleaf, 1977; Senge, 1990; Vaill, 1989; DePree, 1989; Covey, 1991; Lee and Zemke, 1993; Fairholm, 2000a). The spiritual heart of values leadership is all about fulfilling the full range of worker needs in the work groups in which most Americans spend most of their waking hours. Today, more and more people expect work to satisfy their core human needs for individual personal wholeness as it also provides them economic necessities. Now, workers expect their work—the place where they spend the largest part of their lives in both time spent and intrinsic significance—to provide spiritual support for their deeply held values and aspirations for personal and economic growth.

Spirit refers to the vital, energizing force or principle in the person, the core of self. In its secular connotation, spirit defines life's meaning and the individual's motivation for action. A recent iteration of values leadership, spiritual—or whole-self—leadership is emerging based on a kind of metaphysical work-connected relationship and founded on a higher moral standard, a stewardship relationship, and a sense of unity through community. The reasons for this are also becoming clear as we define spirit to include the emotional center of the individual.

Recent research (Fairholm, 2000a) identifies seven dimensions of workplace spirituality. Each represents an approach the values leader can take to help followers get in touch with their spiritual centers and use the power resident there to foster work-community goals. The most frequently defined dimensions of spirituality coming from this research include the idea that spirituality is an inner conviction people have of a higher, more intelligent force impacting their lives. More pertinent to this discussion is the idea that spirit is the essence of self that separates humans from other creatures. People rely on their core spirituality for comfort, strength, and happiness. It is the part of individuals that searches for meaning, values, and purpose in life (Leigh, 1997). One's spirituality includes a personal belief system (Braham, 1999). It is an emotional element in one's self-definition—a feeling. And, a final dimension is that spirituality is demonstrated as individuals act out the experience of the transcendent in life.

Spiritual leadership is coming to be seen as a variant of values leadership. It describes the need human beings have to be accepted as whole persons with many needs, capacities, talents, and goals. It deals also with the personal vision for their future, including their work community but encompassing all other communities of interest both leader and led evolve and act to make real. Sharpening traditional leadership skills will not be very useful to the leaders who want to center on the spiritual dimension of leadership. Their tasks are of the mind, of the soul and the spirit. This focus asks leaders to get in touch with themselves in intimate ways to bring themselves into close association with their core selves and the values that define them as unique human beings. This knowledge is an essential first step in honing skill in changing followers by building a community where the intimate spiritual values and needs of members can be addressed, in fostering high moral standards and seeing the work community and its members in stewardship terms.

Building Community

Spiritually centered values leaders build a community of united followers as the locus of their leadership. At least the following ideas help describe a work community and together constitute the gist of the community-building technique.

Valuing

Leadership here becomes a task of values clarification and values displacement of incompatible individual values (Bjerke, 1999). It is a task of prioritization and reprioritization of work-community member values and generally creating and maintaining a common set of values shared by both the leader and all stakeholders that guide work community member action. Often the mechanism for full self-change is shared vision and a culture that trusts members to behave according to these shared values and vitalizing vision (Bjerke, 1999).

Fostering Trust

Increasingly leaders are coming to see their role as a task of creating a trust culture to undergird both personal and institutional growth (Bedell, 2001).

Transforming People

Spirit leaders recognize that all change is people change. It is not laws or rules that change society, it is the cumulative result of individual people who change in conformance to a shared vision and shared values that changes the organization for the better (Plas, 1996). At a personal level, it is sacrificing part of an individual's deepest being so that devoting effort to group-defined tasks is not a loss but a fulfillment of personal goals that enhances the self (Yearout, Miles, and Koonce, 2001).

Meaning-Making

Spirit leadership is creating workplace mechanisms that communicate meaning (Plas, 1996), not merely that inform or order.

Ethics and Morality

Spirit leaders use methods of leading that highlight ethical values and moral standards. These leaders link their interior world of moral reflection and the outer world of work and social relationships.

Servanthood

Spiritually motivated leaders reject self-interest and focus on creating service relationships (Braham, 1999). Rather than attempt to dominate followers, values leaders go to work for them—providing all things necessary for follower success.

Building Trust

Spiritual leaders build trust (Bedell, 2001) or tear trust relationships down by the cumulative actions they take and the words they speak—by the culture they create for themselves and their organization's members (Palmer, 2001).

Being Trustworthy

These leaders are also trustworthy. They know that if they want someone to trust them they have to tell the truth, act on that truth consistently, and then patiently wait for the relationship to mature (Bedell, 2001).

Sensitivity to the Spiritual

Spirit leaders recognize that spirituality is at the heart of much of the values leadership literature popular today (Senge et al., 1994). Values leaders provide environments that both recognize and feed the spirit in us all while we are directing work activity (Tesolin, 2000).

Nourishing the Spirit

Spirit leaders create workplace systems that satisfy members' needs to feed their spirit through work by teaching them how humanity belongs within the greater scheme of things and how harmony can be realized in life and work (Heerman, 1995).

Living a Higher Moral Standard

Not all values are of equal consequence or meaningfulness. Most people hold a variety of values, some they can and do compromise in some situations but others that they will not violate in any circumstance. Some ideas and ideals just cannot be compromised. Rather, they must be defended. Values leaders prefer to compete with others about some values rather than accommodate them. Indeed, they sometimes are outspoken and deliberately confrontational of alternative value systems. Values leaders apply their values, especially their core spiritual ones, in overtly moral ways (Serven, 2002).

The infrastructure of values-based leadership is founded on an idea of morality. The measure of values leadership is not structural, it is ethical (DePree, 1989). The key operational elements of values leadership revolve around moral and ethical issues and condition what leaders do and their approaches and attitudes. The elements of this kind of moral, ethical leadership include the following factors.

Value-Setting

The values systems leaders create provide the basis of the sanctions systems that specify the moral behavior of community members and determine its measures of success. Shared values determine a work community's ethics. They are part of any self-analysis both leader and led engage in as they observe and reflect on their actions and judgments of all aspects of life (Covey, 2001).

Integrity

Values leaders rank the value of integrity highly. Integrity demands self-discipline, a strengthening self in terms of the leader's inner code of right and wrong (Terry, 1995).

Visioning

Values leaders build consensus and lead democratically via a shared vision that creates meaning for others (Kouzes and Posner, 1987). In this way leaders create an ethical underpinning that provides the context for shared values, meaning, and moral focus for community members.

Enabling

Spiritually sensitive leaders provide systems and processes that motivate, involve them in appropriate networks, and then free them from situational constraints that may hamper their growth (transformation) toward full effectiveness (Plas, 1996).

Risk-Taking

Values leaders challenge traditional work processes (Kouzes and Posner, 1987) and try to produce real change that meets their workers enduring needs regardless of the risk.

Stewardship

Values leaders view their role in the organization as that of steward. And the basis of stewardship is self-directed free moral choice. Every steward has the same rights and is subject to identical limitations in the exercise of self-direction. This sharing of power preserves harmony and good will. The leader is a steward also and subject to the same limitations and advantages as other stewards. They ensure that every steward has a single voice in sitting in council with other stewards and a single vote in the power of consent. Stewardships preserve oneness by procedures that enhance common consent. In this way each steward is protected against unjust or dominating leaders.

Stewardship is not a single guiding principle but a part of a triumvirate that includes empowerment and partnership, as well as stewardship. The principle of stewardship brings accountability while partnership balances responsibility. It is a sharing of the power of governance where each member holds control and responsibility in trust for the work community as a unit. It is a relationship system based on mutual accountability. Stewardship operates at the whole-person—spiritual—level of existence and interrelationship. Membership in a stewardship community asks the leader not only to lead the stewardship community but also to play a role as a member of that community (Rapoport et al., 2001).

A stewardship community lets members make choices about whom to partner with, what products or services to buy from internal or external suppliers, how to spend discretionary funds and time, and how to serve their customers.

The idea of adding a stewardship orientation to corporate leadership is new. Many leaders have no operational experience with this concept and therefore cannot immediately either visualize their steward-leader role in the corporation or their part in building stewardship teams. While the idea may be appealing, many don't know how stewardship works in practice.

Stewardship communities eliminate social distinctions. All stewards are equal. All have equal opportunity for managing their stewardship. All have equal access to available rewards for a well-done stewardship. The steward-leader is also a steward and subject to the same limitations and advantages as other stewards. Every steward has a single voice in stewardship councils and a single vote in the power of consent. Status and hierarchical distinctions are absent (Deming, 1986). No one member is more important to the team than any other. Loss of the contribution of any one diminishes the team and jeopardizes its success since the team is not whole without all members.

The steward-leader's role is that of servant rather than master. By assisting stewards to achieve to their potential, steward-leaders multiply the contribution they otherwise could make. Their role as servants encourages responses from those they serve. They foster cooperation not competition (Terry, 1995). The steward-leader is required to obtain the acquiescence of the stewardship community in giving direction to the stewardship itself. By so doing they gain the use of the best experience in the stewardship community and its maximum creative energy and wisdom.

DISCUSSION ISSUES AND QUESTIONS

Issues

1. Leadership is a part of the usual actions of many people in the organization, not just one.
2. The individual's values system measures his or her definition of truth and of success.
3. The essence of values theory is that values dictate individual and work-community action.
4. The leader's task is to create a community where all members can trust the others to do their part to attain agreed-upon results.
5. Trust is an expectation and a personal obligation to be authentic, trustworthy, reliable.
6. Values leadership has a spiritual—whole-self—component.
7. Spirit refers to the vital, energizing force or principle in the person, the core of self.
8. Leaders build spiritual wholeness by providing a common work-community vision.

9. The infrastructure of values-based leadership is founded on an idea of morality.

10. Values leaders operate in service to rather than in control of those around them.

Questions

1. What are the essential components of the definition of values leadership?

2. Can you identify one leader in your experience you would classify as a values leader? Describe the main characteristics of that person's leadership.

3. What are the ways in which leaders influence the creation of trust (or any other) cultures?

4. Based on your personal knowledge of management and leadership, how are management and leadership similar or different? Can the differences be reconciled? Should they be?

5. What are your personal feelings about connecting spirituality and leadership in work communities? Are they compatible?

6. What do you (or leaders you know) do in your work life that responds to your core spiritual values?

7. What does spirituality mean to you? Does this meaning remain constant in personal, family, social, businesses, and other spheres of your life? How is it the same? In what ways is it different?

8. What is the downside of practicing spiritual leadership at work?

LEARNING ACTIVITIES

Activity 1: Self-Assessment—Value Systems

Instructions. Rank the values in each of the two categories with 1 = most important to you, 2 next in importance, 3 next, and so forth. The following is based on Rokeach's work (1979).

Rank your instrumental values	**Rank your terminal values**
___ Ambition and hard work	___ Contribution and a sense of accomplishment
___ Honesty and integrity	___ Happiness
___ Love and affection	___ Leisurely life
___ Obedience and duty	___ Wisdom and maturity
___ Independence and self-sufficiency	___ Individual dignity
___ Humility	___ Justice and fairness
___ Doing good to others (Golden Rule)	___ Spiritual salvation

Scoring key: The values that you ranked highest of the work community are the ones that are most important to you. Consider whether your life and career choices are consistent with your values.

Activity 2: What Does It Mean to Be a Leader?

Instructions. Leadership means many things to many people. Take a few moments and think about what leadership means to you.

1. Ask yourself the following questions:

   What responsibility does it carry?

   How do you do this kind of work effectively?

   What do you need: skills, knowledge, support from others, and the like to be a more effective leader?

2. Using the responses you developed for step 1 questions, develop specific guidelines for a leader in your organization.

3. Compare this listing to the professional leadership literature.

   Note similarities and differences.

   What conclusions can be drawn for this exercise about the true nature of top and inner leadership?

4. Develop a list of leader definitional characteristics you and others might use to guide your leadership.

Activity 3: Spirituality Questionnaire

Instructions. Seldom do working leaders think about their spirituality outside of organized religious contexts. Yet getting in touch with one's spiritual center is a necessary prerequisite to effective work-community action—whether leader or led.

Completing the following questionnaire will help participants organize their present thinking about their spiritual center and how it may apply to the work they do in leading in the middle of the corporation.

Note: There are no right or wrong answers. Some indication of what other professionals have said in response to this questionnaire may be found in Fairholm (2000a).

1. How do you define spirituality?

2. How important is your personal spirituality in shaping your ethics, values and beliefs?

   ___ Very important   ___ Important

   ___ Not very important   ___ Not important

3. How much do you rely on your spirituality in doing your school work?

    ___ A lot   ___ Not much   ___ None

4. Is there a connection between your personal sense of spirituality and your success in leadership situations?

    ___ A significant connection   ___ It depends   ___ None

5. Should consideration of worker or leader spirituality be a part of the school or workplace?

    ___ Yes   ___ No   ___ It depends (on what?)

6. How much do you rely on your spiritual sense in work or school situations?

    ___ A lot   ___ None   ___ It depends (on what?)

7. What are the most important activities in which you engage that inspire, encourage, and renew you?

8. What are your main sources of spiritual support?

9. What are the most important values guiding your actions?

10. What are the most important reasons that spirituality is important in leadership?

Activity 4: Programs Focusing on the Whole Person at Work

Instructions. Make an appointment to interview the personnel director in your organization about the range of regular and special programs and services offered to employees.

1. Specifically, what programs and services are offered that deal with tasks other than directly related to the job. Examples might include those listed here. (Note: Do not identify these programs to your interviewee. Try to direct questions to elicit these and other programs if they are offered.)

    Tuition assistance toward a college degree—including courses that have no direct benefit to the corporation.

    Employee assistance programs—addiction or marriage counseling and the like.

    Exercise and general health and fitness programs.

    Leisure services—discount tickets, memberships, sponsorship of sports teams.

    Chaplin services or other programs and services.

2. Distinguish between programs offered executives and those for line employees. Find out why the organization does each of these things. What corporate purpose does providing these services serve?

3. After the interview, analyze your data and prepare a report of your findings. List each service and the reasons the director gave for offering each one.

4. Summarize your findings in a brief statement of the extent and purposes of other than direct job-related programs and services for employees. Your summary should include

   The range of such programs.

   The reasons they are offered.

   The purposes they serve for the corporation.

   The purposes they serve for employees.

   Other factors brought to light by your research and analysis.

CHAPTER 3

Inner Leadership

Leadership skill is crucial to leaders who work in the vast middle ranges of the corporation, the agencies of government, and all other social institutions. Yet the literature is largely silent about leadership in the interior. Nevertheless, it is often here that the best leadership happens. Certainly quantitatively more leadership takes place in the multiple work communities in the middle of the corporate hierarchy than it does at the top leader level.

Unfortunately, the leaders in the middle of the corporation do not always get the credit they deserve, nor have they received due recognition historically or theoretically. The top leaders get the credit, and those in the middle—who do the work—are largely ignored. This is true in all social institutions—business, government, the arts, and education. History focuses on the top leaders and the big events. The big problems and the famous leaders get the headlines and the chapters in history books.

Notwithstanding the public acclaim garnered by top leaders, success or failure in most situations rests on a cadre of lower-ranking officers and their followers. The work of the many leaders in the inner levels in any large-scale organization does more to determine both CEO and overall corporate success than does that of top leaders. These leaders are the people who create new futures for themselves and their work communities. They design new programs policies and operating procedures. These inner leaders also implement that policy, oversee process activity, and assess work done against planned outcomes. They deal directly with corporate staff on a one-to-one basis, assess human potential, and integrate human capital with money, material, and technical resources.

DEFINING INNER LEADERSHIP

Inner leadership has a dual definition: part structural, part personal. It describes the type of leadership that takes place in the middle of the organization, whether a business, government agency, or any other social institution. It also deals with the impact of the leader's core values that guide all leaders, as well as their followers. Neither of these two definitions of leadership is routinely discussed in textbooks, classrooms, or boardrooms. Nonetheless, quantitatively (and perhaps qualitatively) more leadership is exercised by middle-level leaders than by the figurehead top leader. If, by chance, reference is made to the work of inner leaders, it is assumed they have the same objectives and use the same and techniques as top leaders do.

This assumption is faulty. Inner leaders occupy a unique culture, unlike that of their bosses. They foster dissimilar goals. They use some distinct leadership techniques and they apply others skills differently than do CEOs. These different points of view, goals, and ways to lead are the subject of inner leadership, or leadership in the middle. An understanding of the inner leader's perspective may help the many leaders in the middle of the organization be successful. CEOs also need to learn about the methods inner leaders use to get their way in groups so they can better collaborate in corporationwide work.

The conventional wisdom says that there is usually only one formal leader in each work group; the rest are followers of that chief executive. The fact is, every work community has many leaders besides the chief executive. Indeed, forming alliances—partnerships, really—between the CEO and these second-level leaders may be the wave of the future (Moxley, 2000). Traditional definitions suggest that inner leaders are followers of the boss. That may be true, but unfortunately the idea of "follower" has negative connotations for most people. Americans are conditioned to think of followers as passive, while operational experience contradicts that view (Miller, 1992). Many followers are routinely compelled by their work to be aggressive and courageous, to assume responsibility and be willing to challenge their bosses.

The public perception, nevertheless, favors the up-front CEO over the behind-the-scenes inner leader. One survey showed that 70 percent of men and 59 percent of women see themselves as leaders ("Do You Consider Yourself a Leader or a Follower," 1994). Only 20 percent of men and 36 percent of women say they are followers. The fact is, as Kelley (1992) says, that today almost everyone takes a turn leading groups. Indeed, followers are key to all social action and success for there can be no leadership without followership. Corporate success in meeting productivity and profitability goals is keyed far more to the work of good middle-level leaders than it is to excellent CEOs.

Because number-two leaders are not often in the spotlight, it is easy to think of them in generic or homogeneous terms. This is a mistake; they vary tremendously in education and experience, in goals, and in talent. They are not robots. They have their own visions, to which they pay attention and their own measures of the importance of the group's work and the level of effort they are willing to expend in its accomplishment.

The inner leader's perspectives on these things are often different from, sometimes even counter to, the official corporate vision. Given these facts of leadership life in the middle of the corporation, it is these interior leaders, not the chief executive officer, who constitute the heart of corporate leadership today. Studying mid-level leaders, therefore, becomes vitally important to understanding corporate success in today's dynamic and fast-changing work world.

Differentiating Inner Leadership from Top Leadership

At least six dimension of difference between inner and top leadership can be identified. Each is discussed here beginning with the first dimension of differences, definition.

Distinguishing Inner Leadership from Top Leadership

Several characteristics of inner leadership techniques stand out as dissimilar to definitional characteristics often ascribed to top leaders or leadership generally (Suzaki, 2002). The first of these has to do with the core definition of inner leadership. Leadership in the middle of the agency is fundamentally different from the descriptions implicit in more traditional leadership theory. For current purposes, *inner leadership is an interactive relationship between a leader and several followers voluntarily engaged in situations (communities or cultures) where leader and led are united on values terms and trust each other enough to risk self in participation in joint activity.* Some of the aspects of this definition need to be emphasized since they describe a vital facet of inner leadership. Singly and together they differentiate inner from top leadership.

First, leadership is a social, not a structural, phenomenon. That is, it happens in social relationships that are consciously created separate from and sometimes diametrically opposed to formal corporate structural components. These relationships between leader and led are personal and intimate in ways that differentiate them from conventional work units. Once created, they need to be maintained; and, therefore, manipulating relationships is both a part of the distinctive definition of inner leaders and one of their key operational tasks. It is in these intimate relationships that the leader's personal agenda (Crosby, 1996) is realized, not alone but in joint activity with the other members of the relationship. Of course, some CEOs focus on relationships; most focus on the more formal structural forms that help make up corporate organization itself and are easier to create and maintain.

Second, the inner leader's relationships are with followers, and followers are always volunteers. They do not have to follow. Of course, workers must show up, do some work, and be polite. But successful inner leaders somehow attract willing followers to do what they want done. In-the-middle leaders often cannot order their coworkers to do anything—this is especially true of their bosses and peers, who do not have to accept their leadership unless it benefits them to do so. They cannot order these people to comply with and accept their vision. By contrast, the typical CEO sees workers as merely "employees" or, worse, "subordinates," but certainly not as volunteers.

Third, inner leaders intend to change people's lives. While CEOs focus on agency productivity and growth, inner leaders deal with both production and their followers' professional and personal growth and maturation needs. Inner leaders accept the task of developing their followers as leaders in their own right. Focus on this kind of transforming change is a critical aspect of inner leadership. It is influencing others to change and then trusting them to do their best in the absence of the CEO's authoritarian controls.

Fourth, leaders are in service to others. Top leaders think that the employees work for them. Inner leaders know that when they provide their followers with needed resources, time, and plans they (leaders) become servants of their followers—they reverse the pyramid. Their job is to prepare followers to provide high quality, excellent service to clients, customers, and each other. Rather than attempt to force followers to this kind of behavior, inner leaders, prompted by a desire to serve their stakeholders, in effect go to work for them—providing all things necessary for follower success.

Fifth, an element of this definition has to do with the inner leader's followership role. Inner leaders are both leaders and followers of the lead of their bosses, coworkers, and customers when the situation dictates they behave this way. This element is not often considered in the professional literature, yet to ignore the followership role is to ignore half of the idea of leadership. Every member of a work community is both a leader and a follower (Hughes, Ginnett, and Curphy, 1999) at appropriate times. In an era of flat organizations, with many more designated internal leaders than before was common, this is an essential characteristic of inner leadership (Brown, 1977), one most CEOs ignore.

Six, inner leadership is also characterized by mutual interactive trust. The element of trust in any work community is critical to leader success in attaining both personal and work-community ends. Over time, no cooperative work can be done without interpersonal trust. It is a necessary and essential element of any leader–follower situation. It is especially the case in relationships in the middle of the corporation because the leader's followers are people who choose to accept the leader's orders, instructions, guidance, standards—anything. They cannot be forced to do so.

At the core the definition of inner leadership is the leaders' value set. Inner leaders assure their goals are met by using their core values to create a work community, determine its values, and vision, and create a culture to maintain them. These tasks constitute crucial inner leader techniques. Since the CEO, all other in-the-middle leaders, and their workers also have values they want generalized in the group, another of their key tasks is values-displacement techniques in a situation of alternative value-sets and competing subcultures. Values are so important that they can be ranked as a major difference between inner and top leadership.

Inner Leaders Lead to Realize Their Personal Agenda

Obviously, each individual lives in multiple social groups and interacts with a variety of others in all facets of daily living. Their perception of their role is personal, unique for each group member. That is to say, both leader and led view their thoughts and actions from the unique perspective of their own individual values and experiences. Each worker comes to work to achieve personal values outcomes, realize a personal vision, and attain personal goals, not just (often not even) those of the work community. Corporate CEOs may be shocked to learn this about their workers and their subordinate leaders. But it is true—all people come to work for reasons personal to them! Part of leadership is forging values unity in this cauldron of values diversity (Truskie, 1999).

Creating a shared values system from this mix of individual competing values systems, therefore, is the basis of all interrelationships between people. For community to exist, the individual's values must come to be consonant with a system of variously rated values that guide his or her life and actions in the group and that make that action conventional, predictable, and acceptable to peers. This is a part of the definition of community—any community, including work communities.

Members join groups primarily to utilize the resources of the community and their relationships in it to help them get *their* needs met. Of course, work-community members also do the corporation's work, either because they have to or because they come to value it as one of their preference values. Group values constitute a network of known and shared norms that members take for granted and provide the infrastructure of any community. They are the standards by which members judge their own actions and evaluate and rate those of others. Given the truth of this analysis, setting and shaping work-community values become key inner leader tasks. Developing and promoting such a values-based work culture is more important to the work of inner leaders than any formally announced corporate vision or values statement or the policies, systems, and procedures proceeding from the corporation's vision statement.

The task of inner leaders is to create a set of values that support their personal agenda for the work community and generalize it to all members as preferable to their own values constructs or the corporation's formal values system (Crosby, 1996). In this way they unite their followers into a work community around their (the leader's) personal values. Indeed, setting and changing work-community values is the leader's prime job. It involves creating a subculture helpful to the realization of values goals. Unless followers share their leader's values, they will expend effort in trying to satisfy their own values, which, from the leader's point of view, produces waste.

In a situation where the inner leader is not in full control, the most powerful tool is shared values about the work (Bjerke, 1999) because everybody has values, and those values trigger our behavior.

Inner leaders Inspire Follower Obedience

A third unique aspect of inner leadership is that inspiration, not motivation, characterizes the inner leader's relationships with followers. The conventional wisdom is that the CEO's job is to motivate workers. So-called motivation is based primarily on tangible, physical, or economic rewards; and to the degree that top leaders can allocate needed rewards to compliant followers, to that degree they "motivate" them.

The fact is that no one—leaders included—can motivate someone else. Motives are internal to the individual and directed by the individual. Leaders have little to do with creating motivation because all motives are personal. Workers behave in a given way in response to their own inner drives. Thus, the only true motivation is self-motivation. When someone else, through his or her behavior, actions, or words, induces other individuals to act, he or she does something other than motivate them, even if the professional literature describes it as motivation.

So-called motivation is actually one set, or a combination of three sets, of actions or approaches leaders might take. They can create or alter their work community's environment so members can satisfy their own needs while (hopefully) also doing needed work. Or they can do something to awaken a dormant motive or change the priority of a member's inner motives to action. Or, finally, they can excite and inspire other persons to action to satisfy by that action their needs and, optimistically, the organization's. Top leaders can induce follower action most easily by resorting to the first two approaches. Inner leaders opt for the third approach—they inspire their followers to desired action and shared results because they cannot use external inducements to "buy" compliance.

Inspirational inner leaders influence others through emotional, even spiritual, forces or methods. They animate others, stop doubt, and encourage coworkers to act without thinking (Roberts, 1907). They apply action to people's hopes and give them new—renewed—purpose. Leaders in the middle use physical and ideological symbols to mute questions and impel people to act without thinking to realize the leader's desired and outcomes. Inspiration goes beyond facts by putting members dreams into words. It appeals to a need to be part of and engaged with others in lofty enterprise.

Inner Leaders Use Personal More Than Authority Power

Inner leaders use their personal power, not their authority, to get followers to think and act their way. They cannot always use their authority power, the power of their position, to force compliance as their top bosses can. Rather, they rely on forms of power based in their personal capacities, personalities, ideas, ideals, and expertise to get others to follow them. Using personal forms of power helps leaders generate and sustain trust.

Both leaders and led are regularly in relationships where they compete with their colleagues for dominance—the capacity to get their own way in the face of competing action by others. Inner leaders normally find themselves in situations where their understanding of what is happening increases by viewing the relationship in terms of political power. Skill in using power is therefore critical to inner leader success. Expertise in the theory and practice of organizational power politics (Fairholm, 1993) is therefore another critical area for leaders in the middle, one not so vital to the authority-laden CEO (Carson, 2001).

Inner Leaders Learn to Both Trust and Be Trustworthy

Inner leaders use trust to get others to perform the way they want. Trust is not based on authority couched in procedures, resource control, and disciplinary systems. It is based in an eventually proven reality. Leaders may not know a follower will deal correctly with them but, if they trust the follower, they will act as if they do. The idea of interactive trust is seen in friendship, in family and social life, and in the art that reflects life. Because their leaders trust them, followers learn that their work need not be routine and enervating. Rather it can generate hope and eventual success.

Inner leaders lack the degree of legitimate authority of top leaders to publish and enforce their policies and procedures. They get compliance, therefore, because of their trust in others and their own trustworthiness, not their control over the mechanisms of command.

Inner Leadership Concerns the Whole Person of Both Leader and Led

Inner leaders act from the base of their whole selves, their spiritual cores (Ruppert, 1991). They treat their followers as whole people as well. Top leaders mostly deal with that part of followers' capacities directly related to needed tasks as outlined in position descriptions. Inner leaders get followers to give them more than just what is on the position description. They ask for and use all the capacities of each follower. They create relationships based on ideas and values that bond them to followers at their deepest emotional—spiritual—levels. It is their personal core selves—their spiritual values and needs—and not job skills that determine the character of inner leaders' relationships with others.

Summary

These few ideas define and differentiate inner leaders from their CEO bosses, peers, and subordinates. Of course, these differences may be somewhat over-drawn when applied to a specific agency or a particular boss. Still, they define tensions that face both top and inner leaders. As inner leaders accept these differences, this knowledge may assist them to be more personally and profes-sionally successful leaders since these distinctions are critical in working in the middle and in understanding its ideal and practical niceties.

METHODS OF LEADING FROM THE
MIDDLE OF THE CORPORATION

Inner leadership is practiced in all social organizations and the full range of other leadership venues. The relationship between top leaders and their inner leaders and inner leaders and their coworker colleagues can make or break both organization programs and personal careers (Hughes, Ginnett, and Curphy, 1999). Effective inner leadership obviously connotes competent, loyal, and energetic support of the CEO's agenda. It also demands that inner leaders be prepared to function in the unique culture they themselves create in the middle precincts of the corporation.

The differences between top and inner leaders described previously are real. Nevertheless, for a hundred years the professional literature has described the leader as a lone hero demolishing obstacles, leaping tall problems in a single bound. This "hero leadership" model implies that great things are accomplished by one larger-than-life individual who issues orders, gives direction, empowers less well equipped coworkers, leads the way, articulates a compelling vision, and changes behavior patterns with elan (Bradford and Cohen, 1984; Bennis, 1999).

While compelling, this hero model (Covey, 2001) was never the case in practice. Rather, inner leaders rely on the theory of values-based leadership. Of course, some of what inner leaders do is informed by orthodox theory. But the unique culture in which they work makes traditional theory only margin-ally useful, if at all. The inner leader's values form the basis of the work community's vision, the root of behaviors acceptable to that community, and the basis of the leader's influence with others.

The need today, as never before, is for top and in-the-middle leaders to form clusters of close-knit partnerships throughout the corporation (Johnson, 1999). In partnership arrangements control doesn't reside in a single person. Rather, power and responsibility are dispersed, giving the enterprise not one superstar but a whole constellation of costars. These partnerships can be alli-ances in which the pleasure of working together and of being together compensates the inner leader for living in the shadow of the more celebrated CEO hero (Heenan and Bennis, 1999).

Specifying specific skills, methods, techniques, and attitudes of mind characteristic of inner leadership is the focus of this book. To list and describe them here would be redundant. As readers peruse the following parts of the book, they will discover something of the range of inner leadership techniques they must master. The techniques discussed in each subsequent part of this book are presented as characteristic of the major differences between middle and top leadership.

Nevertheless, three points can be emphasized here that will aid in understanding the techniques and methods of inner leadership. The first is that, if there is one generalization we can make, no change can occur without a committed work community and inner leaders. Exemplary top leadership and institutional success are impossible without the full inclusion, initiatives, and cooperation of the core of middle-level leaders. Today's complicated and global problems require complex alliances. Success comes when top leaders recognize that there are many inner leaders on the team who want to work in creative alliance with them.

A second summary point is that good leadership and followership are part of the same process. Both roles let inner leaders exercise the full range of their talents; engage in meaningful, important work; and mature as self-actualizing human beings. Excellent inner leaders follow their bosses and are actively engaged with them (Kelley, 1992). Both top and inner leaders and their core followers come to understand and respect followership as a legitimate, valuable part of work life. Both kinds of leader can expect their people to be responsive when they are candid about the importance of followership and they model that behavior as appropriate (Townsend and Gebhardt, 1990).

Finally, inner leadership is not always merely a stepping stone to the CEO's chair. For many people, the role of inner leader is a deliberate professional choice. Making that choice provides as strong a platform for serving all those with whom the inner leader interacts as the CEO's chair does. For indeed, it is inner leaders as much as, if not more than, their bosses who make the work community function—and they always have.

DISCUSSION ISSUES AND QUESTIONS

Issues

1. Leaders who work in the middle ranges of the corporation use unique skills.
2. Inner leadership has a dual definition: part structural, part personal. It describes the type of leadership that takes place in the middle. It also deals with the impact of the leader's core values that guide each leader as well as each follower.

3. Quantitatively, and perhaps qualitatively, more leadership is exercised by middle-level leaders than by figurehead top leaders.

4. Inner leaders occupy a unique culture, unlike that of their bosses. They foster dissimilar goals, use some distinct leadership techniques, and apply others skills differently.

5. Forming alliances—partnerships—between the CEO and these second-level leaders may be the wave of the future.

6. Followers are key to all social action and success since they provide the strength, power, capacity, and facts top leaders must have if they and their organization are to succeed.

7. Leadership in the middle of the agency can be defined as an interactive relationship between a leader and several followers voluntarily engaged in situations (communities or cultures) where leader and led are united on values terms and trust each other enough to risk self in participation in joint activity.

8. Each person comes to work to get his or her personal values, vision, goals, and outcomes met, not just (often not even) those of the corporation.

9. Values and a values-based work culture, not system or procedure, are most important to our success as inner leaders.

10. Inner leaders inspire follower obedience.

11. Inspiration, not motivation, characterizes the inner leader's relationships with followers.

12. Inner leaders use their personal power more than authority power.

13. Inner leaders learn to both trust and be trustworthy.

14. Inner leadership concerns the whole person of both leader and led.

15. Inner leadership is not always merely a stepping stone to the CEO's chair. For many people, the role of inner leader is a conscious choice.

Questions

1. What are the essential components of inner leadership? How is inner leadership different from top leadership? From middle management? From line workers?

2. Provide one example from your experience of an effective inner leader, and describe briefly his or her typical behavior in relationships with you?

3. In your experience in the middle of your corporation, have you ever functioned as a leader? In which relationships did you find it easiest to lead successfully? Explain.

4. What obstacles do you find most challenging in functioning fully as an inner leader?

5. Differentiate middle management from inner leadership. Are the arguments here similar or different from those proposed in the literature to differentiate leadership from management generally? Specify.

6. Can you be an effective inner leader and not also be a values leader? Explain your response.

7. How do you think your boss feels abut the idea of leadership being exercised in the middle and with the objective of securing the inner leader's goals, not just corporate ones?

INNER LEADERSHIP LEARNING ACTIVITIES

Activity 1: Dimensions of Inner Leadership

Instructions. Understanding inner level leadership is more difficult than understanding some past models. As a way to get in touch with the dimensions of this model, complete the following activity.

1. Concentrate on those elements and feelings involved in the inner leadership model.

2. After you have analyzed your understanding of this method of leadership, make a drawing depicting inner leadership.

   Use pictures, diagrams, colors, words, numbers—whatever is needed and available—to create a visual object that represents what you know about inner leadership.

   Be expressive and creative in your drawings so that what they indicate will aid you, and perhaps others, to understand the dimensions of inner leadership more fully.

3. After you have completed the creative aspect of this assignment, prepare a written analysis and explanation of what you have drawn.

4. Share both the drawing and your analysis with a colleague or friend.

Activity 2: Sitting in Council with Others

Instructions. Read the following short statement and then respond to the questions listed below.

For inner leadership to work up and down the organization, new ways of viewing the leader–follower interaction are necessary. *Counciling-with* followers is a new insight into the relationship between leader and follower. It is essential for this model of leadership that inner leaders learn to delegate even, or perhaps especially, when followers are not fully prepared or the work community is in a change mode.

Sitting in council with followers puts the leader and follower together in an equal, sharing relationship, both committed to realization of the vision and the tasks at hand and both caring for the values of the others. Ideas flow freely as influence shifts from person to person. Any or all may propose or alter ideas, methods, problems, and solutions.

A *counseling* role used typically by top leaders is unilateral action taken by the counselor (leader) toward another person. In a word, counseling is telling. *Counciling-with* followers is, rather, finding out together what is right, proper, and needed. Followers become advisors and inner leaders learn from the followers (Fairholm, 2000a). This shared approach is often discussed in terms of participatory or democratic approaches to management. This technique is based on relationship and meaningful interactions—the essential elements of leadership.

Discussion Questions

1. When talking with coworkers, do I tell them things or encourage a sharing of information?

2. Do I encourage group discussions and facilitate group dynamics? Do coworkers frequently exchange ideas?

3. Do I have the self-esteem to allow others to have good ideas and take the lead at times? What challenges does this approach present? Analyze your typical operational responses to these kinds of challenge.

4. Am I able to synthesize group information and formulate decisions or next steps?

5. What do I need to know or learn to do to increase my expertise in counciling-with coworkers?

Part II

THE TECHNIQUES OF INNER LEADER PREPARATION

America is a nation of doers, not thinkers. Americans value theories and systems that work, not those that are merely intellectually elegant. The techniques of inner leadership flow out of this ideology and define discrete behavior sets that guide leaders in their day-to-day relationships with followers. While the techniques and skills delineating this leadership theory are applied uniquely by each leader, they constitute a generic body of practice any inner leader can productively use. Two kinds of leadership techniques stand out. The first deals with the personal preparation of the leader. The second concerns leader actions to prepare followers to function in a shared values trust culture. Part II focuses the reader on the techniques of leader preparation. Subsequent parts deal with the techniques of inner leader action to induce follower compliance.

Of course, inner leaders use many of the common leadership techniques discussed in the traditional literature. Like all leaders, they allocate scarce resources, recognize and reward outstanding performance (Badaracco, 1989), set corporate goals, and otherwise establish policy and procedural performance and service expectations. They also plan, issue orders, evaluate performance, and encourage workers to behave in terms of set standards and practices. These are essentially management techniques, whether or not they are practiced by a leader, and are not discussed here. Rather, the focus is on the those techniques peculiar to inner leaders functioning in work communities and seeking essentially personal goals.

Preparing for inner leadership is a change process for both leader and led. The key to success is in intimate relationships leaders create with their followers in the work community. These relationships rely on authentic caring for all followers, helping them to become the best persons they can become, learning to be both leaders and followers in what becomes an intimate relationship with other members of the work community and seeing their joint work from the perspective of a future they all help create. Inner leadership is a social activity that takes place in relationships between people, between people and the work, and between leaders and the several communities with which they interact. These relationships become the primary environment within which inner leadership takes place.

Inner leaders have evolved several techniques that set them apart from other leaders or managers. These techniques summarize a growing list of specialized knowledge, skills, and tasks that represent common patterns (Slywotzky and Morrison, 2000) of behavior that differ in significant degree from behavior of top leaders or managers. As they reference leader preparation to lead, six of these attitudinal and behavioral paradigms—techniques—are unique to inner leader success: learning to authentically respect all stakeholders, learning to help followers, fostering change and transformation, learning followership, maintaining a relationship focus, and taking a horizon perspective.

CHAPTER 4

Technique 1: Authentically Respecting Stakeholders

Inner leadership involves some complex and unique concepts. In essence it relies mostly on using the common values most people intuitively accept. One of these values is respectful, caring, even loving, behavior toward followers. Respecting coworkers is critical to the leader's success. Successful inner leaders have internalized feelings of respect and enjoyment in working with all stakeholders in the common enterprise, and they show it. Leaders who treat members of their work community with old-fashioned courtesy and respect reap rewards of increased member commitment (Johnson, 1999), better productivity, and increased involvement.

RESPECT FOR FOLLOWERS

Of the various focuses of preparation inner leaders need to internalize, perhaps the most critical is learning to respect (Lombardi, 2000) all their coworkers. The key to success in using any of the techniques described in this part is in the need for leaders to prize each person and the capacities of each individual stakeholder. Respecting all the people with whom they are in interaction is critical to success here. Inner leaders have adopted the philosophy (Crosby, 1996) of inner leadership and have internalized feelings of respect, caring, and enjoyment—even love—in working with others in the common enterprise.

Leaders Love Followers

Caring is defined as feelings of concern or interest for another (Fiedler and Chamers, 1974). It is a part of the idea of consideration, one of the two traits of leadership coming out of post–World War II research. The other is initiating structure (Bass, 1981). Respect also implies caring. It is nothing more than the Golden Rule in the workplace. But the caring must be authentic. When leaders trust their followers by letting them function without tight controls, they create a follower perception that leaders really respect and care for them (Gibb, 1978). Trusting followers see the leader as open, interested in them, and worthy of their reciprocal trust. While openness is risky, leaders' willingness to be open enhances their inherent trustworthiness. Caring leader behavior communicates the leader's willingness to serve the needs of followers, as well as corporate goals.

The most significant definitional characteristic of inner leaders is that they relate to every person in their work community in ways that enhance that individual. This kind of leadership requires specific behavior that actualizes people values. Inner leaders respect their followers enough to seek opportunities and create systems to share planning, decision making, and work methods determinations with them. This caring behavior includes common courtesy toward others, listening to understand, and otherwise showing consideration for the ideas, actions, and opinions of others (Braham, 1999). It is seeking out stakeholders and counciling-with them. Leaders who value those they work with have a penchant for close interaction with them. The several specific techniques leaders use to operationalize this people-oriented values leader model ask leaders to esteem the uniqueness and capacities of each of their stakeholders. The central techniques are described in this chapter. They are elaborated in the activities following this discussion and, indeed, through this book.

Trusting Followers

Hertzberg's (1966) research confirmed that Douglas McGregor's theory Y (1960) ideas were correct. When inner leaders treat employees as McGregor specified in his theory Y—with a basic respect and confidence in their ability and desire to work to a high standards of effectiveness and responsibility—they are more productive and hard working. Implicit in this factor is the idea of mutual trust. Trust is vital to any organizational action. It is the lubrication that allows all parts of the organization—and all individuals—to interact smoothly (Fairholm, 1994). Leaders must trust their followers, and the followers must trust their leaders if they are to lead. Inner leaders rely on the good will of their followers to do what is needed. Force, authority, formal structural roles, and other negative sanction systems cannot substitute over the long term for basic mutual trust relationships.

More and more, leaders are called upon to develop trust relationships with their followers (Palmer, 2001). Such a relationship is built on many things, among them is the need to articulate clear goals, sound policies, and a basic love and respect for others (Lombardi, 2000). Leadership based on core spiritual values of leader and led take place in a culture supportive of relationships characterized by factors like these, factors that are sensitive to the needs of both the followers and the leader. Leaders care for their followers, they respect them, and they like them as friends (Caill, 2000).

A Whole-Souled Concern for Others

The character of stakeholder groups is changing. Highly educated workers are becoming the norm. They are more aware of general conditions in society and of the specific development patterns in their organizations. They are also aware of and work to achieve their own potential and satisfy all their needs, if possible, at work. They want to use all their capacities in ways that benefit them and their several communities of interest—family, career, religion, social group(s), and friends. And they expect their leaders to be proactively helpful in this effort.

Followers seek development of their own capacities and talents for success in each of these communities, either directly or as by-products of their work. Leading this kind of coworkers asks leaders to consider them as a whole, not just as discrete bundles of skills, knowledge, and abilities they need to do some work. The leader's role is expanding to encompass concern for this kind of growth of the total person of each stakeholder who wants to lead, and increasingly is capable of leading, the corporation—or parts of it—him or herself. As these workers become the norm in the workplace, inner leaders will have to share their leadership with these almost coequal stakeholders. Learning how to do this is a new leadership technique for many, one for which few have received formal training in the required skills.

Helping Followers Improve Themselves

Equally important in leader preparation is the acquisition of the skills useful in changing other peoples' values and behavior. Helping followers mature is essential to the idea of inner leadership. Inner leaders see each follower, customer, and client as unique. They relate to each person in ways that enhance that individual (Lombardi, 2000). This kind of leadership requires the leader to adopt a mind-set that values people and that actualizes their common values. It is egalitarian. The leader seeks out opportunities and systems to share planning, decision making, and work methods determinations with each individual to add to that person's personal capacities to make a contribution and to help them mature into their best selves.

Focusing Self and Group

Part of this caring technique is focusing the attention of the group members on what they (the leaders) think is important. Centering the group on behavior that reflects the vision the leader has set defines a key element of inner leadership skill. The key here is that the vision is intended to realize the leader's needs whether or not it also realizes corporate needs.

The literature is beginning to describe a variety of behaviors common to this new leadership. Bennis and Nanus (1985) identifies four major skills inner leaders demonstrate as they behave in their relationships with coworkers of all kinds. He says leaders have acquired skill in managing self, the work community's attention, its meaning, and its level of trust to help insure they accomplish their personal aims. They exercise these skills so followers can fully participate in doing the work the leader wants done. People want to make a difference, and if leaders let—help—them do it, they gain adherents to their vision objectives.

METHODS OF BUILDING CARING RELATIONSHIPS

Inner leaders communicate their respect—caring and love—in every action taken and in every word spoken and deed performed. They convey their concern for followers through multiple acts. They are responsive to the values followers hold, their beliefs, and their feelings (Crozan, 1989). Respectful, caring behavior also includes allowing others to function independently insofar as is possible within the work community's values and vision. Locke's (1991) research into professional leadership failures cites unconcern, insensitivity to others, and disregard of the humanness of their coworkers as major causes of leader derailment. Successful leaders behave in opposite ways.

Most people want and need a degree of independence to perform their work on their schedule and in their way. Within the known constraints of the technique or of the parent work organization's policy, inner leaders strive to allow workers to show some creative independence on the job as a way to increase group solidarity and productivity. Caring facilitates this kind of guided autonomy that includes helping stakeholders become capable of doing more than they formerly did.

Respecting Followers

Caring about people is nothing more than a highly developed concern for others. Inner leaders feel about leading their stakeholders the same way that craftsmen feel about their craft. Real craftsmanship, regardless of the skill involved, reflects genuine caring; and real caring reflects the leaders' attitudes about self, about their fellows, and about life generally. Caring is an inner leadership technique that, if present, permeates all aspects of the work community—its people, clients, suppliers, and customers.

Caring presupposes respect. We cannot communicate caring and at the same time humiliate a coworker, a client, the work unit, or the program. Caring implies unstinting support. Caring techniques operationalize the Golden Rule in the workplace. Leaders who care about their followers give time and attention to workers and to what they do. Caring inner leaders listen to colleagues, customers, clients, and constituency groups. They treat them as respected colleagues who deserve their time, attention, good will, and honest concern.

Leaders living by this inner leadership philosophy use the simple technique of treating coworkers and customers as adults and as trusted friends. Treating coworkers as adults means treating them as fully functioning mature colleagues capable of self-directed activity. As they treat coworkers as adults, leaders become partners in the mutual enterprise (Johnson, 1999). Thus, inner leaders listen respectfully and patiently to their coworkers (Braham, 1999). They value workers as individuals, not as interchangeable parts of the industrial machine. They expect extraordinary things from ordinary workers, and the workers usually deliver extraordinary results. The leader's respect for others may be tough-minded and still communicate caring and respect (Lombardi, 2000). Caring leaders can still expect competence, but they honor it when it is given. Treating coworkers with respect implies a willingness to prepare them and to set reasonable and clear expectations.

Recent literature is almost unanimous in defining leadership in terms of loving and caring for followers. Caring behavior comes from deeply held beliefs and perceptions about people, who they are and their essential goodness. Caring—love—is a definitional attribute of interpersonal excellence. Inner leaders come to love their coworkers, the services they jointly provide, their clients, and all the people with whom they work. Caring is central to leadership. Inner leaders are excited about what they do and whom they do it with. They nurture their colleagues out of a genuine concern for them (Clement and Rickard, 1992).

Courtesy

Central to inner leadership philosophy are a few communal values most Americans intuitively accept. One of these is common courtesy. Perhaps it should be called uncommon courtesy since, in many organizations, it is so seldom practiced. Nevertheless, inner leaders who treat others with old-fashioned courtesy reap rewards of increased commitment, more productivity, and fuller involvement because, simply, courtesy works.

Inner leaders place value on people, not solely on control fads—like Quality Circles, Job Enlargement, Organizational Development, Human Relations, Total Quality Management, and the like. These fads have often been relied upon to induce followers to behave in predetermined ways. This is a top-down focus relying, primarily, on the leader's power. A better approach, one seldom used it seems these days, is courtesy. Courtesy is an alternative to these control system fads. It focuses not on authority for compliance but on cooperative interaction to accomplish mutually held values by mutually prepared people who like each other.

Being Friendly

The inner leadership model prioritizes consideration for the emotions and needs of stakeholders. Leaders respect the talents, feelings, concerns, and values of workers, constituents, and their citizen-customers. Treating others with courtesy means seeing them as friends as well as coworkers or subordinates. Friends have fun with each other. They joke, laugh, cry with each other. Inner leaders respond to this follower human need as they listen to their coworkers, smile at them, and otherwise encourage a friendly atmosphere. While CEOs may, on occasion, deal with employees in these ways, they typically subordinate these actions for action intended to control their workers' behavior, not to accommodate their feelings.

Listening

Inner leaders are avid listeners. They listen to customers, employees—all stakeholders. Listening is characteristic of inner leaders. In fact, leadership is a process of intimate relations with followers, the purpose of which is to unleash the followers' capacities (Peters and Austin 1985). Active listening responds to this follower need and to values that reflect respect for and regard for them. Leaders actively try to understand their stakeholders (Tesolin, 2000). Listening lets them gain raw impressions—that is, unfiltered or interpreted data—from customers or employees. It lets leaders focus on strengthening their followers as they hear and try to understand their innovative contributions and, as appropriate, allow them to implement them. In such cases, followers grow, and both they and the work community prosper.

Several listening styles can be discerned from experience. Some listeners are judgmental, evaluating the speaker's words and ideas. Others are interpretive, attaching meaning to ideas immediately, sometimes prematurely. They run the risk of biasing others' ideas vis-à-vis their own prejudices. Some listeners are supportive, confirming and encouraging others' ideas (Braham, 1999). Still others are probative, seeking answers to the what, why, and where of the speakers' ideas and information. Another style is giving attention and empathetic responses to the speaker in an effort to show you understand what is being said.

Inner leaders, however, characteristically practice a special kind of listening called naive listening. Naive listening is listening as if you have never heard the idea being expressed before. It is a technique for maximizing concentration on what is being communicated. Naive listening is a new way to think about listening. It is an active process of paying respectful attention to others to find out fully what they want to communicate to us (Fairholm, 1991; Cashman and Burzynski, 2000). It is, simply, listening with an open and accepting mind to find out what the speaker is saying. After the correct information transfer takes place, the leader can then accept or reject the communicated data based on its merits. But naive listening provides the correct information upon which to base later judgments.

The key to naive listening is to listen to understand. This kind of listening asks leaders to remember key words, resist distractions, review key ideas, and be open and flexible. It asks them to refrain from evaluation until the end of the idea, to remain mentally and physically alert, to take notes, and to stop talking. You can't learn with your mouth open. Naive leader listeners ask questions, prepare in advance for the topic being discussed, listen empathetically, and routinely restate the talker's key points as a check.

DISCUSSION ISSUES AND QUESTIONS

Issues

1. Inner leaders have internalized feelings of caring, respect, and enjoyment in working with all stakeholders in the common enterprise, and they show it.
2. Caring—defined as feelings of respect, concern, or interest for another— is a part of the idea of consideration; one of the two traits of leadership coming out of post–World War II research.
3. Caring leader behavior communicates the leader's willingness to serve the needs followers have.
4. Inner leaders respect their followers enough to seek out opportunities and systems to share planning, decision making, and work methods determinations with individuals.
5. Leaders who value those they work closely with have a penchant for close interaction with them.
6. When inner leaders treat coworkers with a basic respect and confidence in their ability and desire to work to a high standards of effectiveness and responsibility, they are more productive and hard working.

Questions

1. Have I developed strong listening skills?
2. Do I acknowledge that listening as a key element of successfully fulfilling my leadership role?
3. Do I listen as if I have never before heard the information a coworker tells me?

4. Do I listen for the values the speaker is communicating, as well as information?

CARING LEARNING ACTIVITIES

Learning to be an inner leader engages the individual leader in specific caring behaviors. The following may be useful to both individual leaders and to leader trainers to gain experience and comfort in caring for followers.

Activity 1: The Caring Dictator

Introduction. How the leader demonstrates caring in his or her relationships with employees is as varied as the number of leaders studied. From the following case situation emergent leaders can see how caring is and can be employed in the workplace.

1. Read the case situation carefully and make notes of possible aspects of answers to each of the analysis questions at the bottom of the case.

THE CARING DICTATOR

Jeff Smith, president of Zion Corporation, is successful. Zion owns 206 franchises of the Sonic Accelerator retail chain, which generate $76 million in revenues for the company. Smith's stores make 21 percent more than the national average, and turnover is incredibly low for retail industry, with a supervisor's average tenure at 13.8 years. Smith knows what he wants, how to keep his employees, and how to run his business for high profit.

In a work world in which everyone will tell you that you need to be soft, participative, open to ideas, and empower employees, Jeff Smith appears to be an anachronism. He runs his business on the principle of "my way or the highway." He tolerates little deviance from what he wants and from his instructions and training. He is absolutely sure he knows the best way, and more than one employee is scared to disagree with him. He likes keeping people a little off balance and a little uneasy so that they will work harder to avoid his anger. Smith even has his own "Leadership Commandments," and he will fire those who break any one of them twice. The eighth Smith commandment is "I will only tell you one time."

Smith's stores run like clockwork. He does the top-level hiring himself and is reputed to spend as long as ten grueling hours with a prospective manager and his or her spouse. He wants to know about their personal lives and financial health and looks for right responses and any signs of reluctance to answer questions. Smith says: "I want them to understand this is not a job to me. This is a lifetime of working together. I want partners who are going to die with me." If you are one of the selected few, you are expected to be loyal and obedient. Once a quarter, you can also expect a Smith "loyalty" meeting, where he will take you away with other supervisors to a secret location with no chance of escape. You can expect to be blindfolded, put through survival exercises, and sleep in tents before going to a luxury resort to discuss business.

For all their stress, trouble, and unquestioning obedience and loyalty, Zion employees and supervisors find a home, a family, a community; and a place to grow. If you have problems with your husband, like Sara, the wife of one of Zion's supervisors, you can call Jeff. He will listen to you, chew your spouse out, and send him home for a while. Smith says, "I don't want you to come to work unhappy, upset, about anything, because I don't think you can be totally focused on making money if you're worried." He pays his employees considerably above national averages, plays golf with them, and gets involved in their personal lives. Smith wants to create a bond that lasts. A few years ago, he spent $200,000 to take 138 managers and their families to Cancun for four days. They got training on better time management and marketing techniques and on how to be better spouses.

Smith also likes to have fun. Practical jokes, including gluing supervisor's shoes to the floor, are common. But he also works hard. Eighty-hour weeks are common, and he starts his days earlier than most. He is not above taking on the most menial jobs in the stores, and he is willing to show the way, no matter what. His presence, energy, and unbending confidence in his way make converts. Smith has created an organization that is consistent and simplifies everybody's life.

2. How would you describe Jeff Smith's leadership style?
3. Why is he successful? Would you work for him? Why? Why not?
4. Suppose Jeff came to you, a leadership coach, and asked for your help. What would you tell him? Develop a "leadership development plan" for Jeff suggesting changes in his leadership approach you think are better than the one he now uses. Analyze what he is doing well and what needs change.

CHAPTER 5

Technique 2: Maintaining a Relationship Focus

Leadership in the complex and multidifferentiated interior world of the corporation brings the inner leader into intimate association with many constituencies other than the traditional core of immediate followers implied in traditional leadership theory. Leaders must relate to and satisfy the needs of all the work communities and individuals who have a stake in the success of the inner leader's work community. These stakeholders, not merely that part of the corporate structure formally assigned to them, define the scope of the inner leader's concern. Leadership in the middle regions of the corporation encompasses a complex array of interests, forces, attitudes, actions, pressures, and values (Suzaki, 2002). Leading from the middle asks the leader to acquire different skills, knowledge, and abilities, and capacities that in effect redefine leadership in that relationshipful venue.

Inner leaders accept the notion that they need to be concerned with all the communities that affect their activities. This is a new idea in leadership and is specific to the role of inner leaders. Several forces drive inner leaders toward a stakeholder concept of leadership. For one thing, the driving value in many corporations today is service. And, rapid technological change and the shift to global markets result in short product life-cycles and increased risk of erosion of competitive advantage.

DEFINING THE LEADERSHIP OF RELATIONSHIPS

Inner leaders, focusing as they do on work community values, show a commitment to build relationships (Crosby, 1996) in both their internal and the larger corporate contexts for the long-term benefit of all stakeholders, including themselves. These leaders find it easier to gain the support they need from their constituents if they build intimate personal long-term relationships with them. Followers vested in such relationships who know they will share fairly will be more willing to sacrifice to insure the work community's survival and prosperity. Stakeholders who have evidence that affirms that the leader views relationships with them as long term and responsive to their evolving needs develop greater loyalty and are willing to provide support during periods of economic, social, or environmental adjustment.

Gardner (1990) sees leadership as a relationship characterized by a process of persuasion and example by which leaders induce community members to collective action in accordance with the community's purposes. Undoubtedly, inner leadership is a people-oriented task. Understanding the needs of both parties in this relationship is essential to success. Inner leaders can no longer (if they ever did) be content to learn only about their side of the equation.

Implicit in the leader–follower relationship is the idea of trust. Mutual interactive trust is vital to any work-community action. It bonds all parts of the work community—and individual members—and lets them relate to each other smoothly. Workers want to trust their leaders and inner leaders rely on the good will of workers to do what is needed. Force, authority, formal structural roles, and sanction systems cannot substitute for relationships based on mutual trust. Inner leaders, more than top leaders, are called upon to develop trust relationships with their followers, for that is the only kind of relationship that can maintain itself intact over time and against the attacks of stress, change, and technological encroachments. Such trust relationships are built on many things, among them are the need to articulate clear goals, sound policies, and a basic respect for others. Trust takes place in relationships supportive of factors like these, factors that are sensitive to the needs of both the followers and the leader (Yearout, Miles, and Koonce, 2001).

Affiliating with their coworkers in relationships engages inner leaders in more than system, structure, and strategy formation. It involves them also in shaping the social, emotional, and spiritual dimensions of interpersonal work alliances. These latter aspects of work life are more significant and far more susceptible to orchestration by leaders to the benefit of both leaders and followers and to realize goals of the work community they lead.

METHODS OF DEVELOPING
LEADERSHIP RELATIONSHIPS

Building successful relationships with coworkers helps insure that both they and the inner leader are more productive. Strong interpersonal relationships increase mutual trust, strengthen competence, enhance self-confidence, and reduce the expenditure of negative energy on protecting self. Productive relationships reduce fear and increase happiness. They encourage interdependence and allow coworkers to rely on each other more fully. They reduce the risk to self-image by being open. Such relationships enhances creativity and facilitate introduction of new ideas. Successful relationships support common values and reduce the risk inherent in expressing deeply held values.

Developing Workplace Relationships

Several techniques can be identified to help inner leaders build and maintain strong, mutually beneficial working relationships as the basis for joint work activity. Building strong, trusting relationships also requires that followers come to admire the inner leader. Useful work relationships develop as inner leaders act to create certain characteristics of effective relationships in their work communities, among them the following:

Confidence: Relationships are based on confidence and more (Gibb, 1978). They follow unquestioned belief in and reliance on the inner leader based on evidence or experience. Confidence is also developed when the inner leader is seen as worthy of the followers' trust and is seen as reliable. This is a kind of expression of faith in the integrity or strength or the potential behavior of the inner leader (Yearout, Miles, and Koonce, 2001).

Open communications: Open interpersonal communications builds relationships (Santovec, 2001).

Shared feelings: Relationships define a condition in which members are willing to share their intimate feelings.

Predictability: Relationships also develop out of situations where individuals can predict with some accuracy what their colleagues will do or say, given a specific behavior, situation, or result.

Low risk: Relationships are is created when the inner leader can decrease the vulnerability one member has to other persons in the relationship (Handy, 1976).

Integrity: Trust flows from followers' confidence in the leader's ability, integrity, and ethical fidelity.

Values based: The inner leader's values also influence the development of strong relationships. It is only through direct interaction with the leader's values that followers can develop a deep conviction about the leader or about his or her basic worth.

Reliability: Relationships are strengthened when the inner leader guides followers to believe that what the leader says will eventually come to pass. Relationships form and grow when others have confidence in the dependability of the leader's words or actions.

Truth: Relationships mature as experience proves the essential truth of the follower's initial perceptions about joining in the relationship. It diminishes by the reverse. As people or things are proved to be less than we expected or different from our initial perceptions, we withdraw from the relationship.

Expertise: Relationships develop as followers trust the inner leader's competence and expertise. Followers expect that those they interact with, especially their leaders, will be competent to perform in their roles.

Voluntary acceptance: Joining in relationship with the inner leader is voluntary, noncompulsory, a free-will choice.

Trusteeship: Followers freely interact with their leader when they see that the inner leader assumes a trustee relationship toward them and the work community generally.

Trust: Willingness to relate to the inner leader and the members of the leader's work community results when individual members believe they can bank on their word, promise, or verbal or written statements (Gambetta, 1988).

Recognition of the worth of followers: Relationships come together when followers have confidence in the fact that their inner leader values them as people of worth, when they realize that they really matter as individuals (Britton and Stallings, 1986).

Productivity: Relationships form when followers believe their leaders can make them effective. Effectiveness is based on the willingness of participants to place themselves in the inner leader's hands, to rely on the leader for some or all of their individual success.

Problem solving: Followers relate to the inner leader when that leader is seen as an effective problem-solver. Only in this circumstance will followers voluntarily allow their leader (or anyone else) to have significance influence on decisions affecting their work life.

Assigning meaning: As inner leaders assign meaning to people, ideas, words, events, or the work community itself, they can develop relationships with others who also seek that meaning.

Free and open information flow: Effective relationships require bilateral transmission of information and understanding. Free-flowing information systems permit reciprocal influence, encourage self-control, and avoid abuse of the vulnerability of members.

Enabling: Followers join their leaders in work relationships when they are given power, authority, and responsibility enough to function independently within the constraints of the work community's vision and values. When the relationships inner leaders create with their followers encourage creativity, intelligence, willingness, and drive, followers will join together in the common work.

Collaboration: As inner leaders develop organizational structures and endeavor to align followers with tasks using commonly agreed-upon goals, mutual interaction, common language, and symbols, joint problem-solving and shared decision-making relationships form.

Contribution: Followers want to make a contribution to worthwhile activity. They will join in relationships when their inner leaders encourage them to work in ways that allow them to make a strong contribution to the work community's tasks and to themselves.

Developing Trust Relationships

Mutual interactive trust is a critical element of any effective work relationship between inner leaders and those led. Handy (1976) says to trust is to take a chance on the other person. Trust increases the truster's vulnerability while simultaneously increasing the strength of the relationship. Rogers (1964) asserted that leaders can causally link trust to increased originality and emotional stability in their relationships with people. Trust is cyclical. The more leaders trust their followers, the more trusting the relationship becomes. And, alternatively, the more they distrust others, the more distrust is present in the relationship.

While the advantages appear to be numerous, developing a trusting relationship requires maturity and perseverance. It also takes strength. An inner leader cannot demand trust of another. Trust must be earned, developed. Trust is a gift given freely by coworkers because it is based in their confidence in and respect for the leader.

Relationships Obligate Both Parties

Joining in a relationship with followers asks leaders to accept an obligation to the followers, as well as to expect followers to obligate themselves to them. The sense of obligation members of a relationship feel is the foundation of successful relationships. While work-community theory assumes, but largely ignores, the idea of interpersonal relationships, nevertheless it is integral to leader–follower interactivity. Typically, asking followers to be obligated to their leaders and to the in-place structural and process systems is understood and accepted. Less clear, but equally powerful, is the obligation inner leaders assume merely through the act of accepting leadership responsibilities.

DISCUSSION ISSUES AND QUESTIONS

Issues

1. Inner leaders work in relationships built around some common interest directed by the leader.
2. The relationship is composed of a leader and a follower reiterated for each member of the leader's work community.
3. The relationship is the primary environment within which inner leadership takes place.
4. Small group theory helps inner leaders understand the relationship context within which their leadership takes place.
5. Inner leaders build relationships to gain the support they need from their constituents to prepare them for long-term success.
6. Stakeholders who have evidence that affirms that the work community views its relationship with them as long term and responsive to their evolving needs develop greater loyalty and may be willing to provide support during periods of economic, social, or environmental adjustment.
7. Understanding the needs of both parties in the leader–follower relationship is essential to success.

8. Implicit in the leader–follower relationship is the idea of trust. Mutual interactive trust is vital to any work-community action. Workers must trust their leaders.

9. Affiliating with their coworkers in relationships engages inner leaders in more than system, structure, and strategy formation and involves them also in shaping the social, emotional, and spiritual dimensions of interpersonal work alliances.

10. Strong interpersonal relationships increase mutual trust, strengthen competence, enhance self-confidence, and reduce the expenditure of negative energy on protecting self.

11. Relationships are based on more than confidence; they follow unquestioned belief in and reliance on the inner leader based on evidence or experience.

12. It is only through direct interaction with the leader's values that followers can develop the deep conviction about the leader or about his or her basic worth necessary to form an intimate relationship.

13. Relationships mature as experience proves the essential truth of the follower's initial perceptions about joining in the relationship. The reverse diminishes it.

14. Joining in relationship with the inner leader must be voluntary, noncompulsory, a free-will choice.

15. Relationships come together when followers have confidence in the fact that their inner leader values them as people of worth, when they realize that they really matter as individuals.

16. When inner leaders assign meaning to people, ideas, words, events, or the work community itself, they can develop relationships with others who also seek that meaning.

17. Effective relationships require bilateral transmission of information and understanding. Free-flowing information systems permit reciprocal influence, encourage self-control, and avoid abuse of the vulnerability of members.

18. Joining in a relationships with followers asks leaders to accept an obligation to their followers, as well as to expect followers to obligate themselves to them.

Questions

1. Do I regularly take time to assess the relationships that exist in my office?

2. Do I recognize the natural coalitions that exist in my work community? Do I use them to my advantage?

3. Do I invest the time to develop professional-quality face-to-face and other relationships with my coworkers?

4. Have I developed enough people skills to effectively relate with others?

5. Do I really grasp the power of trust to keep relationships and work communities together?

6. Do I take the time to watch the processes, interactions, and relationships in the office?

7. Do I encourage work community, inspire cooperation, mentor, and otherwise shape member behavior to agreed-upon goals often via one-on-one relationships?

8. Do relationships have a place in measuring my work community's performance?

9. Am I able to diagnose relationships?

RELATIONSHIPS LEARNING ACTIVITIES

Activity 1: Worthiness of Occupations Worksheet

Instructions. Followers must trust the leader before they will be willing to enter a relationship with them.

1. Below is a list of fifteen occupations. Your task is to rank these occupations in the order of their trustworthiness.

2. Place a number 1 by the occupation you think is ranked as the most trusted, place a number 2 by the second most trusted occupation, and so forth through the number 15, which is your estimate of the least trusted of the fifteen occupations.

3. Place your ranking in the left hand column labeled "Your Ranking."

Your Ranking	Consensus Ranking by Your Work Community	
_____	_____	Executives in large corporations
_____	_____	College professors
_____	_____	U.S. Army generals
_____	_____	Clergymen
_____	_____	Used car salesmen
_____	_____	Physicians
_____	_____	Labor union officials
_____	_____	Lawyers
_____	_____	Auto repairmen
_____	_____	Law enforcement officials

_____	_____	Judges
_____	_____	Politicians
_____	_____	TV or appliance repairmen
_____	_____	Psychologists
_____	_____	TV news reporters

3. Now rank these fifteen occupations as you think the members of your work community would rank them.

4. Place this ranking in the second column labeled "Consensus Ranking by Your Work Community."

5. Compare the two rankings.

   About which occupations are you in most agreement with your work colleagues?

   About which occupations are you in most disagreement?

   What, if any, are the implications of these similarities and differences?

   Does your analysis of this questionnaire say anything about the ease inner leaders may have in building relationships in this work community? Explain.

Activity 2: Maintaining a Relationship Focus

Instructions. If information is the lifeblood of organizations, then the arteries and veins through which the information flows are relationships. The new sciences teach us that objects are known only as they relate to others. Inner leaders focus on relationships in all aspects of work-community life because the work community differs from a mere collection of individuals in that members have an influence on each other (Goldstein, 1961). Participation with, inclusion of, and respect for people become a natural part of inner leadership. Indeed people hunger for that kind of community.

Discussion Issues

1. Your coworkers are the "parts" of your work community, and your relationships with these people are the essential building blocks of a flexible and sustainable team? How do you operationalize this fact in your interactions with individual followers?

2. Do you realize that your vision alone has little value as a descriptor of your work community and that it is the members of the work community that have values and it is they who connect with your vision? How does this realization translate into your specific actions in relations with your followers in assignments of work to individuals? Planning? Program evaluation?

3. All systems are composed of elements that relate in meaningful ways to each other in unique, nonlinear ways. This demands that your leadership focus on developing interpersonal trust and a concern for the "whole-souls" of the people you lead. Do you focus as much time on developing intimate relationships with them that emphasize shared meanings about key work-community values, objectives, and methods as you do assigning work to your coworkers? Be specific in identifying actions you take to build rapport with your followers around task or meaningful relationships.

Activity 3: Building Your Network of Relationships

Instructions. Read carefully the following short statement:

When we build a new relationship, we cannot predict or control exactly what will happen. Yet when we encourage large numbers of new relationships, we know that the flow of information across the organization increases dramatically and doesn't necessarily adhere to departmental or functional boundaries. Encouraging new relationships is fostering and using chaos in the most positive sense.

In traditional organizations, information is often closely guarded—perhaps because managers feel that sharing this information would be dangerous or because they do not want to distract employees from their work or even because access to information is seen as a source of power. But this attitude is counterproductive at a time when flexibility, adaptability, and the ability to rapidly implement new ideas are all essential to success. Several analysts have noted that most successful inner leaders spend 80 to 90 percent of their time out of their offices, talking to all sorts of people in the work community. These successful leaders understand well the value of a wide network of relationships, even though there is no guarantee that any one specific relationship will be useful.

When you build relationships in this way, you are not just getting to know individuals; you are also getting to know the work community itself. You are learning about different perspectives, finding out about events and trends. You are constantly monitoring what is happening and how things are working. This informal stream of information is critical to leadership in the middle of the corporation.

The way you network will depend on your personality and how you function in your role as an inner leader. You may stop by people's workstations or invite them to your home for dinner. The key is that you are out networking in the work community.

1. Take a position either in opposition to the ideas expressed here or in support if it.
2. Develop an argument supporting your position using materials from this chapter, your experience, and library references.
3. Prepare a short essay elaborating on your argument and illustrating them from your work experience.

CHAPTER 6

Technique 3: Learning to Help Followers

Preparation to lead the next generation of workers will require current and would-be middle-level leaders to know their followers as well as they know themselves (Covey, 1997) so they can help followers integrate complex work-related ideas and programs. These leaders must be able to relate individually with workers, peers, clients, and citizens in close, intimate helping contacts. They must learn to be knowledgeable in the complexities of an increasingly global work world and with multicultural coworkers. They must learn to become comfortable with power, its use and acquisition. And, they must actively take steps to pursue training and gain experience in these areas to facilitate change in themselves and their followers and in joint programs and systems. Leaders' personal values and the actions taken in response to them constitute leadership, so they must get in touch with their core values and philosophical orientation to work life. Effectiveness in maturing these and other techniques affects the success of visions set, results obtained, and leadership itself.

LEARNING TO DEVELOP FOLLOWERS

Inner leadership is a process of close interaction between the leader and each coworker reiterated for each leader–follower relationship. The purpose of this interaction is to help coworkers—to change them, enhance them, and inspire them to fuller, more complete use of their unique talents in doing the leader's work. It is a teaching and development task. The leader's words and actions combine to influence all stakeholders to desired performance by making full use of the abilities, interests, and capacities of each. The inner leader's task is to help followers learn to do without him or her. Leadership is instructing others in how to lead themselves (Wildavsky, 1984). Leaders need to prepare themselves for this helping (follower developmental) activity. Some of the dimensions of this helping responsibility are explained in this chapter.

METHODS OF HELPING OTHERS DEVELOP

The inner leader's helping role is like any other helping role. It is a task of providing followers what they need to be successful in their own terms, as well as those of the work community. Several elements of this helping relationship can be identified. Techniques for helping followers develop into their best selves involve all the techniques described in this book. This brief review here of these developing-of-others techniques only previews more detailed and comprehensive skills included in the following chapters.

Frequent association with stakeholders in joint planning and decision making about many or most aspects of the common work is becoming a sine qua non of leadership in today's changed workplace. This is especially true of leaders in the inner realms of the corporation. Inner leaders use new techniques of leadership, the specific elements of which included visioning, counciling others, and teaching. They also ask the leader to learn political negotiation skills to facilitate persuasion of growingly independent followers. These techniques operationalize values implicit in this theory. They define its technique and condition its success. And they determine the nature of leadership in the twenty-first century.

Facilitating Participation

Helping followers do needed work is perhaps the best single method of helping them since participation in the work community developmentally engages members' inner spiritual selves, as well as their physical and mental capacities (Braham, 1999). Inner leaders find ways to tap their coworkers' need to exercise their whole selves and to increase their personal sense of responsibility through involvement. In this way group members come to recognize that their leaders really want and encourage them to make a full contribution of their capacities to the tasks set by the leader (Plas, 1996). Full involvement increases members' sense of responsibility and ownership in the group and its results. It produces an atmosphere that welcomes challenge and encourages innovative input. Such a corporate culture is characterized by active listening and open discussion. It recognizes spirit and emotions as essential and equally needed along with intelligence, creativity, commitment, and expertise.

Participation is a core element in any work community that fosters ideas like core values, creativity, growth, individual maturation, and personal satisfaction. For many followers, participation has come to be almost a right (Plas, 1996). Advocates say work groups that emphasize participation have greater flow of ideas, solutions, and results. Inner leaders expend great energy and resources in building a community of like-minded people focused on common goals and values that celebrate individual and corporate contribution.

Rosenback, Pittman, and Potter (1997) say many followers are generally committed to high performance and building effective relationships with their leaders. They say followers can be divided into (1) those who do what they are told, (2) contributors who are known by the quality of their work, (3) politicians who manipulate their relationships, and (4) partners committed to high performance and effective relationships. Inner leaders help their followers become partners. Helping followers be partners asks these leaders to become experts in assisting coworkers participate to their fullest capacity.

Helping Followers Be Comfortable in Face-to-Face Relationships

The act of leadership takes place in these intimate helping contacts reiterated throughout the work-community hierarchy. Effective inner leaders ensure that their followers are comfortable in these intimate helping relationships. Essentially, the leader's work is done face to face. It is helping individuals in specific, direct, and unique ways. The notion of leadership as a detached, impartial, objective controller of collectives of people is faulty. Inner leadership is personal and intimate. It deals with helping followers to change at their values core as well as in their routine behavior. This helping is seen in many small acts involving the leader and individual followers. A useful way to view inner leadership is as a series of intimate helping contacts.

Helping Followers Sit in Council with the Leader

In preparing to lead others, inner leaders first must search their inner selves and assess their environment to find values that they can share with followers and that will energize both leaders and followers alike. Once accepted, these values link group members into a focused unity, a community. That is, leaders can help followers most through shared adherence to accepted values with work-community members. Accordingly, they "sit in council with," as opposed to "counsel" others. In counseling sessions, leaders direct and control the discussion and the outcomes agreed upon. "Counciling-with" (a coined term), on the other hand, finds the leader and followers in a relationship, with each member mutually able to direct the discussion and determine courses of action taken to attain shared values and agreed-upon outcomes. In doing this, the leader joins in common cause with stakeholders in the conduct of the community's work. The personal skills and abilities needed for this kind of leader activity are unique—they ask the leader to think about and value stakeholders in unique ways and to develop skills that facilitate broad and independent follower actions.

Sitting in council with their followers is a critically important technique inner leaders learn as they help followers become their best selves. This development technique is, simply, making the effort to intimately involve stakeholders in what has been called leadership tasks. Just as leaders must learn to lead using this kind of joint-action approach, so too must followers be taught to accept the special responsibilities associated with joint accountability for the work community's work. The approach asks followers to accept individual responsibility for the key decisions and actions taken by the community. No longer can they just let the leader take the burden alone. It asks leaders to be willing to let go of their "right to decide" and let followers do this traditionally leadership work.

Counciling-with describes a mutually affecting relationship in which both leader and followers engage in joint consultation, deliberation, and advice-giving. The counciling-with relationship puts the leader and follower together on an equal, sharing basis. Both—either—may propose the agenda, present ideas and methods to solve work-community problems, or suggest new or altered program plans. Counciling-with relationships operationalize team concepts and are the mechanism for team leadership.

Counciling-with implies intimate association, close interaction, and mutual respect. It is a demonstration of the leader's respect for individual stakeholders. It is also a specific technique that all followers must master. No longer can they merely seek and accept the leader's counsel about a task at issue. Counseling is telling and advising. It is directive and totalitarian (managerial) in its essence. The leaders' task is to teach followers to counsel them so that decisions can be made in a joint counciling session where both leader and led share decision making more or less equally. As inner leaders council-with their followers, they engage often in interactions where they consider each participant a partner in suggesting items for discussion, arguing for acceptance, and determining decisions. It is a definitional characteristic of inner leadership (Johnson, 1999).

This follower-development technique involves face-to-face contact with a wide variety of stakeholders, as much as possible at their work sites. As inner leaders learn to council-with their followers, they facilitate stakeholder involvement and personal and professional development without which neither followers nor the corporation can fully succeed. Learning themselves and then teaching followers to be comfortable in face-to-face relationships is another technique leaders must teach their followers.

Creating Meaning for Followers

Bennis (1982) and Gaertner and Gaertner (1985) see leader preparation as a kind of meaning making. They call it intention setting. Intention—often translated into a vision—focuses the work community and gives it meaning that ensures accomplishment. Leadership in this connection is a vision-setting activity. Building a vision, communicating that vision, and then acting on it are the benchmarks of inner leadership. They also assume creation and implementation of programs reflective of that vision (Barbour and Sipel, 1986). As leaders help followers understand the underlying meaning behind their common work, the work community and its members are assured of continuity and success.

Visioning is the leader task of focusing stakeholder attention on what is important. Visions come out of the personality and experience of the leader. Visioning is a personal aspect of leadership that sets the leader and his or her organization apart from any other leader or work community. Setting the vision, ensuring broad-based understanding, and living the vision in all work done is the hallmark of the values model of leadership.

Teaching Followers

Teaching followers is a fundamental leadership helping technique. It places prime responsibility on the leader for follower success. The leader becomes a teacher and coach of individual followers with the goal of changing them in their essential selves. This technique of helping others by educating or training them places emphasis on the role of the leader, not as goal-setter or controller but as instructor of others. Leaders need to teach new values, new skills followers need to use on the job, and the priority followers need to give to common tasks. This leader-as-teacher role permeates all that the leader does and all relationships entered into.

Teaching Followers the Politics of Work

The sense of the discussion in the literature on leader skills is that leadership is a problem of ensuring coordinated activity. It depends more on the leader's capacity to perceive the true nature of a situation, of the people, and of the communities of interest than it does his or her task expertise. Inner leaders learn to select the appropriate circumstances in which to introduce change. They are politically sensitive experts in office politics.

Inner leadership is a political, more than a technical, role. It concerns people, feelings, and relationships. Skill in creating and using formal relationships is less important than skill in diagnosis of the political surround. Data from the study of inner leadership in Virginia (Fairholm, 1991) confirm the applied character of leadership. It is immediate, intimate, and action oriented. It confirms that these political and socioanalytic skills will be valued more in this century than they were in the last one.

In the inner levels of corporate action, leaders accept the need to define the action situation, assess strengths of participants, and form them into a workable whole. The inner leader needs to be able to sense the nuances in relationships. He or she must be able to act to focus work community resources at the right time. These are political skills. Technical competence is not as important to successful inner leadership as are these political skills. Many of the skills of follower development are political skills, such as skill in negotiating support, developing coalitions, and engineering acceptance. An ability to assess the work situation along these lines is one of the critical skills both leader and follower must master. Inner leaders must also be expert in teaching organizational power politics to stakeholders (Fairholm, 1993).

Building Follower Confidence

Confident people are dependable, deserving of their colleagues' confidence. They are predictable and stable. Followers will follow their leaders only as they prove they can be confided in. Interactive self-confidence is the basis for the quality of leader–follower relationships, perhaps the most important of all the challenges inner leaders face. Their leadership is keyed to the confidence they inspire in their followers. Followers must trust their leaders before they will follow them. Such relationships are empowering to both the leader and follower (Bennis, 1982). Demonstrating confidence is motivating, invigorating, and exciting. Gaining the maximum out of stakeholders only happens when they have confidence in their relationship with their leader. Securing that situation is part of the inner leader's task of helping followers.

Helping Followers Achieve Emotional Maturity

Bennis and Nanus (1985) describe leaders and followers in terms of maturity, that is, people with emotional wisdom. This maturity manifests itself in behaviors that accept people for who they are and try to approach people or problems in terms of the present (not the past). Emotionally mature leaders treat followers as adults even if risk is involved. Adults need scope, responsibility, and independence. They can also do without constant approval. Past theory and practice don't describe this kind of leadership. Inner leaders are focused on broad-gauged concern for the people, as well as the programs led. They prioritize preparing people to be self-governing (Kulwiec, 2001).

A Final Point

Inner leadership is a balance between (1) ambition (power, fortune, profits), (2) competence (expertise, knowledge, training), and (3) conscience (ethics, values, ideals). The best way to identify and nurture these capacities is through experience in work-community settings. They are not individual, thoughtful skills but an active orientation toward leading. The individual matures them in the arena of work-community interaction.

DISCUSSION ISSUES AND QUESTIONS

Issues

1. Preparation to lead the next generation of workers will require middle-level leaders to know their followers as well as they know themselves.

2. Inner leadership is a process of close interaction between the leader and each coworker. The purpose of this interaction is to help coworkers change—to enhance them and inspire them to fuller, more complete use of their unique talents in doing the leader's work.

3. The inner leader's task is to teach stakeholders to do without him or her, to lead themselves.

4. Inner leaders find ways to tap their coworkers' need to exercise their whole spiritual selves and to increase their personal sense of responsibility through involvement.

5. Participation is a core element in any work community that fosters ideas like spiritual values, creativity, growth, individual maturation, and satisfaction. For many followers, participation has come to be almost a right.

6. Inner leaders, like all other committed employees, strive to build successful relationships with their bosses and stakeholders.

7. Inner leaders help their followers become partners, which asks leaders to become expert in helping coworkers participate to their fullest capacity.

8. Inner leaders "sit in council with," as opposed to "counsel" others. Counciling-with implies intimate association, close interaction, and mutual respect.

9. Inner leadership involves face-to-face contact with a wide variety of stakeholders, as much as possible at their work sites.

10. Leaders teach followers the politics of work.

11. Leaders build trusting relationships which are empowering to both leaders and followers.

12. Leaders create meaning for followers.

13. Leaders help followers achieve emotional maturity.

14. Visioning is the leader task of focusing stakeholder attention on what is important.

15. The inner leader is a teacher of his or her followers with the goal of helping them improve their essential selves.

16. Inner leadership is more a political role than a technical one. It concerns people, feelings, and relationships. Skill in creating and using formal relationships is less important than skill in diagnosis of the political surround.

QUESTIONS

1. Describe the elements of helping leadership.

2. Assess the cultural constraints on the idea that leaders need to be followers at some times in their work in your work community. What are the major blocks to you being a follower as well as a leader?

3. What are the advantages and disadvantages of sitting in council with your followers? What strengths and weaknesses do your followers now have that would facilitate counciling-with them?

4. Describe as many ways as you can that you (a leader in the middle) teach your followers on a day-to-day basis. In what other areas do you need to emphasize your teacher role?

5. Provide examples of situations where your main task was one of making meaning for your followers. What specifically did you do? What else could you have done?

6. What is the impact on work-community cohesiveness if a given inner leader spends too much time as a follower rather than a leader?

LEARNING ACTIVITIES TO DEVELOP FOLLOWERS

Learning to be an inner leader engages the individual leader in specific behaviors. The following may be useful to both individual leaders and to leader trainers to gain experience and comfort in developing their followers.

Activity 1: Credibility Scale

Instructions. One of the key elements of inner leadership is the leader's credibility with his or her coworkers. Having credibility allows coworkers to trust the leader enough to undertake necessary actions with sincerity. Following are some elements of credibility.

Rate yourself on each of the items using the following scale:

1	2	3	4
Never	Occasionally	Often	Always

_____ 1. I state my position clearly.

_____ 2. My coworkers and/or subordinates always know where I stand.

_____ 3. I listen to other people's opinions carefully and respectfully.

_____ 4. I accept disagreement from my coworkers.

_____ 5. I try to integrate my point of view with that of others.

_____ 6. I encourage and practice constructive feedback.

_____ 7. I encourage and practice cooperation.

_____ 8. I build consensus out of differing views.

_____ 9. I help my coworkers develop needed skills.

_____ 10. I provide frequent positive feedback and encouragement to stakeholders.

_____ 11. I hold myself and others accountable for actions.

_____ 12. I practice what I preach.

Total: _____

Scoring key: Add up your rating for all twelve items. The maximum score is 48. A higher score indicates demonstrations of behaviors that build credibility.

Are there any items for which you have a low score? If yes, those are areas that you need to target in order to build your credibility. List items with a low score. What can you do about them? Focus on clear and specific behaviors. Develop short-term and long-term goals. When will you know that you have improved? How will you measure yourself?

Activity 2: Are You a Team Leader?

Instructions. Inner leaders build work communities and engage members in working successfully in these communities. This instrument will help you determine your present capacity to lead such communities.

Rate yourself on each of the following items using the scale provided here:

1	2	3	4	5
Strongly disagree	Somewhat disagree	Neither agree nor disagree	Somewhat agree	Strongly agree

_____ 1. I enjoy helping others get their jobs done.

_____ 2. Leading others is a full-time job in and of itself.

_____ 3. I am good at negotiating for needed resources.

_____ 4. People often come to me to help them with interpersonal conflicts.

_____ 5. I tend to be uncomfortable when I am not fully involved in the task that my work community is doing.

_____ 6. It is hard for me to provide people with positive feedback.

_____ 7. I understand organizational politics well.

_____ 8. I get nervous when I do not have expertise at a task that my work community is performing.

_____ 9. An effective inner leader needs to have full involvement with his or her team.

_____ 10. I am skilled at goal setting.

Total: ____

Scoring key: Reverse score items 2, 5, 6, 8, and 9 (1 = 5, 5 = 1). Add your score on all items. Maximum possible score is 50. The higher the score, the more work-community leadership skills you have.

What are the implications for you of your score?

Compare your score with that of others. What does your relative ranking in the work community tell you about yourself?

CHAPTER 7

Technique 4: Fostering Follower Change and Transformation

Successful inner leaders have mastered the techniques of undertaking planned actions that produce appropriate responses on the part of their followers and in their personal sense of themselves. That is, inner leaders are follower change agents. Fostering change is getting people to sacrifice to behave as the leader desires when they are under no obligation to do so. It is a persuasive task, developmental, growth producing, and other-directed. It is more a teaching and counseling technique than it is a directive role. It is a service role, one that involves commitment and sacrifice by both leader and follower. And the results are change in the essential character of the inner leader, each member of his or her work team, and the larger communities within which they both work and live.

DEFINING TRANSFORMING LEADERSHIP

Fostering change and transformation in the work community goes beyond shared responsibility and connotes a relationship protective of the purposes, methods, and resources of the group. Inner leaders may, on occasion, support individuals in taking innovative activities that risk community resources. Most often, their role is to preserve and protect the integrity of the group while they take action to develop it into something they think is better—for the group and for themselves.

Thus, much of inner leadership is an influence process aimed at transforming—or changing the nature and character of—coworkers, community structure, and operating systems. Inner leaders inspire and preside over an encompassing change process that impacts them personally, as well as individual stakeholders and the work community itself. Transforming inner leaders try to advance the needs of their followers so that they align with their own goals and aims. In doing this they pay attention to the individual by understanding and sharing in the realization of followers' developmental needs. Influencing others to change involves trusting them to do their best (McMillen, 1993).

In the process of leading on the basis of their intimate values, inner leaders create a new scale of meaning within which followers can see their lives in terms of the work community. They engage the heart (Conger, 1994; Kouzes and Posner, 1987) of each community member. The leader's role is to transform the basic focus of the lives of followers and of their institution in ways that enhance both. Inner leaders have always done this, but the profession has only recently recognized transformation as a "new" role for them. In this transforming role, inner leaders take an active part in helping followers change to become their best selves. Part of that transformation is helping to change followers into leaders and transforming the firm into a different social institution.

This transformation technique includes ideas of both creativity and innovation. Inner leaders, however, most often foster innovation among work-community members because any follower can innovate, while only a select few are naturally creative. Inner leaders prioritize innovation and give everyone in the community space to innovate. They encourage work-product champions (Peters and Austin, 1985), people who take personal ownership of a specific service program or product line and shepherd it through to completion.

The innovation change technique sees the inner leader's role as seeking personal transformation as well as changing followers (and the institution) to achieve the shared vision. This is a process of converting both into something more than they previously were. Innovation is worthwhile because innovative people and work communities are especially apt at responding to change in their environments. Innovation, for inner leaders, defines true leadership. Inner leaders use innovation to try to change the work community to fit the world. Managers, on the other hand, often try to change the world to match the work community.

Understanding the Process of Change

Change theory dates from the pioneering work of Kirt Lewin (1994) in the first decades of the twentieth century. He proposed a simple, four-step change process:

1. Create dissatisfaction; sensitize the work community to the need for change
2. Unfreeze the status quo
3. Movement
4. Refreeze at the new, higher level of performance

Others have embellished this model, but its intrinsic logic is compelling and no one has substantially improved upon this construct. They have only added detail to one or another of the basic processes of change. Lewin's model is a simple, yet useful, method of assessing a change plan to determine its chances for success. This uncomplicated change model provides leaders with insight about when and how to begin a change event. It also suggests the forces in any situation that may impact on the change or desired results from that change.

METHODS OF PRACTICING TRANSFORMING LEADERSHIP

Leading change involves leaders in initiating change and accepting changes made by others that foster social, psychological, spiritual, or technological improvements, competitiveness, and innovation in coworkers and or programs. The goal in each case is to change peoples lives at the core. From earliest recorded history, mankind has responded to the human need all persons have to be concerned for, and a contributing part of, the development and growth of their fellows. Service to others is the primary mechanism inner leaders use to instill transformational change ideals in individual work-community members. Selfless concern for others is the mark of the mature person. It is the prime measure of success for the inner leader.

Inner leaders' techniques of personal and follower change and transformation revolve around two orientations. First, inner leaders see the workplace as an authentic community designed to encourage growth in both leaders and followers. The focus of much of the leader's work and the end product of work-community activity is to provide members an expanding array of experiences in doing cooperative, productive work, work that is better today than it was yesterday. Inner leaders develop and implement programs designed to apply and interpret productivity goals in the light of the work communities' current assignments, problems, and situations.

Second, inner leaders see the work community as a prime environment within which the members can gain experience in creativity, innovation, and independent vision-directed leadership action. These work communities are the most effective places to apply ideals of interpersonal relations as jointly leader and led sit in council with each other to plan, organize, and carry out needed work. Here the leader can find opportunities to model desired standards and behavior, as well as find opportunities to let others practice similar leadership conducted under his or her watchful care.

Transforming Attitudes

Inner leaders have cultivated the change attitudes described in the following sections.

Seeing All Change as People Change

The traditional wisdom is that to change people or social institutions we must change the structure of human relationships or of common work practices. Past change models presuppose that altering the work-community structure or instituting new work processes and systems will automatically change members to conform. This method is used in all sectors of society—business, government, and politics. People assume that introduction of new programs, new people in charge, automation, new hardware, or other innovations will effect a change in the quality of life and the standard of living of a society and the productivity or satisfaction of the workers in a given work community. So leaders impose this kind of external physical change and then manage, control, and direct followers to do what the new, altered system requires of them.

The facts of work-community change suggest something quite the opposite. Thoughtful analysis of the major changes in individual, work community, and social life highlights the fact that another, more effective change strategy is, in fact, in play in almost all change situations. To change the work culture, leaders must first change the individual workers. When workers change, the change brings about alteration in the collective circumstances of the work community.

The work environment changes most usefully as people change their values, their beliefs, their assumptions, and their expectations. It is not laws, rules, electronic equipment, or even leadership expertise that changes society. It is the result of many individual workers who voluntarily *choose* to accept a new value, a new behavior (Bjerke, 1999), or a new attitude that changes work environments. The only authentic, lasting change occurs when individuals independently change themselves. As workers change, their formal structures and institutions will follow.

The challenge for inner leaders is to foster this change and to direct it through articulation and maintenance of common core values acceptable to and internalized by work-community members who are helped to produce desired results. Inner leaders know that the fastest, most effective, and longest-lasting way to get institutional change is to deal frontally with the people to get them to accept new community values and expectations. Of course, changing the circumstances can eventually change people's minds and hearts. But this is a secondary strategy that ignores values and attitudes in favor of the artifacts of the work culture, not its essence.

Prioritizing Innovation

Fixed production practices without adaptation to new circumstances lead to a reverence for form without regard to content. Given the modern work community, the need is for innovative solutions to both continuing and new programs and services. Innovation is intrinsically different from creativity. It defines the actions of putting known ideas to work in new ways. Innovation has two aspects: (1) newness in the sense that something has never been done before by this group or work community, and (2) newness in that something has never been done before by anyone.

Creativity on the other hand, is a new idea-formulation out of known facts. A creative achievement arises when a person attempts to resolve a tension between intuition and discipline—between impulse and caution. Creativity comes from an internal negotiation between what intuitively seems to be correct and what the constraining forces of technique, tradition, and materials may require. Of course, creative ideas and insights are important, but there are many fine ideas that are easier to find and equally valuable to the inner leader and the work community in helping people and programs improve.

Transforming Skills

Inner leaders have also honed the change skills reviewed here.

Encouraging Change

Inner leaders keep their relationships with followers free of judgment and evaluation. This characteristic permits workers to recognize that the locus of responsibility lies within themselves, not outside, in the work community, with other people, or with an indeterminate "them." Only then can followers be really free to independently change to make more full use of their inner capacities. Leading change is essentially a task of helping individuals change themselves. Inner leaders initiate helping contacts, the goal of which is for the leader to help each follower modify behaviors that both see and recognize as needing change.

This kind of transformation in people happens when leaders understand that the purpose of change is to help followers to become more whole—complete. It results when leaders understand that, by and large, followers want to use that personal wholeness to aid themselves in their work. Most followers are motivated not by outward trappings, bonuses, or challenges to greatness as a company. Rather, they—all people—make personal change as they see in that changed behavior the chance of making meaningful contribution to others through their work and in the process grow themselves.

Teaching Followers

A prime focus of this transformational leadership technique is teaching others. The objective of the teaching is to produce leaders from followers who are capable of governing themselves in terms of mutually agreed-upon vision-directed activities. Some teaching behavior is done as the leader models desired follower behavior in his relationships with them. Other behavior, such as coaching, inspiration, and setting high-quality service priorities, employs more traditional teaching and training methods. The most evident characteristic of this follower-changing leadership technique is that inner leaders serve as almost private instructors for their followers. A second powerful implication of these techniques is that leaders also build a learning culture that encourages desired performance in stakeholders. This learning culture is also a teaching tool. It facilitates realization of the leader's values-based ideas and methods and excludes, as far as is possible, other possible follower actions.

Helping followers grow and change places a prime responsibility on the leader for ensuring that followers are successful. The leader's goal becomes changing them in their core selves. Helping followers change places emphasis on the role of the leader, not as goal-setter or controller but as a guide to followers to help them make their most useful contribution to work-community success. Inner leaders teach new values and skills followers need to use on the job and alternative priorities followers need to honor to attain the work-community's vision. This leadership teaching role imbues all that the leader does and all relationships entered into. Simply put, this model asks the leader to learn to be a teacher.

Leading Change

Inner leaders who do not keep up to date about the change going on in their work community will find themselves in the backwater of corporate life and estranged from their coworkers, for by definition they are key participants in any work-community change process. They are both agents of change and authority figures. Successful inner leaders are fully involved in the change process, sometimes as direct participants and other times as change catalysts facilitating growth in members and change in the work community. They have legitimate roles to play in every change event. The leader authenticates what the work community does and how it does it. As others in the work community desire to accomplish changes, they look to the inner leader they volunteer to follow to ratify their plans, or they see a need to persuade the leader to accept their ideas. The inner leader's concurrence is implicitly understood to be necessary before a change can be implemented.

Changing Followers' Spiritual Selves

The purpose of personal change and transformation techniques is to help followers change their inner, spiritual selves so they can behave toward others in more authentically helpful ways. Leaders can do much to create a situation where concern for followers' freedom of action is a recognized part of any work-situation values system. Inner leaders provide opportunities for service to those with whom they work—opportunities as personally fulfilling to their followers as the responsibility to seek growth-producing opportunities for themselves. As followers come to understand the lessons of followership and determine for themselves in what actions and which situations they grow most, their leaders also mature. This kind of reciprocal atmosphere of personal concern can exist in every interpersonal contact. Some specific things leaders can do to make the results of their service more satisfying for the follower include the following:

1. Inner leaders learn something of the needs for personal and spiritual development of individual followers. They can then assign followers to tasks and duties that will bring out their latent qualities and talents.

2. Inner leaders are alert to the problems resulting from too-frequent changes in follower assignments. Followers need time to learn their duties fully and feel a sense of accomplishment before moving on to other tasks.

3. Inner leaders discuss openly those aspects of a follower's personal development potential that may result from the work assigned. This can be a regular part of the agenda for individual performance evaluation interviews with followers or be the subject of special group or individual meetings.

4. Inner leaders recognize that many of the interpersonal contacts followers have with stakeholders are, or can become, training experiences helping them relate better to their own work. As leaders give their followers tasks that let them practice behaviors and skills that need development as part of their work-community assignment, the followers gain valuable experience that will aid them in their developing job competence. In doing this, as the inner leader considers followers' core needs in assigning tasks to them, followers can gain needed experience, satisfaction, and confidence in their own maturing capacity.

5. Inner leaders assign followers to work with others—other work-community members, customers, or clients—based on similar or complementary interests. Matching personality types will increase the learning potential of both individuals.

Fostering Innovation

Inner leaders provide the resources needed to effect change. Innovative work communities are characterized by the presence of "resource slack." (The term "resource slack" means the presence in the work community of surplus assets.) These surpluses might be in the form of flexible leadership styles or available staff time that can be directed to other than just routine work. They might also mean the availability of money or other resources to apply to developing new ideas for service delivery or other goals. Where there is this kind of surplus, the risk of trying something new is reduced. Inner leaders have learned to provide time and resources to innovation to an essential activity without depriving other programs of needed assets.

The relationship between innovation and the presence of resource slack is crucial to change and cannot be overemphasized. This situation is a different idea from resource allocation that is traditionally the case. Most often leaders strive for economical use of resources They try to eliminate waste and return unused resources. But the innovative work community needs just that sort of "duplication and surplus" to be innovative.

Inner leaders need not be personally innovative—although that characteristic can be an advantage. However, they must be able to recognize innovative people and be willing to underwrite their activity if the work community is to prosper. Ideas are of no value whatever if they are not used and capitalized upon. There are several things inner leaders can do to encourage innovation in their follower core. For example, they make an effort to find people with open, inquisitive minds and stimulate them by their attitude and material support. They encourage followers to think about and propose alternative ways to meet the program goals of the work community.

In addition, inner-level leaders expend effort to keep the work community's communications channels open and provide as much information as possible to all followers, since determining beforehand who of the follower core is innovative is impossible. Effective inner leaders also ask questions of followers and continuously elicit their opinions and suggestions as to ways to do their job—or the job of anyone else—better. And they teach their followers how to develop their ideas and how to present them in ways that will demonstrate the idea in its most useful light. Many people are cautious about exposing their ideas openly. They fear ridicule and shy away from the potential of being found wrong, or "interfering" by their colleagues.

The leader's work in encouraging techniques of innovation is to help followers feel free to discuss alternatives in a nonthreatening forum. There are many forces in play that restrict innovation: fear, uncertainty (Carson, 2001), tradition, possessive feelings of "my turf," and the general conservative mindset present in many work communities. Inner leaders take an active, encouraging role in soliciting and promoting follower innovation as they seek to overcome built-in inertia to change.

DISCUSSION ISSUES AND QUESTIONS

Issues

1. Inner leaders know that all change is really changing people and intentionally engage in changing other persons' lives.

2. Change is a natural principle of life that includes physical, intellectual, spiritual, and behavioral change.

3. Leadership is an influence process aimed at transforming or changing the nature and character of people, structure, and system.

4. The process of change is to create dissatisfaction, unfreeze the status quo, make a change, and refreeze at the new, higher level of performance.

5. The evolving work community needs not so much creativity as it needs innovation, the actions of putting known ideas to work in new ways.

6. Dealing with change involves leaders in initiating change and accepting changes made by others that foster social, psychological, spiritual, and technological improvements.

7. Inner leaders have a legitimate role to play in every change event. Their task is to get followers to want to change themselves.

8. Innovative work communities are characterized by the presence of "resource slack," the presence in the work community of surplus assets.

Questions

1. Do I recognize that change is a natural and inevitable characteristic of work communities?

2. How often do I link the changes the office is going through now with the changes it will have to face in the future?

3. Do I encourage innovation as a work-community strategy? Or do I face change reluctantly and hesitantly?

4. Have I trained my coworkers to embrace the uncertainty of change?

5. Do I have the skills to implement planned change efforts in my workplace?

6. Do I recognize that work-community change is different from personal transitions?

7. How have I helped people through their transitions? Do I plan for the people side of change as I plan work systems change?

8. Do I realize that leading people through change takes as much or more time than managing work-community change processes?

TRANSFORMING LEADERSHIP LEARNING ACTIVITIES

Learning to be an inner leader engages the leader in specific behaviors. The following may be useful to both leaders and to leader trainers to gain experience and familiarity in learning how to change others.

Activity 1: The Group Change Process (from Kirt Lewin, 1994)

Instructions. The traditional model of change can be traced to the work of Kirt Lewin. Working in the 1930s, Lewin and his students developed a generic change model suitable to explain change and predict participant behavior in most interpersonal situations. An expanded model of this change process includes the following steps:

Contemporary Model for the Leadership of Change
1. Identify Forces for Change
2. Recognition of the Need for Change
3. Diagnosis of the Problem
4. Identification of Alternative Methods
5. Recognition of Limiting Conditions
6. Selection of One Method
7. Implementation of Program
8. Evaluation of Program

1. Think of a significant change you experienced in the past six months or year.
2. Describe that change using the Lewin model.
3. Analyze that change using the change model by responding to the following questions:

Was the change successful?

Did followers in the client system accept the change? Were they enthusiastic? Or not?

What steps were left out?

What steps did they emphasize?

Did the change agents do anything overt to show that they responded to this important part of change management?

What specific behavior or actions did they make?

Was the client community—the followers asked to change—aware of this step? That is, did the change agents make the reasons for their actions clear to followers?

How would you have improved on the tasks of leading this change event?

List the things you have learned about change that you want to apply to your next change situation.

Activity 2: Change Management

Instructions. Technological developments, restructuring, reorganizations, downsizing, or changes in company policies, procedures, or philosophies all place pressures on work communities to change to stay dynamic. Inner leaders—all professionals—have to face and accept these changes. They must also aid in the change process and help others feel comfortable with the adaptions they need to make. All change resolves itself into a process of changing people—their values, attitudes, knowledge and behaviors. One way to lead people change is to use the following model. The process includes four steps.

1. Write a short personal case study describing a recent change in your recent work experience.

2. Couch your description in terms of the people change model shown in Figure 7.1.

3. Assess your success. How did adherence to this model (even though it might have been blind adherence) affect success?

4. How can you relate any less-than-successful results to failure to effectively follow this model?

Figure 7.1
Model of People Change

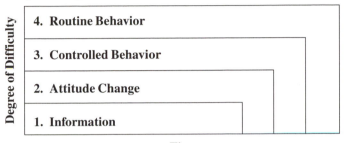

CHAPTER 8

Technique 5:
Learning Followership

Companies go to great lengths to cultivate corporate leaders. They focus on the roles and responsibilities of the leader as a figurehead, spokesperson, or even the emotional heart of the corporation (Bolman and Deal, 1995). Little, if anything, is mentioned about the other half of leadership: followership. Of course, a major part of an inner leader's job is to help followers be self-governing, independent leaders in their own right (Kulwiec, 2001). But success in doing this requires that they also assume the role of follower of the lead of their newly self-governing followers. Neither traditional theory nor leadership development programs typically include instruction in how to be a follower of others' leads.

DEFINING FOLLOWERSHIP

Given the complexity of modern corporate structures, every leader is a follower of someone else even as others follow him or her. Both the professional literature and operational experience attest to this fact. Therefore, being an effective follower is as important professionally as being an effective leader. Hollander (1978) suggests that we must consider followership as one functional part of leadership. But there is another significant element of the idea of leader as follower: making the followers.

Part of leadership is to build other leaders within the work community. Leaders build followers. They are concerned with follower growth. They enlarge their followers, their capacities, knowledge, and skills. They enlarge their expectations: and when followers become expert, the leader assumes a follower role from time to time as the expert guidance of given followers is needed by the work community. The problem is that the conventional wisdom is that followership is not as desirable as leadership. Many leaders accordingly ignore this vital role or, worse, eschew accepting that role.

The relatively minor status of followership accounts for some of this reluctance. Misconceptions about followership are prevalent in our society. Some of this lack of understanding stems from our language (Hughes, Ginnett, and Curphy, 1999). Dictionary definitions focus on the ideas that a follower role is somehow less than other roles. They define followers as "in service" to others, as passive receivers of the ideas of others, or as imitators of someone else. These definitions connote a reactive role rather than a proactive one. In fact, these ideas define only a minor part of followership. Followers often have a strong desire to lead and do so whenever the situation warrants.

Because followers are not often in the spotlight, it is easy to think of them as automatons. This is a mistake (Hughes, Ginnett, and Curphy, 1999). Followers vary tremendously in education and experience. They often command much organizational power, and they often are governed by an internal locus of control (Rotter, 1971). Inspiring them to want to do what the inner leader wants, therefore, becomes a dynamic—constantly changing—leadership task.

In becoming followers of their own followers, leaders assume a proactive role intended to help accomplish needed work-community results. Traditional definitions ignore the fact that every work community is growing and altering continuously. Inner leaders, of course, lead in this transforming process; but so do followers. Leaders understand that the needs of both parties in the leader–follower relationship are essential to success. Leaders can no longer (if they ever could) be content to learn only about their side of the equation. Inner leaders learn leadership partly through experiencing followership first hand (Carson, 2001).

Being a follower is part of all leaders' professional interaction and contributes to work-community success (Kelley, 1992). Followership is not blind obedience (Miller, 1992). Most corporate success comes about because of people who have been willing to follow. This is true of leaders too. Another example from sports helps illustrate this concept. A football team's star runner isn't the key to a powerful running game. Rather, it is dependent on the offensive linemen, whom most people would not think of as team leaders. Yet a distinguishing characteristic of a great running back is his ability to follow his blockers as they lead out in the play.

Similarly, few top leaders can claim to have personally developed the strategic plan for their corporation. Nevertheless, the main elements of this plan that will guide the corporation and its chief leaders into the future are the result of the work of anonymous followers. These behind-the-scenes inner leaders effectively establish the character and purposes of the organization.

They bring about change directly through their research, report writing, and negotiation skills in initially "selling" their part of the master plan to the boss and in subsequent implementation tasks.

By helping their followers gain experience in leading, inner leaders can produce profound and encompassing results in their workers' efforts. Perhaps more than any other single factor, this kind of behavior by inner leaders will help the work community get beyond theory and realize deep, lasting change (Dering, 1998). Too often outside observers attribute corporate success to leaders when, in reality, it is dependent on the technical expertise of others (Barnett, 1996). Good middle-level leaders recognize the importance of subordinating themselves to the expertise of their in-the-middle peers and subordinates. That kind of followership is also good leadership. Both leader and follower roles, therefore, are emphasized by effective inner leaders.

METHODS OF FOLLOWING THE
LEADER'S FOLLOWERS

Successful inner leaders must master two techniques: leadership and followership. Being a good leader also mean that as the situation warrants it or the needs of a follower dictate it, the leader will subordinate himself or herself to a follower. Thus, inner leaders sometimes allow followers to lead out in a given phase of a joint task. Followership places the inner leader in a collaborative partnership with other members of the work community. Subordinating their judgment to their subordinates' is part of the inner leaders' role and assumes that there will be situations when these leaders will lead and times when they will be called upon to follow (Carson, 2001). This is not an abdication of leadership, a passive acceptance of another's lead, but a proactive and often courageous act of leadership. Only when the leader's past actions have created a partnership, when the leader and the follower are united by a common sense of purpose and direction (Carson, 2001), does the leader master followership.

Followership is a fundamental skill that should be a part of any effective leadership development effort. The idea of inner leadership as service suggests that people lead because they choose to serve (follow) others. Being a leader asks us to both serve one another and to serve a higher (work- community-wide) purpose (Senge et al., 1990). Inner leaders have to lead *and* follow or get out of the way.

Mastering Followership Techniques

Learning the techniques of followership is a key part of inner leadership. Good leadership demands of each leader preparation, practice, hard work, and appropriate attitudes. Mastery of those leadership attributes first come as leaders see other leaders act in these ways and then model their leadership after these examples. The people inner leaders choose to model may be friends, teachers, or some one of the great present or historical hero leaders they honor by copying their behavior. Whom the leaders follow and what principles of action they emphasize determine the course of their leadership life and what kind of leaders they become.

Of course, inner leaders need to learn to follow their bosses so they can honestly teach their followers to also follow them. Acceptance of the follower role helps leaders develop the ability to respond willingly and openly to their bosses. As inner leaders accept instruction, they gain greater wisdom through observation and emulation based on acknowledgment of the skills and talents of their bosses. These actions awaken a sense of assurance that the boss is, in fact, worthwhile and someone from whom they can learn.

Good leaders accept the challenge to greatness inherent in the follower role. They are excited by the challenge and willing to subordinate external influences of peers, programs, and prestige in accepting unreservedly the follower's program and leadership as their own. As leaders submit to the authority of coworkers whom they recognize as worthy of emulation, they open themselves and their work community to progress.

The following paragraphs describe some of the attributes, behaviors, and characteristics inner leaders acquire through their followership experiences that prepare them for effective leadership.

As they follow others, inner leaders are able to overcome routine and change their past ways of working and even the nature and character of the work they do. Following the lead of others actually changes them. They become different people as a result of acceptance of the demands of service to others. They are removed from their ordinary pursuits and become leaders and models of the highest potential in leadership.

Follower leaders get personally involved with the programs of their work communities. They immerse themselves in these programs. They become doers of the work, not just overseers of it and in this process learn more about their common work and about themselves.

Inner leaders pick outstanding people to model and follow. In this way they learn intimate details about coworkers and are better assured which coworkers are prepared to practice leadership successfully before they subject themselves to those followers' guidance.

Inner leader followers learn to look beyond the surface reasons to see the basic nature of the situation. They learn the nature of the program or procedure but strive also to see through outward appearances and discern the character and worthiness of their associates and the ideas and practices being promulgated. Then they use this knowledge as a way to help others.

Effective inner leaders explore their own thoughts and attitudes, compare them with those of their followers, and alter their behavior as needed. They do not succumb to the temptation to rationalize.

Inner leaders in their follower role try out ideas and information received from their leaders-in-training to discern their utility in helping the work community succeed. They reject the dross and integrate the good parts to further prepare them for future work-community (and leadership) success.

Following their coworkers' lead causes inner leaders to be more receptive to other people. They learn to treat all coworkers with equal respect and dignity. Contrary to a popular misconception, advancements in the corporation are not always based on office politics (Serven, 2002). Leadership advancement often comes out of demonstrated competence, respect for coworkers' needs, and a desire to more fully serve coworkers and the community vision.

Followers of others learn to listen with understanding. Active listening requires leader-cum-followers to concentrate on both oral (conversational) and emotional (feelings and attitudes) levels in their communications with others (Braham, 1999). Real understanding comes as the individual is able to expand his or her capacities. Only as inner leaders accept other people as equals and come to the relationships with an open mind can they expect to learn and grow (Cashman and Burzynski, 2000).

In follower roles, inner leaders are often in a better position to find out the truth about work issues. And as they apply this truth in their actions, they gain freedom to direct the work community along desired paths. As followers, inner leaders are in a better position to seek advice from all those around them. Truth and wisdom are not always resident just in one sophisticated, experienced worker—even if that worker is the leader. They can be and often are present in almost anyone.

Following others lets inner leaders recognize that just because they have the title of leader does not make them superior to other workers. Followership teaches these leaders to accept the fact that personal maturation comes in direct proportion to one's contribution.

Followership asks inner leaders to ignore much of the personal acclaim that might come as a result of the adoption of their ideas or plans. Followership is an exercise in humility. It challenges leaders to anonymous service. Unselfish service is the mark of the successful follower—and the successful leader in the middle of corporate action.

Followership is not constraining of independent action. Rather it is an opportunity for the inner leader to use his or her experiences, expertise, and personal capacity to actively advance the work community's agenda. Followers typically engage in prospering the work of the work community. And in doing this they do many things on their own initiative, things the putative leader may not have even thought of in first announcing the program and making assignments for its execution.

Being followers helps inner leaders be more conscious of their need for further training, of what they yet need to learn. They know that success in one branch of work community knowledge does not always immediately transfer to success in another.

In follower roles, inner leaders get the chance to view their special qualities and talents—and those of colleagues—as corporate assets and acquire a sense of responsibility toward their proper use. They learn to view these coworker strengths as a trust and to recognize the need to be vigorous in their use. They understand that talents not used, or improperly used, pay off for neither themselves nor their work community. Further, they come to know that life requires consistent effort. An occasional "big push" will not serve their needs or those of their community members.

Being followers lets inner leaders learn to respect others, to not ignore or belittle their fellows. They come to recognize the accomplishments of others and their dependence on the accomplishments of many as the basis for their own success. While what an individual coworker does may be important, it has greatest relevancy in context of the pioneering vision and work of all other work-community members—both present and past.

Followers find it easier—necessary—to practice the common virtues. They recognize that the work community is powerful only when they use their talents in helping others. Inner leaders learn in their follower roles to be considerate, slow to anger, and good tempered. They learn that they can manipulate the principles of human relationships only on these terms. They come to understand that their individual effectiveness depends on their character as they become free from pride, vanity, and arrogance. Then their lives change and they begin to be spiritually minded (Caill, 2000).

Inner leaders learn in their years of following the leads of others to use the qualities of personality and practice described here. It is a part of their preparation for effective leadership and a significant part of practical leadership.

DISCUSSION ISSUES AND QUESTIONS

Issues

1. "The other half of leadership" is followership. Successful leadership requires leaders to sometimes be followers of the lead of members of their work community.

2. Good leaders—great leaders—recognize the importance of subordinating themselves to the expertise of others. That kind of followership is also good leadership.

3. By helping their followers gain experience in leading, inner leaders can produce profound and immediate results in their workers' efforts.

4. Because the conventional wisdom is that followership is not as desirable as leadership, some leaders ignore this vital role—to their detriment.

5. Followers often have a strong desire to lead and do so whenever the situation warrants.

6. Skill in followership requires active participation, including a willingness to offer advice, assistance, input, support, and opposition when appropriate.

7. Every worker is both a leader and a follower.

Questions

1. Am I consistent in all my actions to implement plans in which followers participated in developing?
2. Do I show respect and caring for each follower? Do I take the time to voice my interest in them?
3. Do I engage with my followers in all the techniques of leadership described in this book?
4. Do I form a unified, cohesive work community where the followers are interdependent?
5. Do I foster an attitude of continuous improvement, encourage member motivation, foster initiative, and accept feelings and attitudes as legitimate?
6. Do I communicate the meaning of the ideas I share with followers as well as just the facts?

ACTIVITIES USEFUL TO THE LEADER'S ROLE

Activity 1: What Is Your Followership Type?

Instructions. You can use this self-rating to rate yourself and your organization's leaders. For each of the following items, rate yourself using the following scale (you can also use the items to rate the leaders in your organization):

My ranking _____   Ranking for my organization _____

1	2	3	4
Always	Never	Occasionally	Often

_____ 1. I enjoy working on routine tasks.

_____ 2. I am looking for new ways of doing things

_____ 3. I have trouble delegating tasks to my subordinates.

_____ 4. I like my subordinates to share the same values and beliefs.

_____ 5. Change makes me uncomfortable.

_____ 6. I encourage my subordinates to participate in decision making.

_____ 7. It is hard for me to get things done when there are many contrasting opinions.

_____ 8. I enjoy working on new tasks.

_____ 9. I feel comfortable giving power away.

_____ 10. I consider myself to be a risk taker.

Scoring key: Reverse scores for items 1, 5, 6, 7, and 9 (0 = 3, 1 = 2, 2 = 1, 3 = 0).
Need to Control Score: Add items 1, 2, 5, 8, and 10. Your score will be between 0 and 15.

Total: _____

Need to Be Controlled Score: Add items 3, 4, 6, and 9. Your score will be between 0 and 15.

Total: _____

CHAPTER 9

Technique 6: Taking a Horizon Perspective

Inner leaders spend their time in dealing with new problems and in creative and innovative activity. They are engaged in thinking beyond the day-to-day activities of work accomplishment. They, more than their bosses, are embroiled in thinking about horizon issues. They engage in "problem-finding" more than problem-solving activities. This is very different from managing a precise system with prescribed roles, tasks, and service results. It is equally different from the top leadership tasks of planning and strict plan implementation.

DEFINING THE LEADER'S HORIZON FOCUS

All people pay attention to something. Inner leaders select and consistently pay attention to the tasks and values they want and need. In doing this, they communicate a consistent message to followers, clients, suppliers, and the larger community (Cashman and Burzynski, 2000). Paying attention—focusing self and work-community members—is a major inner leadership technique. This proclivity is a key to defining inner leadership.

Zaleznick (1977) defined future thinking as the capacity to see connections, to draw inferences that aren't obvious, that may also be unprecedented. The dictionary says it is an immaterial mode of seeing or conceiving. Horizon thinking is thinking through the work community's central purpose, redefining it, and establishing it clearly and visibly. Bennis and Nanus (1985) define horizon thinking as a task of creating a mental image of a desirable future. This kind of thinking synthesizes and translates the leader's aspirations into community aspirations. A future focus transcends prescribed or commonly accepted corporate goals—set by the top leader—and substitutes an intimate, focused future in line with the inner leader's values and the values of work community members.

A future time-horizon is more global in scope and more encompassing than traditional futures thinking. Inner leaders focus on these kinds of "horizon problems." Since the future is not and cannot ever be precisely defined, their work is becoming largely nonprogrammed. These tasks involve integrating disparate ideas and issues in and about their work communities. As the work world changes, middle-level leaders find they spend less time on day-to-day problem solving and more on simulation of a future no one has experienced yet.

Inner leaders create a future for their work community. In continually communicating that future vision, they focus follower attention and energies on attaining this future state of being. Inner leaders develop in their followers a sense of continuity and significance in order to see the present in the past and the future in the present (Bennis and Nanus, 1985). They make tomorrow as real and operational as today. They cultivate an ability to search for a consensus that will inspire individual effort, not for adequate decisions to direct them. They have learned to deal comfortably with ambiguity in people and program and time and place.

Inner Leaders Have an Integrative Perspective

Horizon thinking asks inner leaders to integrate disparate ideas, goals, systems, and experts. As the work community becomes more multidifferentiated, inner leaders develop ways to integrate the work and expertise of an exploding array of stakeholder experts. They demonstrate an attitude of acceptance of the many seemingly unrelated parts of the work community and client system. They generate an open-minded perspective about their work and their community's role in the larger societies of which they are a part. And out of all this they create a vision of the future state of the work community and the larger community they serve.

A key task of the future-oriented inner leader is integration, is "getting-it-all-together." Leaders in the middle engage in focusing the disparate elements of their work community. They spend time and energy in integrating and focusing the community in an increasingly complex and multidifferentiated system of organizations, programs, and clienteles. In paying attention, inner leaders focus stakeholders' energy, attitudes, and resources on what they think is important.

METHODS OF HORIZON THINKING

Horizon thinking asks inner leaders to emphasize some experiences over others and in this way more sharply focus the work community's cultural integration process. It is another process that helps change the way people think about their work, their coworkers, and their joint purposes. Creating a unique community future involves leaders in several important mind-changing tasks. Among them are setting the values base for mutual interaction and thinking strategically about the work community and its future that may be different from the values shared at present. Horizon thinking is systematically shaping a desired future work context—culture, organizational structure, and work processes and goals—within which members can trust others and expect others to trust them. It becomes a task to inspire and encourage others to be their best selves through innovation, intuition (Tesolin, 2000), spontaneity, compassion, openness, receptivity to new ideas, honesty, caring, dignity, and respect for people (Cashman and Burzynski, 2000).

The Visioning Process

While inner leaders can choose from a variety of methods of shaping their work community's future, the objective used is simple. It asks the leader to create the future for the work community rather than letting the future just happen. Of the several ways to create a desired future, the following is suggested as an illustrative outline of this process. This iteration involves five phases:

1. Leader preparation
2. Scanning the forces of change
3. Creating the horizon future
4. Sharing that future state of being with others
5. Marshaling work-community member action.

This process represents a unique technique of inner leadership. The horizon thinking technique is evolving and dynamic. Nevertheless, we can describe it in general terms. Its mastery is implicit in success for the inner leader.

Leader Preparation

Horizon thinking is a tool of both work community and leader action. While it applies to all community members, it originates from the creative insights of the middle-level leader. It entails an attitude change to commit unreservedly to define a specific future for the work community and to the idea of focusing on one or a few alternative future priorities, values, and processes instead of others. Unless the commitment is genuine, this technique will fail. The task of future creation also involves communicating that future and using it in all the leader does. It is expensive of the inner leader's and the organization's resources—especially initially.

After a creative future is defined, the task is fundamentally one of inner leader discipline. That future becomes the standard by which all else the inner leader does and says is measured. The inner leader must also prepare the work community to participate in defining its collective future. Prior to actually beginning work to create a new future for the community, followers must be readied to be effective and to feel comfortable in sharing decisions, plans, and methods of work-community operation. In preparation for this follower training, leaders typically have thought through the future they desire and used that as the benchmark for collaborative interaction.

Scanning the Forces of Change

Creating a community's future is preceded by seeking out and understanding the forces for change in the larger corporation, the immediate work community, and the broader cultural environment surrounding it. Creating an appropriate future for the work community requires inner leaders to probe deeply into the factors impacting the work community and the various communities it serves. They must scan these communities to find answers to basic questions of institutional purpose and place in the larger corporate community and the general society and among professional colleagues. Inner leaders scan the environment for clues to what unique role the community can fulfill. This scanning process seeks answers to questions like these: "What is our role, our service, our 'business'?" "What does the law say about us?" "Who are our clients, our competitors?" "What is happening in the larger community, in technique, in public opinion, in the courts, in the legislatures, that affects our mission?" It also seeks answers to questions like this: "What is being said by our professional colleagues, our customers, futurists, opinion makers, politicians that affects us?"

Part of this environmental scanning process involves examination of the leader him or herself. Future-building is a complex interaction of the leader's personal values and orientation and those of work-community members. Which core values become part of the final future created depends on this interaction. Scanning, therefore, must equally explore inner leaders' experiences, values, biases, behaviors, and other characteristics that set them apart and make them unique. These factors in the "leadership environment" are equally as important, as are facts about the work community and larger communities of interest of which they are a part.

Three factors are critical here. First, care is needed to ensure that the scan is not colored by existing perception of the present. The scanning needs to be a continuous process. And inner leaders can enhance scanning by encouraging broad participation by all stakeholders—coworkers, clients, customers, and subject matter experts, as well as by themselves.

Creating the Future

Using scan data, inner leaders then create a future for their work community. Creating a future deals with change. This kind of change is incorporated into goals and centers on people. An effective future statement extends beyond the leader to all followers and to collateral communities. At least the following characteristics of an organization's future statement are important. These statements should reflect the leader's core purposes for the work community. They should define and articulate a feasible and challenging goal. The futures statement articulates a goal that has a larger significance than the immediate work objectives, task accomplishment, or profit. It deals with horizon ideas. The statement of a work community's future is a value-laden statement of what it wishes to become. It is not who the members are, nor even how they are doing. It is a statement of what the work community will seek, the purposes it will foster, the nature and character of its product mix, its service philosophy, and its essential self-definition.

Once articulated, the futures statement alters the nature of the relationships between the inner leader and community members. It provides a common purpose around which members can coalesce in doing their separate jobs. It becomes a mechanism to improve solutions to conflict. Such a statement keeps both leader and followers focused on the larger issue—their mutual horizon idea. A futures statement constitutes the raison d'être for the work community's activities. It also serves as a standard for reaching decisions. And it makes clear the directions of the community. It defines their ends and means results.

The procedure for creating a statement defining the work community's future is essentially the same whether it is for a work unit, a department, or the full corporation. The following phased approach outlines a procedure to arrive at a futures statement for a work unit in the middle of the corporation.

1. Identify what the work community does for its clients, the corporation generally, and society. Analyze the work unit's past as well as current experiences, programs, and activities and select its central activity. Inner leaders may have to reinterpret existing goals statements or look at the essential nature of the community's essential tasks.

2. Identify the leader's interests, skills, and areas of commitment. The future created by the inner leader is an outgrowth of his or her cumulative experiences and includes assessing his or her formal education and training, examining avocational experiences and capacities, and assessing leadership skills, styles, and abilities.

3. Identify the work community's clients and customers. Stakeholders come from both inside and outside the community. The futures statement must encompass the needs and interests of all stakeholders or vital parts of the work community will be excluded.

4. Match external client needs and internal personal capacities and interests. This phase of the process involves developing a listing of values, deeply held beliefs, and traditions held by the work community and individual members.

5. Write out a futures statement. Working alone or with followers, inner leaders commit to writing their mental image of a desired future state of being that incorporates the central reason for their being and the guiding values of the community and its leader. Based on this analysis, they may initially develop several versions of the vision.

6. The next step is to select the futures statement with the most "fit."

7. Present it to the work community stakeholders. Persuade them of its usefulness, secure their understanding and commitment, and relate it to the full corporation, clients and customers, and subordinates.

8. Determine relationships of the futures statement to work-community concerns. The inner leader needs to understand all relationships and how the statement relates to each element of the interpersonal relationships network.

Sharing That Future State of Being with Others

Creating a new future is one thing, communicating it quite another. The task of the inner leader is to inculcate that perception of the potential future and its intrinsic values in the minds and hearts of all stakeholders. Inner leaders give it continuous attention by words, pictures, speeches, training, pamphlets, posters, plans, and other actions that help realize that future. Sharing the future is a continual process of teaching others and unleashing the discretionary power resident in the workforce. This task of persuasion is the essence of the inner leader's job (Gareau, 1999).

Sharing the new future involves the leader in communication. But it is communication to persuade (Cashman and Burzynski, 2000), to change the values and the behavior of stakeholders to conform to the new future. This kind of sharing is done in personal contacts, in work-community meetings, and in both formal and informal contacts with stakeholders. The new future definition of the community is an outgrowth of the experience and values of the leader. Inner leaders communicate that level of commitment to stakeholders (Johnson, 1999). In a way, inner leaders do this to act always authentically within those values. Inner leaders, in many ways, model the work community values. They personify them.

Marshaling Work-Community Member Action

Taking action to implement (make real) the future thus created and not other goals, is the final phase of horizon thinking. It is focusing attention to reflect coworker's action toward that future. Action to carry out the defined future involves all actions the leader takes. Implementing it is seen in the words spoken and the people they are spoken to. It is seen also in policies adopted, procedures implemented, programs adopted, changed, or discarded. It is seen in promotion decisions and in firing policies. It is part of space allocation, benefits programs, and salary schedules. In short, all the inner leader does is part of the task of making real the new potential future.

The Scenario

A scenario is another way to define alternative futures for a work community. A scenario is a description of an imagined future state of affairs. Scenarios usually portray several possible futures rather than predictions about a single future event. Scenarios have unique characteristics that make them an excellent technique inner leaders might use for this purpose. Scenarios are of greatest value when dealing with extended future possibilities. They may be presented in various forms or combinations of forms: narratives, feature newspaper stories, data tables, graphic displays, videotape, computer games, and so on. A scenario is a kind of future "picture" that incorporates a plausible set of relations not likely to be evident from traditional forecasting techniques.

A scenario can include a wide range of variables—technological, informational, skills, public interest—depicting a broad spectrum of possibilities. It may invoke new value systems or standards for the examination of these variables, values, or standards that might seem undisciplined or inappropriate if used in other activities. A scenario is created by inner leaders (with or without help from their followers) who believe they can envisage a path into a future. Scenarios use information available about the future topic but should not be limited by that information. They describe one or more plausible paths from the present to the future period contemplated. They describe critical events on that path and call attention to policy and planning issues. Finally, scenarios recognize that a plausible future may not at present seem either likely or even socially desirable.

Scenario Writing Guidelines

The role of the scenario is to set forth plausible alternatives in a way that helps the inner leader focus attention on actions that will need to be taken at various times in the future. That is, each scenario should be judged in terms of the following five criteria:

1. *Relevance*: Does the scenario deal with an important aspect of the futures in a way that permits further development?
2. *Usefulness*: Does it provide insights, sensitivities, an idea, structural framework, or suggestion that can be used now or in the future to guide policy and leader action?
3. *Originality*: Does the scenario present ideas that are new or deal with old ideas in new, creative ways?
4. *Consistency*: Do the conclusions of the scenario follow from its assumptions?
5. *Communicability*: Is the scenario interesting, and can it be understood by persons who do not have specialized training in the topic or field of interest?

Techniques of Scenario Development

There is, of course, no single, correct way to write a scenario of the future of a given work community. Some hints, from others' experience, follow.

In writing a scenario covering the next thirty or forty years, leaders need to know what the constraints on the future are going to be and where to get such information. Three kinds of data are useful in knowing what the constraints on the future might be. The first might be called *trends*—forces from the past and the present that are pushing society in certain directions. The second thing is a consideration of *events*—the things that interrupt the trends—inventions, natural disasters or war, death, disability, or sudden creative insights. They are the unpredictable elements of the future. Along with events, inner leader need also to look at *images*. Images of the future are what people think the future is going to be like.

Analysis of trends, events, and images helps inner leaders determine what the major alternative futures might be and plan for these alternatives, rather than for any one of them. Then they develop scenarios to indicate what the major alternative futures might be and produce some scenario or sets of scenarios for each of these major alternative futures. For example, some suggest that the two dominant conflicting images of the future of American postindustrial society today are those of continued growth and development versus some sort of conservator society or steady-state society. The interplay of these competing futures can be expected to be a major conflict in the evolving future in America and most of the industrialized world. Other important factors are, of course, possible. Scenario writing helps inner leaders articulate critical forces and bend them to their purposes.

The scenario writer can consider several different types of scenario writing. One, which can be described as future history, involves taking real events in the past and decisions in the present, showing how those decisions might be made, and then working out a plausible set of consequences. A second type of scenario involves a kind of looking backwards from an imagined future. In this format, the reader is somehow transported into the future where someone asks how the world got this way. Another technique can be compared to a conglomerate. This is a technique whereby the reader is—suddenly—somewhere else; and as he or she examines the environment, things begin to make sense. The fourth form has been called decision consequences. In this technique a problem is presented, and readers are asked to vote on one of several alternatives. The future with the most votes becomes the accepted one. This is a very good way to get people to see the importance of considering the consequences of making certain decisions at the present time.

Strategic Planning

Strategic planning is a mechanism for identifying critical issues that face the work community as it moves toward its future. It is also a tool for developing strategies to cope with these issues. The purpose of strategic planning is to integrate inner leaders' actions and enable them to capitalize on synergies. Strategies are the sources of primary cohesiveness in the work community (Eadie, 1983). Strategies may be formed at several levels: global, functional program areas, and implementation. They support directed organizational action (or hamper efforts at excellence) at each level.

The old idea that strategic planning should be done in an ivory tower is bankrupt. Fewer than 10 percent of Americans effectively execute the strategies they or their consultants devised (Kiechel, 1984). Now, more internal leaders are taking responsibility for strategic planning. The idea is that the best strategic planning can be done by those leaders who are most intimately associated with the work of the organization. The challenge in strategic planning is to turn leaders into strategic thinkers. The technique provides leaders a language of strategy to use in doing it themselves.

DISCUSSION ISSUES AND QUESTIONS

Issues

1. Inner leaders engage in "problem-finding" more than problem-solving activities.

2. They select and consistently pay attention to the tasks and values they want and need. This focusing—of self and work community members—is a major inner leadership technique.

3. Inner leaders develop and articulate a horizon goal, a clear, attractive, compelling view of what life, their work situation, and the individuals involved can or should be like.

4. Horizon thinking synthesizes, vocalizes, and translates the leader's aspirations into community aspirations.

5. Horizon thinking is a process these leaders use to create continuously a successful future for the work community.

6. Horizon thinking provides both leader and led with new perspectives from which to view their work, their operating systems, and their longer-term goals and outcome objectives.

7. Horizon thinking involves the leader in creating a future for the work community rather than letting the future just happen.

8. Creating a community's future involves seeking out and understanding the forces for change in the immediate work community, the larger corporation, and the broader cultural environments surrounding the work community.

9. From data obtained by scanning these environments, inner leaders develop a picture of the work community thriving in the vortex of the change forces identified.

10. The futures statement is a clear, compelling statement of what the work community should be and do in the future.

11. Sharing the future involves the leader in communication to persuade, to change the values and the behavior of stakeholders to conform to the future.

12. Inner leaders sometimes use scenarios—descriptions of one imagined future state of affairs—as a way to communicate their community's future to others.

13. Strategic planning is also a mechanism for identifying critical issues that face the work community as it moves toward its future.

Questions

1. How often do I link the changes the office is going through now with the changes it will have to face in the future?
2. What are the basic assumptions underlying horizon thinking?
3. Do I include recognition of the major larger cultural forces that may impact any horizon thinking I might do to help prepare my work community for the future?
4. Someone has said that the leader can "create" a future for his or her organization. Do you believe this is true? Why? Why not?
5. List several obstacles inner leaders face as they try to create a unique future for their work community that may differ from that set for the corporation or by other communities to which the leader's community is linked. How do these factors affect the leader's success in horizon thinking?

ACTIVITIES USEFUL TO THE LEADER'S ROLE

Activity 1: Scenario Writing Exercise

Instructions. A scenario is a description of an imagined future state of affairs. Scenarios are a creative way of dealing with future possibilities. They may be presented in various forms or combinations of forms: narratives, feature newspaper stories, data tables, graphic displays, videotape, computer games, and the like. Scenarios include multiple variables—technological, informational, skills, public interest—and depict multiple possibilities.

1. Using the guidelines contained in this chapter—relevance, usefulness, originality, consistency, and communicability—create a future scenario for your work unit covering the next twenty-five years.
2. In preparing this scenario,

   Read, study and follow the techniques for scenario writing discussed in the text.

   Select a scenario type (future history, looking backwards, conglomerate, or decision consequences).

   Research relevant trend data, significant events that have happened or may happen to impact data trends, and what significant (trend-shaping) people think about what might happen—their images of the future.

   Develop several alternative future scenarios.

   Analyze the implications of each scenario.

Select one alternative future.

3. Prepare a report describing your scenario for the future of your work community.

4. Present it to your bosses or others as you see appropriate.

PART III

THE TECHNIQUES OF
VALUES LEADERSHIP

Inner leaders prioritize traditional American values (Terry, 1995) that foster a return to community—like respect for life, freedom of action, unity, justice, and happiness, along with a few other operationally useful values. These values are espoused by most Americans and anchor a unifying value system acceptable to most leaders and their work-community colleagues. In this way they create moral meanings for work-community members. They carry a burden of ethical responsibility, the center of which is service to their stakeholders. They create values systems that prioritize both work community productivity and worker satisfaction.

The values they set are statements of the oughts, formulations of the desirable each person sets for him or her self. They represent settled ideas about the way one measures experience and relationships. They are also the prime cause of individuals' behavior. The leader's values characterize much workaday experience and give meaning to that experience. Inner leaders see their work as articulating meaningful values systems that define their own leadership and the work ethic of their community of coworkers. These tasks are not as daunting as it might first appear. Most adults have internalized value systems that serve them throughout their lives—including their work lives.

Inner leaders serve followers' values needs as together they work to serve the common good. This kind of leadership is the reverse of much of past leadership literature. Rather than attempt to dominate followers, inner leaders work to provide all things necessary for followers to transform themselves and successfully complete their work tasks. They enhance their followers' moral selves as they also help confirm followers' beliefs in their own inherent self-worth.

The values-oriented techniques discussed in this Part separate inner leadership from other workplace functions. Basing their leadership, as they do, on values, inner leaders are able to achieve successes unlikely if they used more values-sterile approaches. These values techniques reflect vital elements of the specialized knowledge, skills, and techniques that define the leader in the middle and not at the top. They circumscribe inner leadership and establish its context—a context full of values connotations (Klenke, 1996). These techniques include orchestrating meaning within the group, emphasizing values, creating a higher moral standard, servant leadership, and celebrating success.

CHAPTER 10

Technique 7: Orchestrating Meaning in the Work Community

DEFINING MEANING-MAKING

Orchestrating meaning involves the leader in creating and communicating meaning to workers about the organization and their joint work (Plas, 1996). Inner leaders concentrate their full attention and that of their work community on the vision they have created for their community, that is on what they—as leaders—think the vision means and the value they attach to it. Engineering meaning takes place via every action leaders take, every word spoken and every decision made. The most visible expression of community meaning-making is in the vision statement leaders create and promulgate throughout their work community.

Making-meaning is a symbolic role that applies unique meanings to words, objects, ideas, work processes and policies making them specific to that work community in a given time frame. The task is one of reflecting core values in the community's icons, its symbols of itself (Peters and Austin, 1985). These symbols become referents to desired performance and to relationships with others. They are based on the inner leader's values. These symbols define the true meaning and character of the work community more than do organization charts or policy manuals.

The Technique of Meaning-Making

The scope of the vision statement sets the work community's outer limits of possibility. A vision is a present declaration about the community's intended future that also connects members with their collective past. Visions are charged with meaning and have meaning only as followers see them as true—both today and tomorrow. These truths about their collective future must be grounded in basic human truth. Life, liberty, justice, unity, and the quest for satisfaction and happiness are examples of such truths. They compose the values-set guiding collective work effort. Values like "being the best," or seeking "high quality," or "excellence" or "broad market control" are not of the same caliber. In creating a meaning structure based on the leader's core values, inner leaders demonstrate several common behavior patterns. Bennis and Nanus (1985) suggest they include managing attention, making meaning, engendering trust, and acquiring self-knowledge (Carson, 2001).

Leadership in the middle of the corporation is about the sharing of intentions. Engineering meaning in groups is more likely to be helpful when it comes from inner leaders with strong character. These leaders attend to choices made by all persons in relationship with them. Meaning-making tasks are about persuasion, about right or wrong, about finding shared understanding (Bennis, 2001). They are not about coercion or force. Inner leaders train, educate, and coach followers in vision-directed tasks. They ascribe a compelling meaning to the common work, one that gives followers a reason to self-motivate and get involved in appropriate networks. Once understood, this common understanding of why the community and its work are important frees followers from situational constraints that may hamper their growth or transformation to full effectiveness. Followers respond to their leader's values and the meaning they attach to actions and events as the leaders base their leadership on wholeness, shared values, and concern for the human side of life—not just on the materialistic paradigm characteristic of past leadership models (Caill, 2000).

METHODS OF PRACTICING MEANING-MAKING

Operational efficiency in the middle of the corporation is based on democratic leadership. Inner leaders base their relationships with coworkers on values that honor and extol democratic interaction between leader and led. The reason is pragmatic. Work-community members do not have to follow the inner leader, they *choose* to do so. Unless the work community supports and facilitates followers' realization of their goals, members will not respond to the largely personal appeals for cooperation from their leader. Making meaning for what are essentially volunteer work-community members asks the inner leader to master several techniques. These techniques help followers see the leader's intent and purpose for the joint work as useful to them. Among the meaning-making techniques inner leaders use are focusing follower attention, creating a vision, setting expectations, and using symbols.

Focusing Follower Attention

Inner leadership asks the leader to think inwardly—to think past today's problems toward the possibilities of what the work community and its members are and can become. Inner leaders challenge the work-community members to become more than they now are, to redefine themselves, to make a difference in both their personal and professional lives. Meaning-making is seen in conscious actions the leader takes that focus stakeholders on and reinforce the work community's self image. Indeed, all that the leader does reinforces this image. It is part, for example, of promotions given, rewards dispensed, people hired, speeches made, orders written, and all other leader actions.

Fundamentally, meaning-making is nothing more than continually paying attention to what the leader thinks is important. Everyone pays attention to something. Leaders select and consistently focus attention on what they want and need for themselves, for the work community, and for stakeholders. Paying attention also involves communicating a consistent values-laden message to all coworkers, clients, suppliers, and the greater communities of which this work community is a part.

On one level, creating a meaning is simply a matter of priority. What leaders pay attention to, what they focus on, determines whom they lead and how committed followers are to them and the values promulgated. Mid-level leaders must importantly pay attention to the right values, that is, to the few values most community members will accept and respond to. Among the core American values most relevant to leadership in the middle are the following (Fairholm, 1991):

1. Respecting and valuing the intrinsic humanness of all people.
2. Honoring each person's need for satisfaction and happiness.
3. An intrinsic desire people have to be united with others in working toward something good that is also greater than themselves.
4. A need to be treated fairly.
5. A desire for justice in their relationships with coworkers.

Paying attention to human needs, for quality services, to innovate (be creative), to trust and be trusted, to excel in something, for enthusiasm, for self-esteem, and to be passionate about their work is also central to successful inner leadership. These familiar needs must be part of the values mix inner leaders adopt and reflect in their relationships with community members.

Creating a Focused Vision

Leading in the middle ranges of the corporation is much more a function of the individual leader's personal agenda and the relationships he or she develops with followers than it is a subset of corporate direction and planning (Crosby, 1996). Many now see it as a kind of psychological contract in which the leader and follower cooperate voluntarily according to agreed-upon core values and a common view of what the work community is and can become. Indeed, the inner leader's vision defines this work community's values-laden meaning and purposes. The power of the leader's vision comes from the power of the values, experiences, and assumptions developed by both leader and led over time. Work-community members come to feel related to the community's vision statement and to feel connected on a personal, even spiritual, level.

Creating a work-community vision, therefore, is a function of what the leader is as a person and what he or she prioritizes in terms of his or her work life. His or her statement of the work community's vision becomes a vital part of his or her meaning-making task. Understanding the technique of visioning, therefore, becomes a key inner leader skill. Visioning is more than goal setting. It involves activating the emotions, as well as the mind. It has a strong values connotation that reflects the leader's spiritual core and therefore is a more-than-rational statement of personal and community intent.

Visioning is analogous to setting the superordinate goal that Pascale and Athos (1981) discussed or what Bradford and Cohen (1984) called overarching goal-setting. Creating a vision statement involves the inner leader in creating an attractive, powerful, challenging, and compelling statement of the future for the work community, valuing that vision through his or her actions, and programing its implementation. In also involves the leader in communicating the vision context (meaning) to all members of the work community—not just as a sterile statement of future intent but as a central, guiding purpose toward which they can bend their mutual efforts.

A vision is a challenging, unifying, unique, and creditable statement of what the work community is and can become. The vision statement can be articulated in only a few words that summarize what is unique and special about the work community. It is a guideline all members can use as a focus for what the work community stands for. Illustrations of work-community vision statements might include the following:

1. A personnel department might decide to focus on providing training and procedures that would enable managers to "manage humanely in a growing organization." A suitable motto or slogan might be "personal concern."

2. A payments department manager might select a vision to "work with clients with an attitude of solving their problems with imagination. Their slogan could be "creative service."

By themselves, these statements can be meaningless; it is only when the inner leader believes in and constantly talks about them and uses them in all his or her interactions with followers that they come to life; they become inspiring to all members of the community.

Creating a creditable vision statement asks inner leaders to follow a general pattern of thoughtful action including the elements listed in the following section.

Characteristics of a Work Community's Vision Statement

Useful vision statements reflect the work community's core purposes. They articulate a clear, challenging, broad-based, and feasible goal. This vision outcome has a significance beyond the immediate work objectives. Acceptance of it alters the nature of the relationship between the inner leader and work-community members. It provides a common purpose. It allows for a better resolution of conflicts. It keeps the leader and led focused on their larger issue—horizon goals. It constitutes the raison d'être for all the work-community activities. It serves as a standard by which decisions are reached. In sum, a well-crafted vision statement makes clear the directions of the group, it defines the community's horizon outcomes and gives them meaning.

The Importance of a Vision Statement

The inner leader's job is to create and articulate a vitalizing vision that challenges the work community to go beyond its current level. A vitalizing vision becomes a vehicle for change and growth, a result not often attained unaided by the inner leader. It alters the leader's relationships with coworkers and provides a common focus for work-community activity and energy use. Clear, simple, and broadly known visions make conflict resolution easier by tying conflict to agreed-upon overarching goals competing parties can relate to. Such a vision keeps the leader and followers focused on the larger issues of concern to the work community's survival and growth. They provide the basis for inspiration of followers and sustain attention on excellence. Vision statements have a stretch quality to them. Effective vision statements are made by leaders who understand their members, tie the vision to members' specific work tasks, and use it to secure member commitment. In the absence of a vitalizing vision, the leader falls into a maintenance role, which role has a management orientation.

The Process of Forming Vitalizing Visions

The process of forming a vision for a work community of any size is the same. In the final analysis, the task is the duty of the leader. Members can help, but the responsibility for creation of a meaningful future is manifestly a task of leading, not following. It asks inner leaders to create and then validate a vision and to articulate, interpret, and apply it to all aspects of the work community's work. The leader must ensure that the vision statement meets the characteristics criteria noted earlier.

Preparation is necessary to ensure effective, directed action. The steps are first to prepare the group. Well before the first visioning meeting, inner leaders have prepared their followers to be effective and comfortable in sharing decision making, planning, and specific methods or work processes. Also, before the work-community members get involved, inner leaders write down several possible vision statements that are consistent with the overall work-community work processes, goals, and mission objectives. These draft vision statements are more than a restatement of the work community's purposes. They are distinctive and suited to the specific unit's purposes. They must imply a larger significance than work tasks. And each must be challenging.

Followers are useful to help refine the draft vision statements written by the inner leader. The work-community members' roles in this process are not a sham—a way to get the leader's vision accepted—it is a vital part of the process. Members can provide additional values, knowledge, and perspective the inner leader lacks. Working together in this way they can ensure that the final vision will better meet the community's needs.

Making meaning via visioning takes thought and creativity. The process involves—both for the leader's preliminary visioning activity and for subsequent collaborative effort—the following kinds of activities:

1. Identify what the work community does for its clients, the corporation itself, and society.
2. Select a central activity of the work community. In any work community, there are a variety of possible central purposes. The inner leader needs to look beyond routine activities and probe deeply into underlying purposes. This is a task of reinterpreting existing work-community goals; looking at the nature of the unit's tasks, technique usage, and possible techniques it may use; assessing available technical expertise needed of self and coworkers; and looking at the relative abundance or scarcity of needed resources.
3. List the output produced—documents, information, services, goods, and so on.
4. Identify the leader's interests, skills, and areas of commitment. (Visions are personal as much as they are institutional.)

   Examine current and past work experiences.

   Examine formal education and training.

   Examine avocational experiences and capacities.

   Assess present leadership skills, styles, abilities.
5. List relevant capacities, skills, and knowledge.
6. Identify the work community's clients and customers.
7. List internal "customers" and key relationships.

8. List external constituency groups and key relationships.

9. Match external client needs and internal personal capacities and interests.

10. Write out a vision statement—or motto—based on this analysis. Develop several versions. Write out each alternative.

11. Select the vision statement with the most "fit."

12. Present it to members. Persuade them of its usefulness, secure their understanding and commitment, relate it to the work community and its clients.

13. Determine relationships of the vision statement to internal work-community concerns.

14. Help members to see all relationships and how important the statement is to the work community, its customers, and to you—the leader—so each member will personally buy into it—assuming it meets his or her legitimate needs.

Setting Expectations

As inner leaders set high expectations for performance for the group, they are making use of another technique of meaning-making. Inner leaders' expectations focus and direct vision, values, and standards. Their expectations define the meaning context for their work community. Leaders deliberately engage in behaviors that acquaint followers with their expectations for them and for the work community. Whether the objective of these expectations is simply to direct and control member behavior or to reorient their thought processes, the result is to create meaning for them.

Using Symbols

Another simple, yet effective, technique inner leaders use to make meaning for their community members is by using symbols to communicate their ideas, values, and behavioral standards. Every work community has its symbols of itself. Ideas, words, objects, work methods, and other items are used to represent aspects of the work community's culture, values, and view of itself. These symbols define the character of the work community more than do organization charts or policy manuals. Inner leadership is a function of using symbols, legends, and traditions as much as anything else to direct work-community members in desired ways and in vision-focused directions. By these actions, inner leaders engage the heart, as well as the head and the hands of followers (Fairholm, 2000a).

Every work community has its symbols—things representing aspects of its culture: traditions that define the work community, stories that color personalities, values, programs, and visions. Symbols include physical surroundings, who gets invited to meetings, seating arrangements, the order of the agenda, as well as its content, the location of meetings, and many other factors. Language is also symbolic. Language is a way to focus attention. At Disney, customers are "guests"; at Peoples Express, every employee is a "manager"; and at Wal-Mart, they only hire "associates." Each designation connotes specific attitudes and orientations about workers and their relationships with each other and their bosses. Stories, too, are powerfully symbolic (as in the example of Perdue's chickens). They communicate attention, excitement and values, and corporate vision.

Of course symbols can also communicate negative connotations.

DISCUSSION ISSUES AND QUESTIONS

Issues

1. Inner leaders expend energy in almost every action they take to focus themselves and their stakeholders on what they consider to be critical.

2. Orchestrating meaning involves the leader in communicating meaning to workers about the institution and its work.

3. Meaning-making is a symbol-using task that places new, unique meaning to words, objects, ideas, work processes, and policies making them specific to that work community in a given time frame.

4. A vision is a present declaration about the community's intended future that also connects members with their collective past.

5. Inner leadership involves the leader in thinking inwardly, in thinking past today's problems toward the possibilities of what the work community can mean to its members.

6. The inner leader's vision defines the interior work community's values-laden focus.

7. Creating a work community vision is a function of what the leader is as a person and what he or she prioritizes in terms of his or her work life.

8. By themselves, vision statements can be meaningless; it is only when the inner leader believes in and constantly talks about them and uses them in all his interactions with followers that they come to life and become inspiring.

9. The inner leader's expectations that focus and direct vision, values, and standards define the meaning context of the work community.

10. Inner leaders make meaning via the use of simple symbols to communicate their ideas, values, and standard behaviors.

11. In the absence of a vitalizing vision, the leader falls into a maintenance role, which role has a management orientation.

Questions

1. Do I link day-to-day work with the vision and direction of our work community?

2. Have I taken the time to understand and articulate the essential nature of the work we do and the community we work in?

3. How have I connected the work we do to the values we hold?

4. Are others in the work community able to articulate our purpose and direction?

5. Can those we serve recognize our values and vision through the work we do?

6. Do I take the time and the many opportunities I have to teach followers our vision and values?

7. Have I established a culture that encourages new ideas and independent thought that enhance the organization's vision?

8. Do I help others interpret direction and guidance based on the organization's values and vision?

ORCHESTRATING MEANING ACTIVITIES

Inner leaders engage in specific behaviors. The following activities may be useful to both individual leaders to gain experience and comfort in creating meaning for work community members.

Activity 1: How-Tos for Creating Work-Community Meaning

Instructions. Steal some quiet time by yourself. Imagine your work community at a time in the future being "the best it can be." What would be true about it?

1. Record your thoughts. Listed below are some considerations.

values	levels of achievement
team contributions	leadership and employee development
diverse talents that contributed to success	recognition received
obstacles overcome	partners and alliances created
customer satisfaction	revenue, market-share, growth levels
best practices and innovations	risks that paid off
changes made	teamwork that strengthened the community
flexibility to respond to change	span of influence
symbols of success	

2. The next step is to shape your thoughts into a message or a few thoughtfully crafted statements that will help you share your vision of the future with others and enlist them in it.

Activity 2: Creating a Vision Story

Instructions. Throughout history stories have been a most effective means of communicating. A vision story can serve as an innovative way to communicate a work community's vision and values, so that everyone is included and can see his or her part. To try it, you will have to tap into your creative talent.

- Pick a person, an event, a problem, a happening from the past experiences of your work community.
- Write a story about that person, event, or problem that reflects not only what happened but the way the values, purposes, and ideal processes of your work community helped shape the result. Include in the story descriptions of the risks, struggles, achievements, and rewards encountered along the way to completion of the event or solution of the problem.
- Give the story a title.
- Share it with everyone in your work community.
- Publish it in your work team and elsewhere as appropriate.
- Talk about it often.
- Reevaluate it occasionally.

CHAPTER 11

Technique 8: Emphasizing Values

Everybody has values, and these values trigger behaviors. And the complex of our routine behaviors shapes our life. Inner leadership embodies tasks of articulation and institutionalization of new and enduring values in work-community members. Inner leaders shape values, articulate them to employees and customers, and persuade these people to accept the articulated values as their own so they will do the work their leaders want done. In a word, inner leadership is a values-endowing activity. Selznick (1957) says that leaders infuse the work community with value. The values that seem to work best are those that prize most highly individual work-community members, clients, and their leader.

DEFINING VALUES AS A FORCE
IN INNER LEADERSHIP

Inner leaders succeed by putting their lives and their money where their values are. This may be the only way to lead in the twenty-first century world (Fairholm, 1991). Leading from a foundation of values requires inner leaders with the courage to act even if they risk offending others, leaders who are willing to stand alone on principle and who voluntarily give voice to ideas that are counter to the cumulative wisdom of their work community (Graham, 1994). Inner leaders focus on realizing their values and those of stakeholders, not just on task accomplishment. They lead by changing individual's lives for the better. They do not merely preside over tasks or conduct meetings, they influence followers and constituent groups in a volitional way, not just through formal authority mechanisms.

Values are more basic constructs than rules. They determine a community's rules and rank them. They are the criteria for selecting actions, goals, and methods. Values are learned. Some values are explicit, others are not. They nonetheless trigger some specific behavior and constrain behavior that contravenes preset values. A work community's values are sometimes codified in vision statements or codes of ethics. These statements provide frameworks for transmitting and implementing specific behavior within the work community toward specific goals and results. They are powerful in shaping member behavior and in validating institutional policy. Values define acceptable action, resolve conflicts, determine sanctions systems, and are integral to reward systems. They define the desirable and acceptable for the individual and the work community.

Values are broad, general, and conclusive beliefs about the way people should behave or some end-state they should attain. They connote desirability. Individuals evolve values sets that define for them what is true or beautiful or good about their world. Work communities do this also. Either the putative leader creates a group values set or an informal leader does. Most people's values come out of their early conditioning, experience, and significant events in their lives and are stabilized at a fairly early age.

For Burns (1978) the concept of values is crucial to leadership because values indicate desirable end-states. Inner leaders serve as values clarifiers and as communicators of values in the work community. It is only as inner leaders incorporate these values in their vision statements and actions and use them to arbitrate conflict that they attract and keep followers. Burns suggests that values can be a source of vital change in people and work communities. Core values like justice, equality, liberty, security, and respect for human dignity guide most people. As inner leaders reach into this level of follower needs, they induce them to change.

Hodgkinson (1978) calls attention to values as a key ingredient in work-community interaction. He sees them as akin to work objectives, purposes, and policies. These values become "facts" in the sense they are accepted and acted upon by members. His concern is about the work-community "meta-values" of efficiency, effectiveness, and growth, which he concludes corrupt the work community and its members. While they are a problem for social humanists, the very fact of the power of these values reaffirms them as chief determinants of work-community members' interactions with their leader. Nalbandian (1989) describes the work of inner leaders in terms of values like representativeness, efficiency, individual rights, and social equity. Rokeach's (1979) work identifies values held in common by members of various social disciplines. He identifies eighteen core values and another eighteen values that are instrumental in attaining the core values. These relatively few values guide inner leader actions and behavior on the job. While more research is needed to make these tentative findings explicit, there is indication that values condition much specific professional behavior.

The Values Focus of Leadership

If past leadership theories focused on values at all, they focused on those of efficiency and control. These are fast becoming obsolete as inner leader values, though they still have utility for many chief executives. Rather, inner leaders form relationship patterns that rely not on values of external control but on those that give social and personal meaning to the collective work done, aid collaborative decision making, facilitate shared planning, and foster mutual responsibility for work-community success. Inner leadership is a task of creating and then maintaining work community cultures that support the larger corporate culture's values and the dominant values of its leader.

Experience suggests that successful work communities are those that are defined by values that focus on workers as customers and that help stakeholders become their best selves. It is characteristic of our evolving society today that most workers have more than one choice about the tasks they want to perform or how they will receive help form coworkers or from which colleagues they will accept help. They are demanding to make their own choices about what they do, how they do it, and whether they will accept an order and obey it.

Hard work by itself is not as important anymore (perhaps it never was) as is making a positive impact on results. Values focusing on hard work and on performing work processes, not on attaining results, are only creditable in situations where the work involves repeatable work steps. In today's world, customers' product needs and wants change and mutate almost daily. To accommodate this reality, the work community must become more flexible and responsive. Inner leaders cannot afford complex, staid, slow-to-change workers or systems that cannot easily respond to the increasingly special, unique, constantly changing demands placed on them. Rather, they rely on developing and promulgating shared values to link work, workers, and evolving results.

Forces Shaping Leadership Today

Several forces in society interact to shape the values construct leaders use. At least three forces seem relevant to inner leadership. First, the workforce is changing. People working in the corporation—all social groups—today are older, more educated, more diverse, and more wanting (Plas, 1996). Their approach to work also is different from that of their supervisors and bosses. Whereas older corporate employees typically reflect the Protestant work ethic of hard work, dedication, and loyalty, today's worker brings what might be called a bureaucratic or process work ethic characterized by a focus on work per se.

Second, contemporary workers see work as only one of several important aspects of their lives, not as a life-defining "calling." Today, job demands are less powerful incentives for getting workers to do what is required. Job tasks must compete with family, leisure, religious, and social elements of their lives and work does not always come out the winner.

Finally, today's workers often come to the job expecting their work to be much more responsive to their personal predilections than did their predecessors. Workers today have at their fingertips more information about the work they do, the firm they work for, and their industry generally than ever before. They also have knowledge—largely from idealistic media programming—of what is possible in the ways of personal perquisites, benefits, and support. Armed with this dubious knowledge, they come to the job wanting and expecting a work situation vastly different from the one their bosses envisioned as new hires twenty or thirty or forty or more years ago. Leaders in the middle of these new workers' demands cannot rely on sterile system; they must bond people together at the level of their (that is, both leader and led's) spiritual core values.

Workplace Values

Two perspectives on the place of values in work-community life are possible. In one, the individual leader's values are preeminent, and work communities are formed to serve these values. The other viewpoint suggests that work communities themselves also have values that supersede those of individual members. The sense of much of the leadership literature is that values dictate work-community action whether they emanate from the inner leader or from the community's membership. They dominate work-community action, dictate reward systems, and measure individual and community success. Thus, control over values is perhaps the most significant tool inner leaders have to work with.

Much of the contemporary discussion about values still deals with the traditional value of work-community health and survival. It can be summarized by the statement that what is good for the work community is good (Scott and Hart, 1979). Supporting this overarching attitude are values of rationality, efficiency, loyalty to the work community, and adaptability. Individual values are largely ignored. Indeed, a purpose of leadership according to this construct is to displace incompatible individual values with the work-community values just listed.

An alternative construction of the contemporary workplace is possible. In this construct, each work community is bound together by a different set of values than those of the parent corporation. Each community sets its own informal rules and ethical standards that serve to guide members and shape its belief systems. In this respect, work ethics are like any other community's ethics, they are a kind of group mind-set. The group's ethics system relies on common values held in common by the members of that work community that set them apart from all other groups.

The following paragraphs summarize the values basis for much of the ethics practiced in American work communities. They seem, however, to fall into several clusters of values centered around ideas of integrity, freedom and fairness, family values, service to others, and personal growth and development (Badaracco and Ellsworth, 1989).

Integrity. A key work-community value appears to be integrity—wholeness and internal unity. Integrity involves the inherent knowledge of right and wrong the ability to avoid the wrong, and the willingness to stand up for what is right. A macro perspective of integrity includes abiding by the laws set forth in our formal legal system. A microperspective includes living by known and set values, showing fairness and candor in evaluating a follower's work, and being consistently congruent in words and actions. The integrity value involves ideas such as honor, courage, truth, and continuous learning. It is a combination of discipline and freedom. It is key in any definition of work ethics; indeed, it defines them. Integrity is a prime value guiding leaders in the middle, where they are on more equal terms with followers and cannot hide behind formal authority or the intricacies of complex systems.

Freedom. Inner leaders base their relations with coworkers on respect for their freedom and independence and on treating others with fairness and justice. Values of fairness, justice, and independence have special utility in work situations and help prepare the culture for effective action.

Family Values. Values like family closeness, love, trust, and charity are also important workplace values. The Golden Rule of treating others as we want to be treated is at the core of these values. Faith in God and man, looking out for the other person, working for what you believe in, nonviolent respect for the sanctify of human life, happiness, enjoyment of life, and respect for others comprise for many their core family values. Inner leaders know that their coworkers want to be able to exercise these values in their family associations but also to have them recognized and respected in the workplace. Inner leaders who incorporate security for family, health and well-being, happiness, and fellowship into their work community's values are responding to powerful ethical needs of their followers.

Service. Inner leaders practice the service value and use it as a bonding tool to secure coworker acquiescence. Service—that is, helping people realize their own power and using that newly realized strength to win improvements in their situations—is an important part of the complex of work-community values. This value embraces ideas of commitment, perseverance, and persistence in rendering service through work. Inner leaders see work as a place and a way to demonstrate kindness and goodness and communicate this value to coworkers. Belief in their own ability and that of coworkers and feeling that work is a place where both leaders and led can live up to their potential for service define this values cluster.

Growth. The opportunity for personal growth and self-development is also a part of the values mix inner leaders live by and seek to share with followers. These leaders see a need for opportunity to experience the full meaning of life in their workplace relationships. They want to find opportunity to continue their pursuit of truth and learning at work and foster similar actions by their followers. They see work as a time to find ways to let their talents mature and then use them to make positive contributions to society. Personal growth is a combination of discipline and freedom. Those leaders and those work communities that foster these values and provide this regimen may add to their fund of enabling tools.

The Ethics of Inner leadership

There is an ethical connotation in inner leadership. These leaders articulate and confirm a clear work-community ethic. They use values in defining and focusing work-community effort toward acceptable and ethical goals using means consistent with these underlying values. Inner leaders differ from top leaders in recognizing and even emphasizing this ethical dimension. Unfortunately, theory, literature, and reported practice are remarkably free from overt statements of values, except reiterations of the conventional wisdom of efficiency, effectiveness, and control.

Except for efficiency, many top leaders, like managers, advocate a values-free workplace. The result is that the rise of management systems coincides with the demise of ethics in America. Many business entities and their top leaders have ignored ethics and the values premises upon which they are based. Hart (1988) suggests that society has assumed that, since we formed our nation on the basis of certain "unalienable rights," present practice should still reflect them. While they profess them as benchmarks, many leaders and most theories ignore them as integral aspects (conditions) of leader behavior. Even a cursory look at ethics in America leads to the conclusion that many workers have taken ethics—and their values-basis—for granted. The result is a loss of ethical integrity.

In the long term, we can solve the really hard problems facing our work communities only if we behave ethically. Staff selection and training, culture maintenance, vision setting, and other tasks that ensure work-community success all have ethical dimensions. Top leaders have largely ignored ethics. So also has most contemporary leadership theory. The inner leadership model prioritizes ethical behavior defined by the group's values.

METHODS OF USING VALUES

As noted, values are standards that are learned and internalized from the various institutions of society, not just from work cultures. An individual's values change not only as a result of changes in self-concept and with increasing self-awareness but also as his or her environmental context changes. This change is sometimes externally motivated but often is motivated by a need for self-actualization. People change their values when they feel dissatisfaction with their current values as they are applied in their several social contacts.

No one, including inner leaders rises, like Venus, with a full-blown values system that lasts a lifetime. Each individual naturally undergoes continual change as the result of everyday living. Traditional theory suggests that our value programming is relatively rapid in the early years of our maturation but slows until, by our majority, it is set and changes slowly thereafter. Many suggest that setting our values and changing them over time is an intensely personal undertaking, one not normally usurped by corporate leaders. Indeed, except for parents, the clergy, and maybe a few other intimate associates, those with whom one has relationships, many believe, should not be party to values changes—certainly not people in one's work community. Inner leadership—and simple observation of real life—suggests that this perception of values change is faulty to the extent of being pointless.

Setting and Changing Values

Contemporary research is concluding that pressure to shape an individual's values set comes from many sources—parents, ministers, teachers, leaders, friends, colleagues, leaders, and significant life events. It also affirms that many people share many of the same values and that these values can be known and altered both by individuals and by people external to them. Rokeach (1979) suggests that our list of desired terminal values is formed out of the ideas we come into contact with and the larger-scoped beliefs we come to accept. That is, the profession we select, the level of religiousness we adopt, our ethnicity and the ideology we subscribe to dictate in large part the end-state values we honor and toward which we seek to gauge our life.

The power of values lies in the scope of their impact on individuals' attitudes and behavior. Values thus become operational standards that are important not as abstract ideals but in their use as guides to what individuals think about, how they think about it, and how they behave toward others. Individuals select unique sets of values among alternatives after considering the probable effects of the alternatives on their lives. Therefore, one can say a particular value is "owned" when the individual acts consistently in terms of it and publicly acknowledges it.

For something to be a value for someone, it must fulfill the following criteria:

- It must be chosen freely from alternatives.
- The effects of the various alternative values must be considered.
- It must be acted upon by the person.
- It must be acted upon repeatedly.
- It must help the person achieve his or her potential.
- It must be publicly affirmed by the person.

Unless a value meets all six of these criteria, it is a partial value, a value being formed by a person.

Inner leaders use this values-setting process in setting the work community's guiding values. In essence, it is a task of choosing, acting, and prizing. Choosing is consciously considering and deliberately and freely choosing a value over other possible values, the consequences of each being known. A value becomes set when the individual acts consistently on the basis of it. Initially the action may be tentative and sporadic, but with experiences it becomes the trigger of repeated behavior. Finally individuals must "prize" the value as an effective source of support for their goals of self-development and maturation and share and affirm it publicly.

The Process of Values Change

The need for inner leaders to understand how values are changed and the mechanisms they can use is critical to their success. As noted, the process consists of six parts. Knowing this process, inner leaders can abandon the traditional policy of hands off and begin to shape their work community's values in the same way teachers, priests, parents, managers, and friends—even strangers—have been doing for generations. There are six ideal phases of values change.

1. *Choosing the value*. Except in rare circumstances, the ideal way to choose a value is by voluntary selecting it. That is, the choice is ideally freely made after thinking about alternatives and considering their consequences. Inner leaders create opportunities for their followers to choose values they want them to select by couching them in ways that attract the followers.

2. *Acting upon the value*. Since people select their values after having experimented with them by acting in terms of new values in isolated situations, inner leaders provide work opportunities to let followers exercise the new value in ways that lead to success.

3. *Esteeming*. People adopt a new value if they see it as something to esteem, prize, appreciate, or cherish. For followers to esteem a value, inner leaders must find ways to let followers see that the new value helps them achieve their potential.

4. *Publicly affirming*. Part of inculcating a new value into other people's value sets includes getting them to publicly accept the value as theirs and to attest to its utility for them. Inner leaders take steps to insure that all work-community members know the new value. They build discussions about work-community values into as many contacts with followers as possible and also let followers defend and support the emerging values set.

5. *Acting in isolated situations*. A new value becomes a guiding standard as the leader, or the individual himself or herself, builds involvement in work activities that prioritizes the new value at times and in ways that maximize the potential for followers to have a success experience.

6. *Acting according to a routine pattern.* As experience in using the new value as a guide builds, inner leaders act to incorporate it into all appropriate work-unit actions.

Values Displacement

The sense of values theory is that an individual's values are set fairly early in life and change slowly over a long time. This stable-state nature of human values is disturbed, except for incremental alteration, only by experiencing a significant emotional event. Such an event may be either a positive or negative crisis or a personal catharsis, a kind of epiphany. In fact, any major life event can trigger values change—marriage, divorce, having a child, winning or losing a job, or even reading a book, having a new idea, meeting a personal hero, or some other personally impactful event. And followers sometimes change their values merely by the acquisition of new knowledge. Indeed, the mechanisms for change are multiple.

From the point of view of leading from the middle of the corporation, before there can be purposeful participation, coworkers must share certain values and pictures about where they are trying to go (Senge, 1990). Creating shared-values workplaces is a task of nurturing some values among followers and downplaying others. One's central standard of right conduct comes from core, often spiritual values (Bjerke, 1999). People form these values in the family, in religion, in school, and in other social interaction. More and more work communities are surfacing leaders who lead from this kind of spiritual-values orientation rather than management by objectives, TQM, or some other participatory model. Actually, all these leadership fads, and all the others, find their utility in some kind of sharing of values among group members. Inner leaders lead through shared values. They ensure that, insofar as possible, all coworkers accept the work community's values, goals, and methods. They articulate values that followers also hold, or they help followers shape their values system so they come to desire the leader's values.

Inner leadership, therefore, becomes a task of values displacement (Bjerke, 1999). A values leader displaces unwanted—even if morally okay—values held by the work community or its individual members and replaces them with values the leader honors—values he or she thinks will enhance his or her personal success or that of the work community.

Values and related changes in attitudes and behavior can come about in two ways. They change as a result of changes in the individual's self-conception (self-definition). One's values change also because of increased self-awareness of incongruencies, inconsistencies, contradictions, even hypocrisies, between self-conceptions and self-ideals, on the one hand, and on the other, their present values-related attitudes and behavior.

The general order of the creation of our individual values set is from premoral to conventional conformity to self-accepted values. That is, we move from a value neutral state to conventional community values to a unique and individually set code of values. As noted, the process need not be necessarily slow. Rokeach's (1979) research suggests that it can happen in as little as forty minutes. All that is necessary for someone's values to change is an inner need to make his or her self-concept match his or her desired behavior.

Values-based behavior modification has implications for many human social issues—alcoholism, drug abuse, obesity, and a range of achievement-related tension disorders like unsafe driving or physical inactivity. It has special interest to inner leaders for it is the basis of the leader–follower dynamic, and while key to the conduct of leadership, it has not been discussed until very recently. Research in values change theory suggests that inner leaders can change follower values in a variety of ways such as the following:

1. Creation of a new standard of belief—publication of a code of values.
2. Abrupt destruction of previously held orientations—hiring a new boss.
3. Attenuation or slow withdrawal of effort and commitments—boredom with the status quo.
4. Extension of values held into new situations or spheres of influence—cross-training.
5. Elaboration of held values via progressive rationalization into a new area—training.
6. Specification of more explicit context in which a value is considered applicable—training.
7. Limitation of the use of the value via confrontation with other opposing values—controlling the environment.
8. Explication of an implicit value—persuasion.
9. Constancy, or greater systematic application of a value in many circumstances—adapting new policies and procedures.
10. Intensifying or changing a value from one among many to the center of our life—forcing focus, paying attention to one part of the work.

Long-term values change can be induced by machines, as well as by human experimenters. Such is the power of the mass media in the form of music, television, and the Internet that leaders may and do employ them to bring about value change.

Determining Which Values to Use

Rushworth Kidder (1993) identified several values he says are held in common by people regardless of culture or nationality. According to Kidder's research, knowing these universal values "gives leaders a foundation for building goals, plans, and tactics, so that things really happen and the world really changes. Using these values in their relationships with others unifies the work community, giving it a home territory of consensus and agreement. Knowledge of some universal values gives inner leaders another way to reply when asked, Whose values will you teach? Answering this question, as we plunge into the twenty-first century with the twentieth's sense of ethics, may be one of the most valuable mental activities of our time.

Kidder's "universal" values include:

LOVE	TRUTHFULNESS	FAIRNESS	FREEDOM
UNITY	TOLERANCE	RESPONSIBILITY	RESPECT FOR LIFE

He also implies others such as courage, wisdom, hospitality, peace, and stability.

Some of these universal values seem to be self-evident. They are reflected in the everyday experience of people of good will the world over. People in American society and in most other societies in the world commonly include them in lists of core values. They may form at least a skeleton guide inner leaders use to help create their work community's values in a growingly diverse, complex, and differentiated work world. Based on these few universal values, inner leaders construct a values foundation that appeals to the soul of many. For example:

- Nobody considers it moral to abuse children.
- Nobody considers it moral to rape.
- Nobody considers it moral to steal.
- Nobody considers it moral to commit murder.
- Nobody considers it moral to discriminate.
- Nobody considers it moral to be disrespectful.
- Nobody considers it moral to lie.
- Nobody considers it moral to be dishonest.

On the other hand, people think it is right and proper to

- care for and love family and friends.
- treat all people fairly.
- respect the right of all to free moral choice.
- be bone honest in our dealing with others.
- conduct our lives so others will see us as worthy.

As inner leaders enforce these standards by both edict and expectations they help assure that followers will positively respond.

DISCUSSION ISSUES AND QUESTIONS

Issues

1. Inner leadership bases its utility on the power to excite, motivate, and coopt work-community members who come to share the leader's values.

2. Inner leaders clarify work-community values, displace incongruent individual values, and maintain the set of common values shared by both leader and led.

3. Values are more basic constructs than rules of conduct. They determine rules and rank them. They are the criteria people use in selecting actions, goals, and methods.

4. Traditional leadership tasks and skills are not useful to inner leaders. Rather, their tasks are of the mind, the soul, the spirit, asking them to get in touch with themselves in intimate ways as a necessary first step in changing followers in intimate ways.

5. Inner leadership deals with the whole person, with maturation of the spiritual, physical, and emotional, as well as economic dimensions of stakeholders.

6. Values define acceptable behavior as well as acceptable personal or corporate traits or characteristics.

7. Values displacement is a hallmark of inner leadership.

8. Leaders in the middle of the corporation prioritize traditional American values like respect for life, freedom of action, unity, justice, and happiness along with other values.

9. Values define both expectation and actual experience; and for this reason, the community's values system is an important dimension in defining and differentiating cultures.

10. Values are not rules of conduct; they are criteria for selecting rules that guide actions, goals, and methods.

11. The sense of much of the inner leadership literature is that values dictate work-community action and shape reward systems and measure individual and work-community success.

Questions

1. Do I watch for signs of helpful–hurtful values in my followers, as well as productivity and efficiency ones?

2. Do I understand that personal values are more powerful in shaping corporate action than formal rules and regulations?

3. Do I listen for values as well as information?

4. Have I developed a keen eye for what is happening in the office? Do I take the time to watch the processes, interactions, and relationships in the office?

VALUES-BASED LEARNING ACTIVITIES

Inner leadership engages the leader in specific behaviors to change the value measures of individual followers and the nature of their goals. The following activities may be useful to leaders as they try to gain experience and comfort in displacing the values of their coworkers.

Activity 1: Valuing

Instructions. The individual's set of values is naturally undergoing continual incremental—sometimes revolutionary—change. Yet, for most of this generation, values displacement has been ignored. The reason is the mistaken belief that setting one's values is a personal, private action with which process externals should not engage. The reality is that a lot of people and events impact on everyone's values and serve to change them. Inner leaders bring values displacement "out of the closet" of neglect and into the light of leadership action. They reveal the need for expertise in this preeminent leadership activity.

1. Assume you are the inner leader of a work community in your present work environment.
2. Develop a plan to induce your coworkers to change their values respecting habitual punctual attendance (or any other value you think is needed in your present work situation).
3. Follow the six-step guideline found in this chapter.
4. Include in your plan specific actions you will take in each step and that you will ask coworkers to take to insure that this new value guides the life of your coworkers.
5. Share this plan with a colleague who can help you refine—and maybe implement—it.

Activity 2: Where Do Our Values Come From?

Introduction. Inner leaders internalize one (or a very few) of these founding values in their work-community values set and in their strategic vision statements. The value adopted in the vision is the basis for individual and work-community action. It is the source for inspiring commitment and mobilizing action toward its realization in the life of the work community and its members because everyone has values, and they affect our behavior. But, where do your values come from?

1. Think about your values and their origins.
2. In the spaces provided on page 134, write down as many sources of your values as you can. (Add to the diagram as needed.)

Activity 3: Core Values Ranking

Instructions. Milton Rokeach identified eighteen core or terminal values and another eighteen instrumental values that help us in attaining our core

---

Sources of My Values

1._____	6._____
2._____	7._____
3._____	8._____
4._____	9._____
5._____	10._____

---

values. Use his model to determine what your values are as of today that guide your actions and behavior, both on the job and off.

1. Complete the following two questionnaires for yourself. You may also complete the questionnaire as it applied to your work community or to another coworker.

2. Complete the ranking for yourself first. Then complete the ranking as you see your coworkers (collectively) back home would rank them.

Your Core Value System

Core Values	My Ranking of Values	As My Associates Would Rank Them
A Comfortable life	_____	_____
An Exciting Life	_____	_____
A Sense of Accomplishment	_____	_____
A World at Peace	_____	_____
A World of Beauty	_____	_____
Equality	_____	_____
Family Security	_____	_____
Freedom	_____	_____
Happiness	_____	_____
Inner Harmony	_____	_____
Mature Love	_____	_____
National Security	_____	_____
Pleasure	_____	_____
Salvation	_____	_____
Self-Respect	_____	_____
Social Recognition	_____	_____

True Friendship	_____	_____
Wisdom	_____	_____
_____	_____	_____
_____	_____	_____

Your Instrumental Value System

InstrumentalValues	My Ranking of Them	As My Associates Would Rank them
Ambitious	_____	_____
Broad-Minded	_____	_____
Capable	_____	_____
Cheerful	_____	_____
Clean	_____	_____
Courageous	_____	_____
Forgiving	_____	_____
Helpful	_____	_____
Honest	_____	_____
Imaginative	_____	_____
Independent	_____	_____
Intellectual	_____	_____
Logical	_____	_____
Loving	_____	_____
Obedient	_____	_____
Polite	_____	_____
Responsible	_____	_____
Self-Controlled	_____	_____
_____	_____	_____
_____	_____	_____

3. Identify the three values you ranked highest and the three you ranked lowest of both core and instrumental values for yourself and for your work community. Then respond to the following questions.

   - What did you learn about yourself when you analyzed your highest and lowest ranked values?
   - How do your rankings of your core values compare with the composite of your perception of colleagues' rankings?
   - How were your instrumental values similar to or different from the composite ranking?
   - What does this mean to you about your relationships in this group?

4. Can you make some conclusions about the impact of individual and work community values on

   • your individual fit with the team.

   • the power of values in shaping corporate success.

   • the power of values in shaping your individual success.

5. What can you do as a leader with this kind of information? Be explicit.

Activity 4: The Values Supporting Personal Professional Ethics

Instructions. An effective way of thinking about what you want for the future is to write your own obituary. This may seem a strange thing to do—especially for younger people, or those at the end of their careers, but it is a way of really thinking about what you want to do with your life. Writing your own obituary will take some thinking and reflecting on your part. It should be done in quiet.

1. Write your own obituary. Use any format you desire, but here is a made-up example:

Mr. John Smith died at his home yesterday after a short illness. He was 83. Before his retirement eleven years ago, he was executive vice president of the Sloan Hospital. According to hospital officials, Mr. Smith began his rise to prominence when he undertook research (on his own time) and sold plans for the hospital's expansion into international health care. He was in charge of testing for the project, and when it was successful he was assigned to a key position in the international division. He later became vice president/international.

Mr. Smith was active in civic and service work communities in the city and served on many boards and committees for public betterment. Among other notable volunteer activities was his work with small businesses begun by people of minority groups. He believed that know-how was the biggest lack in making a success of these small business ventures. It is to be noted that the failure rates for our city are much lower than those in other cities of comparable sizes.

Mr. Smith attended Tulane University for three years and later completed his B.A. degree and the MBA degree through the University of Chicago Extension. He and Mrs. Smith were active participants in local college evening classes, taking a wide range of subjects such as geography, foreign languages, geopolitics, painting, and sculpture.

When his two boys were younger, he was active in their activities, including Boy Scouts and Little League Football. (In working with the Little League, he was able to persuade the other parents to deemphasize winning and emphasize sportsmanship and skill.)

Mr. Smith is survived by his wife, Edith, and two sons: Robert J., an attorney in Richmond, and Peter. L., an oceanographer now working in Florida.

Note: Some items are not yet even begun by our Mr. Smith. Please think through what you have done to date in your life *and* what you want yet to accomplish. Include both in your obituary.

2. When you have completed your obituary, lay it aside for a few days.

3. Then review it carefully and analyze why you wrote the words your wrote, why you recorded the events and activities you recorded, and which of the values you hold are reflected in the content of the obituary.

   • Why do you think you would write the words you did in your obituary?

   • What values are reflected in the kind of accomplishments you listed for yourself?

4. List those values you believe form the foundation of your life based on your obituary.

5. Your list may contain some of the following values that other people have listed as the reason for their activities. Which of these values reflect your present values set? (Circle those that apply and write in other values you listed in step 4.)

Achievement	Growth	Joy/Peace	Choice
Health	Security	Wealth	Service
Spirituality	Work	Recreation	Fun
Power	Creativity	Immortality	Brotherhood
Tradition/Culture	Affiliation	Freedom	Independence

6. If any of these values (or others) are the base cause of your writing any part of your obituary document, write that value in the margin near the appropriate phrase or sentence. One activity or event may be caused by several values. If this is the case in your situation, record each appropriate value in the margin.

7. Review your marked-up obituary document and determine which values are most important in your life, at least as they precipitated significant behavior in your past, present, and potential future actions.

CHAPTER 12

Technique 9: Leaders Create a Higher Moral Standard

Most people spend most of their waking life at work and want work to have a moral dimension. Everybody wants to do good work, to work for the common good and contribute to the success of the work community. Unfortunately, too many people have been led to believe that there is one standard for private morality and another for business morality and conduct (Nair, 1994). The fact is that moral integrity argues for one ethical standard, applicable in personal, social, economic, and all other aspects of life. Inner leaders provide that moral standard. Their task is to create it in themselves first, then bring it out in their followers.

Arguably, much government regulation of business and industry is a result of business leaders not accepting personal responsibility to ethically serve their clients. Some corporations, perhaps unwittingly, encourage a spirit of moral turbulence by rewarding executives who achieve economic goals by humiliating people, promulgating questionable policies, or stimulating subordinates through fear. A society driven by "responsibilities" is oriented toward service. One motivated by individual "rights" is oriented toward acquisition, confrontation, and advocacy. The first builds, the second destroys.

DEFINING HIGHER MORAL STANDARDS

The word *ethics* derives from the Greek word, *ethos*, which means more than mere obedience to rule. It is also about character, how one feels about oneself (Blanchard, 1992), and reputation, how others feel about you. Being ethical means being moral. It means doing the right thing for yourself and for the greatest number of people. It is a matter of personal and professional character.

Character is a cluster of related ideas that includes morality, ethics, honesty, and humane values. It is knowing that the actions taken are right, that is, acceptable. Moral leaders learn to know good from evil. They understand that all people have the inalienable right of free moral choice. And they know that the irrevocable law of the harvest—restoring good for good and evil for evil—operates in life, including work life.

Woefully, some jobs ask leaders to sacrifice fundamental values (Gortner, 1991) at the altar of the expedient. Too often leaders are asked to accept a lower work morality as necessary to get things done in the real world of business or government. For example, politicians ask us to judge them on their policies, not their personal conduct. Social activists claim high moral ground for their programs and sometimes use violence to obtain their ends. Business executives do not want their day-to-day conduct examined, but ask instead that others evaluate them on their bottom line performance (the Enron debacle is a case in point). Journalists may maintain a personal commitment to truth but often succumb to the pressure to be first, and rather than wait for the whole story, and publish half truths. Or they print their biases as the truth.

Both the ends and the means of accomplishing the inner leader's program goals are important, not just the ends. Many Americans measure the operational manifestation of morality by the Golden Rule: treating other human beings as we want to be treated. Moral leadership is a process, not just an objective. It is love in action. As we enter the twenty-first century, it is apparent that inner leaders are acquiring a new language of leadership, one where it is again okay to use all of the operative "S" words—soul, sacred, spirit, and sin, as well as structure, standards, strategy, system, and style.

Successful inner leaders have learned that they cannot be successful over the long term unless they base their relationships with those assigned to assist them on moral systems. Follower commitment comes after leaders demonstrate their moral code by their actions to institute procedures, techniques, and work processes that consider moral factors. These factors include how the leader handles differences of opinion about human worth, whether or not they highlight impartial analysis and inquiry, and how much they demonstrate caring for their followers.

The Basis of Morality: Spiritual Wholeness

Our work communities do not function well (Wheatley, 1992) when honesty and personal responsibility atrophy, particularly at the top or when leaders are content to focus for ten or more hours a day on only the mundane tasks and ignore their inner spiritual needs or those of their followers. The soul of the inner leader's morality is love. Love—concern for the well-being of another—constitutes the basis of ethical leadership. Leaders love leading, love their work community's products and service, and love the people with whom they work. Love accesses the healing and energizing powers of the leader's spiritual core and recognizes that his or her leadership is a reciprocal relationship with all members of the work community.

Part of moral leadership asks leaders to create "corporate spirit," a spiritual force that honors high performance, compassion, empathy for others, and individual contribution. It is illogical, therefore, to assume that when leaders come to work they leave at home their innermost core values and beliefs. Moral leaders deal with follower contentment, capacity, equanimity, detachments, and connectedness. When leaders liberate the spiritual content of their leadership, they unleash a powerful commitment to help the less fortunate, to be of service, and to respect those who are different.

Traditional values are waning in those work communities today that have not followed a solid affirmation of moral values. Nothing is filling the values vacuum. The 1970s and 1980s turned vice into virtue by elevating the unbridled pursuit of self-interest and greed to the level of social virtue (Etzioni, 1993). Leaders in the middle are sensitive to the nonphysical. They argue for a return to a society where some things are beyond the pale. All people, including coworkers, want a set of moral virtues, some settled beliefs and values that their work community can endorse and actively affirm—beyond which they will not allow themselves or others to go. This apparent change of position can be seen today in the move to be drug free in the workplace, in the demand to return to values of hard work for a fair day's pay, and in followers' desires for leaders to treat them with the same basic dignity with which they wish to be treated.

Moral Leadership

The higher leaders climb in the corporate hierarchy, the greater their burden of responsibility and their need to reevaluate themselves and their spiritual roots. And the root of spirituality is service. The infrastructure of inner leadership is based on the idea of moral leadership founded on service. It is uncompromisingly committed to the higher principle of selfless concern for others. Spiritual leadership rejects coercion to secure desired goals. It is noninterfering of human freedom and choices, though these choices may entail some painful decisions and shifts in priorities. Elements of moral and spiritual leadership include several elements that inner leaders possess and inspire in their stakeholders.

Sharing Meaning

The inner leadership task is more than physical structuring of people and functions that has occupied business managers throughout time. It includes formal relationships, of course; but, more important, the inner leader provides values, meaning, and focus to that structure. It is leaders (not managers) who focus the power present in work relationships on more than just productivity. These leaders shape the cultural surround within which the work community and its people operate. They provide direction, incentive, inspiration, and support to individuals and work communities if support is to be forthcoming. Inner leaders deal with the intimate core being of their followers as they also deal with their bundles of skills needed to do work.

Leadership is the integrating capacity in complex social interaction. The leaders others volunteer to follow will set the goals and determine the values by which the work community measures accomplishment. These values and goals also define the acceptable process, guiding the interrelationships between leader and led. They integrate the needs and activities of the pluralistic constituencies that look to the work community for support, assistance, and meaning. They tie together the disparate goals, measures of success, and strategic policies that govern work life.

Influence

In effect, true leadership is conferred by followers. The measure of leadership is not the celebration of the mind but the tone of the heart (DePree, 1989). Leadership over volunteers—the only kind of leadership there is—relies on moral rectitude. Moral inner leaders make followers feel powerful and able to accomplish things on their own. The model of spiritual leadership is not command and control. It is confer and network. The leadership process is an influence process aimed at transforming—changing—both people and system. Success in the twenty-first century will depend on how well leaders understand the role, the technique, the values, and the orientation of moral leadership. Inner leaders are influential in the work community and with each member. Unless the influence they exert is morally acceptable, followers will not follow, and leaders cannot lead. They will have to revert to managing others to get their work done.

Risk Taking

Moral leadership is done in activity, and action involves risk. Sometimes inner leaders need to challenge existing work and work community processes (Kouzes and Posner, 1987). They cannot always simply accept current work systems or existing structural relationships. Rather, these leaders are pioneers, often producing real change that meets people's enduring needs regardless of the risk. Inner leadership is intended to convert, change, and transform followers to moral action. And change is always risky.

Risk taking is challenging the process (to use Kouzes and Posner's words), not simply the existing structural relationships but the value system underpinning it. Moral leadership seeks to produce real change that meets peoples' enduring needs. It enhances production and improves operational efficiency. It improves morale in work communities, fosters greater coordination across functional areas, and enhances relationships with and within the larger community and society.

Transformation

Moral leaders are spiritually transforming. They enhance people's moral selves, help confirm others' beliefs in their own inherent self-worth. In the process, they help create a new scale of meaning within which followers can see their lives in terms of the larger community. Successful inner leaders influence change in the values, attitudes, abilities, and behaviors of individual followers. In this sense leadership is transformational of the people and their work community. Transforming leaders try to elevate the needs of their followers in line with their own goals and aims. In doing this, leaders pay attention to the individual by understanding and sharing in the realization of followers' developmental needs.

Moral leadership is a change process that transforms both the stakeholders and the institution itself into something better than they were before. This transformation takes place in a consciously created and managed culture that prioritizes morality and focuses on the spiritual side—the heart—of the individual stakeholders. Of course there is some gamble that leading on the basis of moral standards may not work. Asking the leader to foster a specific moral dogma entails risk. The risk is that members will accept only the outward form, not the inner conviction necessary to true moral change. That is always a risk—that members will accept the tenets as an outward show, not have it written on their hearts. Inner conviction, patience, and predictable moral actions will ensure the leader's success as a moral guide for the work community and its people. If leaders remain focused, if they are seen as authentic, success will come.

METHODS OF PRACTICING HIGHER MORAL STANDARDS

Morality in business is receiving increasing attention in practice and in classrooms. Inner leaders' morals and ethics come out of their individual and community (cultures) values. Moral values define one's life and impacts all interpersonal relationships. Including a moral dimension in their choices and actions helps inner leaders think and act beyond narrowly defined business and political interests. It forces them into the realm of the spirit self. Such leadership will give meaning and purpose to work. Arguably, this is the only way leaders can attract tomorrow's workers to their vision and goals.

Inner leaders see morality as both a process of inquiry and a mode of conduct. It is asking questions about what is right and what is wrong. And it is setting an example for others about the rightness or wrongness of particular actions (Kouzes and Posner, 1987). Being moral is creating a climate of ethical expectation; and the best way to teach ethics is by example, that is, to practice them.

Inner leaders are moral examples. There are some things they prefer not to compromise, adapt, accommodate, or collaborate on where their core values are at stake. Indeed, being moral means inner leaders cannot compromise some ideals, they must defend them. Thus, leaders may sometimes be assertive and deliberately confrontational of alternative value systems. At times, they feel the need to affirm the superior value of their personal, spiritual values over the demands of technical operating system. Morally motivated inner leadership entails principles of action, motivated by an inner sense of the leader's spirituality (see, for example, Burns, 1978; Covey, 1991; DePree, 1989; Fairholm, 1991, 1994, 2000b; Greenleaf, 1977; Lee and Zemke, 1993; Vaill, 1989). Application of the leader's moral values in work situations necessitates a spiritual orientation, one that centers on moral conduct. It is a task of doing good while doing well.

Inner leaders set the standards for behavior for the work community. They create a higher moral standard of personal conduct that serves as a model for follower emulation. The dimensions of the moral standard, of course, vary with the individual leader and with the character of the work community and its members. At least the following elements of leader action to develop their moral side seem relevant to their preparation to lead.

Leaders Exemplify a Higher Moral Standard

Critically, inner leaders are models of morality. They live their moral standards. Living by their moral values asks leaders to first know what their core values are, live by those values consistently, and communicate them to their followers in both word and deed. Living by one's inner truth means putting that truth into practice. Followers work harder when the work community is characterized by mutual trust, respect, concern for each other, and where work community members honor each other as human beings. These ideas are appropriate for the inner leader to learn, as well as the lowest worker.

Leaders Learn to Love Their Followers

Love defines the soul of moral leadership and is the source of its courage. Moral leaders learn to access the healing and energizing powers of love in their own lives so they can pass that attitude—attribute—to followers. Leading with love also means that leaders understand that their passion for the work and their workers comes from the attribute of compassion. They learn that, in the final analysis, leaders serve and support their followers, not the reverse. Moral leaders come to love leading, love their work community's products, and love their followers.

Leaders Learn to Serve Their Followers

All people have multiple needs, only some of which the work community can ameliorate. Today's workers want more balance between their own needs and the work community's (Ruppert, 1991). They want to be active in the several dimensions of their lives: love, family, faith, self-confidence, others. These qualities of life animate and qualify their lives. Inner leaders make sure that they serve other people's highest standards of personal and work community conduct.

Leaders Are Ethically Centered

Inner leaders have developed a sense of ethics based on their core values as a precursor to effectively developing work-community values. That is, the leader's personal core values provide the basis for the sanctions systems that define his or her personal moral (spiritual) center and form the basis of community morality. Some leaders operationalize their personal moral codes in the work community through formally adopted codes of ethics. Others schedule time to formally discuss moral issues and practices. Primarily, the business of being ethically moral is engineered by inner leaders who take charge, set the moral climate, and accept accountability for their own actions and results. These leaders set the standards for performance and morality within their work community and enforce these standards through their expectations. Operationally, moral leadership involves following ethical standards and patiently sticking to their goals and purposes enough that followers can predict the leader's behavior.

Leaders Are Morally Centered

Inner leaders draw on their spiritual cores to build and use a belief system that reflects their own innate goodness, ethics, and morality. And then they consistently live it. Inner leaders listen to their inner selves as they develop a kind of credo that accepts life, reverences it, and gives it dignity. At a minimum, such a life credo includes ideas like doing no harm—doing nothing to make people or matters worse. It recognizes debts, mental or material, to a variety of external others—tradition, family, colleagues, former leaders, current followers, and many others. An articulated credo puts a ceiling on desires and limits the leader's personal freedom. Morally centered leaders strive for integration, wholeness of self, spiritual unity, and integrity. Once attained, this sense of moral certitude lets leaders feeling good about themselves and reflect on the morality of current business questions. It also lets them think about their actions in terms of their inner values and standards of right and wrong.

Leaders Are Integrated

There is a pressing need for stability and spiritual values in America today (Garton, 1989). Living by their inner truth asks leaders to strengthen their personal and work community integrity (Hawley, 1993). Honesty is essential in moral leaders. So is giving attention to their spiritual needs. Inner leaders seek—and find—the authentic nature of their inner spiritual selves and discover and nurture people, situations, and objects that feed their spirits and nourish their souls (Hinckley, 1967). Morality demands integrity of all who govern their lives by high moral standards. Moral integrity is having courage and self-discipline to live by one's inner truth. It is a function of feeling whole, total, entire, complete. It involves the idea of goodness, human decency, fairness, kindness, consideration, and respect (Badaracco and Ellsworth, 1989). Learning to be morally whole—integrated—takes courage. It involves a willingness to say what needs to be said and not needlessly say what may hurt another. It demands self-discipline. It asks inner leaders to spend time in consolidating their inner, intimate strengths and connecting themselves to their inner promptings.

Leaders Develop Moral Judgment

Ethical behavior flows from our ability to distinguish right from wrong and the commitment to do what is right. The measure of moral judgment is summed up in positive answers to two questions: "How would I want to be treated in this situation?" (the Golden Rule) and "How will the decision or action read on the front page of the newspaper?" Moral judgment is the activating mechanism of one's moral character. It is part of the self-analysis leaders engage in as they observe and reflect on their actions and judgments of events. It is a part of all aspects of life. Their moral core is what sustains inner leaders through long periods of emotional drought in a crumbling, corrupt, and oftentimes disappointing world.

DISCUSSION ISSUES AND QUESTIONS

Issues

1. Most people spend most of their lives in work. They want it to have a moral dimension.
2. Moral integrity argues for one ethical, moral standard, applicable in personal, social, economic, and all other aspects of life.

3. Inner leaders work to promote a moral standard for themselves and for their work community.

4. If leaders don't give their core values place at work—the most significant part of life for many, certainly in terms of time—they loose their moral centers.

5. Ethics means more than mere obedience to rule. It means doing the right thing for yourself and for the greatest number of people.

6. Some jobs ask leaders to sacrifice core values at the altar of the expedient.

7. Many Americans measure the operational manifestation of their morality by the Golden Rule: treating other human beings as they want to be treated.

8. It is apparent that leaders are acquiring a new language of leadership, one where it is again okay to use all of the operative "S" words—soul, sacred, spirit, and sin, as well as structure, standards, strategy, system, and style.

9. Successful inner leaders have learned that they cannot be successful over the long term unless they base their relationships with those assigned to assist them on moral systems.

10. Moral inner leadership is done in activity, and action involves risk.

11. Inner leaders are moral examples; and moral leaders prefer not to compromise, adapt, accommodate, or collaborate in areas where their core values are at stake.

12. Love defines the soul of moral leadership and the source of the inner leader's courage.

13. Some leaders operationalize their personal moral codes in the work community through formally adopted codes of ethics.

14. Morally centered leaders strive for integration, wholeness of self, spiritual unity, and integrity.

Questions

1. The measure of moral judgment is summed in positive answers to two questions: "How would I want to be treated in this situation?" (the Golden Rule) and "How will the decision or action read on the front page of the newspaper?" Measure your leadership on these criteria.

2. Do I try to create a community of interest that circumscribes both work community and member values, ethics, and morality?

3. Do I publish, by all possible means, a set of morals and ethical behavior that accurately reflects my vision?

4. Do I provide direction, incentive, inspiration, and support to my work communities and each member?

5. Do I include a clear moral dimension in my work choices and actions?

6. Do I think and act beyond narrowly defined business and political interests?

LEARNING ACTIVITIES FOCUSING ON
HIGHER MORAL STANDARDS

The following may be useful to both individual leaders and to leader trainers to gain experience in integrating his or her personal moral values into workplace actions.

Activity 1: Locus of Moral Control

Instructions. Read the following two sets of statements and indicate whether on balance you agree with Choice A or Choice B.

Choice A

1. Success is largely a matter of getting the right breaks.
2. It is foolish to think that I can really change another person's core values and attitudes.
3. Getting promoted is a matter of being a little luckier than the next person.
4. A lot of what happens to me is probably a matter of luck.
5. Many times the reactions of my bosses seem haphazard to me.
6. Marriage is largely a gamble.
7. Sometimes I feel I have little to do with the evaluations I receive.
8. I have little influence over the way other people behave.
9. It is only wishful thinking to believe that one can readily influence what happens in our society at large.
10. It is almost impossible to figure out how to please some people.

Choice B

1. Promotions are earned through hard work and persistence.
2. If you know how to deal with people, they are really quite easily led.
3. People like me can change the course of world affairs if we make ourselves heard.
4. Getting along with people is a skill that must be practiced.
5. The success I have is the result of my own efforts; luck has little or nothing to do with it.
6. I have noticed a direct connection between how hard I work and the rewards I get.
7. The number of divorces indicates that more and more people are not trying to make their marriages work.

8. When I am right, I can convince others.

9. In our society, a person's future earning power depends on his or her ability.

10. I am the master of my fate.

Discussion Questions

1. What do you suppose are the ethical standards of someone who selected Choice A? Choice B?

2. If you were the leader of someone who is characterized by the statements in Choice A, (Choice B) how could you induce him or her to do what you wanted him or her to do? Be explicit.

3. How would someone characterized by Choice A statements respond to a formally promulgated code of ethics? Choice B?

4. Write a short essay describing what you suppose would be the ethical basis of a leader characterized by Choice A factors.

5. Write another short essay describing what you suppose would be the ethical basis of a leader characterized by Choice B factors.

Chapter 13

Technique 10: Servant Leadership

An essential characteristic of inner leaders is that they provide needed services to followers so they can succeed and in the followers' successes facilitate the leader's success (Braham, 1999; McLaughlin, 2001). A service role asks leaders to change the traditional leadership mind-set that assumes they are served by their followers.

DEFINING SERVANT LEADERSHIP

Two aspects of this service role are important. First, the leader's job is to prepare followers to provide high-quality, excellent service to clients, customers, or citizens. In doing this, inner leaders act to empower followers to enable them to be of service (Bleskan, 1995). This aspect of the service dimension is similar to training and education programs leaders have been doing routinely. If there is a difference in these activities associated with inner leadership, it is in the effort to prepare the follower to be of service on a wider front. These leaders see merit in helping followers broadly develop their capacity to be of service.

Second, leaders serve their followers. The leader's job is not only to encourage and sustain high quality service to customers by all stakeholders but to provide service to all those who have a stake in performing that service. Some have called this task servanthood. The task of leader servanthood is one of facilitating the work of others; serving coworkers as they have needs so they can accomplish their set tasks. Leaders serve followers in ways that ease their tasks and that energize and inspire them to unified action. The leader's service to followers can take the form of personal assistance, resources, training, or encouragement or in any of countless ways that enhance the capacity and resources of the follower.

This kind of servanthood is the reverse of much of past leadership literature. Rather than attempt to dominate followers, inner leaders *go to work for them.* That is, they serve them by providing all things necessary for follower success. Followers' success is facilitated partly through the leader's work to create a useful work-community culture. Leaders also serve followers as they teach core values and desired skills and patterns of work behavior. They serve by providing information, time, and materials necessary for followers to be successful in doing the community's work tasks. Inner leaders also assign goals and plans and inspire and train others to carry them out. Once followers are trained and committed, leaders also share responsibility with them. In effect, leaders prepare followers, provide facilitating help, and then let followers lead themselves within the constraints of the shared vision (Greenleaf, 1977).

Inner leadership requires that the leader establish and maintain a work culture that fosters service as a prime value. This values-displacement activity includes setting standards of conduct and focusing attention and the energy of the work-community members on service quality. The intent is to change coworkers so they internalize the service value in performing their work. Inner-level leaders are involved in creating and maintaining work systems so that emphasis on service results, and they can measure the quality and scope of services provided (Danforth, 1987).

METHODS OF PRACTICING SERVANTHOOD

Servanthood asks inner leaders to practice leadership because they choose to serve others (Braham, 1999). A simple, yet useful definition of service is any act, attitude, or behavior someone does that helps another person. Inner leaders help others by making available to them needed information, time, attention, material, or other resources. They also help by focusing their time and attention on work-community purposes that give meaning to the work. In effect, servant leadership invites leaders to create and facilitate a culture of follower self-leadership. It is attitude—both the leader's and the follower's—that determines whether an act performed helps or does not help. Given this fact about serventhood (Braham, 1999), it is therefore impossible to specify specific acts of service a leader may render to a follower outside the constraints of a specific time and place context. The situation and the present needs of the follower compel each act of service.

Service Techniques

Preparing to serve their followers asks inner leaders to master specific skills and tasks that implement the principles of this leadership technique. The first task in mastering inner leadership centers on the principle of self and follower development. The definitional elements of inner leadership include those of caring, service, and innovation. While productivity is always a part of any leadership action, inner leaders rely for excellent performance on a vitalizing vision that unites stakeholders in synergistic service to one another. This service takes the form of a variety of tasks and skills.

1. A first task is setting and living a consistent set of values that honor the essential humanness of followers and challenges them to cooperative work effort. An important characteristic of inner leadership is that it presumes that leaders and followers are connected by common acceptance of a few values held about who people are and why and how they should relate to one another in social groups. This leader model puts forward a values-set honoring individual members per se upon which the work of the work community will be founded, one that is also suitable for the foreseeable future. Such a set of agreed-upon values cements the work community together and makes in-the-middle leadership success possible. The community's values form the basis of the vision statement and all the actions inner leaders take to energize followers.

2. Inner leaders learn to create, promulgate, and consistently apply a vitalizing vision of what they can become through service to the work community and to their customers. The leader's vision forms the platform upon which all interactive work-community work is done. It interprets the leader's values set and defines the present and future values context, the intent of which is to attract community members (Klenke, 1996). Visioning comes out of the personality of the leader, but unless the vision strikes a responsive chord in the lives of stakeholders, it cannot energize and inspire cooperative action. Any effort to induce followers to attain high quality performance, effectiveness, or excellence must be conditioned by a vision that asks followers to do these things within the context of the vision's values.

3. Inner leaders must become expert in developing and leading a service-oriented work community and in manipulating the ambient work culture. Supporting the work community's values-set and its guiding vision demands that leaders create and maintain a congruent cultural surround within which both leader and stakeholders can find support for actions to operationalize their service values. An effective work-community service culture includes preparation of strategic plans, setting standards of service excellence, and displacement of competing values held by some members of the community. Each of these aspects of culture management need to be placed in the context of inner leadership (as opposed to top leadership).

4. Inner leaders need to prepare to serve their followers by learning to relate in one-on-one relationships with followers to convey desired information, understanding, and job skills. A central need in servanthood is that leaders prepare themselves to be able to feel comfortable in situations where they and other work-community members sit together in council to share planning, policy, and decision-making activities. This is a new technique requiring the inner leader to prepare in terms of values and attitudes, as well as skills and knowledge. It presupposes a leader who respects, cares for, even loves followers. Counciling-with others can be done only as an institutional system when leaders and followers respect the essential humanness of one another and act in response to these values.

5. Inner leaders need to prepare to serve their followers by learning to be teachers and otherwise to communicate needed information. Preparation to serve their followers also asks inner leaders to teach followers to maximize their innate talents in group-sanctioned service to one another and to their customers. Often using coaching techniques, inner leaders expend energy to teach stakeholders to bond with the work community in ways that serve them individually as together they serve the work community's purposes. The result of gaining skill in teaching proficiencies is that followers are enabled to be independent in values-related work activities (Carson, 2001). That is, they learn to act on their own in ways the leader would have them act. The need for supervision is minimized as followers internalize common values and behave in ways that respond authentically to those values.

6. Leadership in the middle asks leaders to also master several techniques that facilitate follower service to the work community and to customers. Some of the specific skills inner leaders need to master in working with their staff include common courtesy, management by walking around, naive listening, using symbols, focusing, and celebrating accomplishment (these skill areas are defined and placed in context of leaders' self-development elsewhere). For example, implicit and explicit in inner leadership is the idea of empowering followers to govern themselves as they pursue service excellence in their work-community activity. The service objectives of inner leaders are two: first, helping stakeholders to produce high quality service to coworkers, clients, and customers as they perform of the work community's work; second, to seek to enhance each member of the work community. Leadership success can be measured in terms of both service excellence and transformed followers who come to be self-controlling, self-directing, and self-governing servants in their own right. That is, the inner leader's role is to teach followers service values and to prepare them to be of service themselves.

7. Successful inner leaders engage in a continuing program of personal change to improve those capacities and values that honor people, shared leadership, and high-quality service in work performance. Inner leaders incorporate a concern for the growth and transformation of followers to the end that these followers will want to use more of their innate talent and intelligence in

doing the communal work. The process of leader change to prioritize a service role is personal and intimate. This mind-set change must precede any acts of service a leader might perform for a given follower or for the work community generally. Inner leaders learn to assess their current service strengths and continually work to improve them,

8. Accepting a philosophy of service is the basis of the inner leader's relationships with all stakeholders. The most important part of preparation to be successful servants of their customers and stakeholders is to accept the service role implicit in the process and philosophy of inner leadership. Both the leader and those led must come to accept this role and the values that form its foundation. This choice is critical to the practice of inner leadership. For the inner leader, it is essentially a task of internalizing the values of shared leadership and mutual interactive development. It is partly a problem of education about and acquaintance with the tasks and skills of service. It is also partly an act of faith.

9. Learning to be of service to stakeholders implies that leaders are willing to let them perform as much of the work as they can, including as much of the leader's work as they are willing to assume. Maximizing their service to followers includes inner leaders in involving staff fully in the work-community's work. Serving followers is letting them perform all the kinds of work that will help them become more fully conscious of the work that needs to be done. It entails helping followers acquire more skill in performing their duties. It involves providing them with situations and conditions in which they can learn about the other jobs done by coworkers and become more expert in doing that work in addition to their own.

10. Inner leaders provide both formal and informal organizational structures that facilitate broad service activity. Structural and procedural mechanisms need to be fashioned to institutionalize shared servanthood. Sometimes new structures need to be introduced into the work community to formalize service responsibilities. These structures usually take the form of small work units that require cooperation and interdependency. Such structures may include task forces, operating committees, or councils of workers. These small groups force members to take responsibility for directly helping attain the work unit's aims—its plans, program designs, and new services or service delivery systems—as well as developing policies and operating processes and otherwise overseeing job tasks. Policies and procedures authorized in the work community also need to be developed that constrain members in how and when to serve others.

11. Inner leaders assure that service rendered is useful, relevant, and timely. The essence of success in this technique is not always keyed to a policy or procedure or an elaborate process. Rather, it relies for success on the attitude of mind of leaders and followers. As both come to accept the role of helper— to each other and to customers—whatever actions they take will be part of this inner leadership technique. Of course, some system of control and account-

ability must also be included in leader–follower relationships to insure appropriate use of human and other resources. The key ingredient is a values construct that prioritizes service.

As inner leaders serve the needs of all of their stakeholders, they model desired service behavior and underline the importance of service in their contacts with those with whom they interact. Then they can be successful.

DISCUSSION ISSUES AND QUESTIONS

Issues

1. A key inner leadership technique is being expert in providing needed services to all stakeholders to make their work successful.

2. Inner leaders serve their stakeholders so they can succeed and in the followers' success facilitate the leaders' success.

3. Rather than attempt to dominate followers, inner leaders go to work for them. That is, they provide all things necessary for follower success.

4. Inner leaders establish and maintain a work culture that fosters service as a core value and includes setting standards of conduct and focusing the attention and energy of the work-community members on high-quality service.

5. Inner leaders help others by making available to them needed information, time, attention, material, or other resources.

6. It is impossible to list universal acts of service a leader renders followers since the situation or the needs of the follower dictate the character of each act of service.

7. A first task in developing a service orientation is setting and living a consistent set of values that honor followers and challenge them to cooperative work effort.

8. Leaders need to gain expertise in working cooperatively with followers in one-on-one relationships with them.

9. Inner leaders need to prepare to serve their followers by learning to be teachers—to transmit desired information, understanding, and job skill.

10. Successful inner leaders continually change to improve those capacities and values that honor people, shared leadership principles, and high-quality service at all levels.

11. Learning to be of service to stakeholders implies a willingness to let them perform as much of the work as they can, including as much of the leader's work as they are willing to assume.

12. Servant leaders provide both formal and informal work community structures that facilitate mutual service activity.

Questions

In responding to each of the following questions, describe and evaluate specific program or actions you take to inculcate servanthood principles in your work community.

1. Have I created a customer-focused service standard in my work community?
2. Do I try to bind my followers to a common cause of quality service and recognize both work community and individual service accomplishments?
3. Do I foster conscious programs to inculcate a strong service and quality work orientation among employees?
4. Do I make the people who actually do the work an in-house consultant team to improve conditions and results?

SERVANT LEADERSHIP LEARNING ACTIVITIES

The following may be useful to inner leaders to gain experience in serving their followers and teaching them to serve others.

Activity 1: Create a Story

Instructions. Much of the work inner leaders do is in aid of getting their stakeholders to perform higher levels of service to each other, to customers, and to the larger community of which they are a part. One way to do this is to create and promulgate stories that highlight service and illustrate its importance in the work of the work community.

1. Think about your work community; its leaders; all stakeholders; and the programs, products, and services they collectively provide.
2. Recall a story (or stories) prevalent in your community that emphasizes service. Recast that story to bring it up to date while still respecting its essential character, values, and intent to highlight service values.
3. If you cannot think of a currently widespread story, create a new story that illustrates and illuminates the service values held by your work community and helps define it as a unique place in which to work.
4. Consider sharing the story with your work colleagues.

Activity 2: "Counciling-With" Others

Instructions. For stewardship patterns to work up and down the organization, new ways of viewing the leader–follower interaction are necessary. Counciling-with followers is a new insight into the relationship between leader and follower that Fairholm (1991) developed a decade ago. Sitting-in-council with followers puts the leader and follower together in an equal, sharing relationship, both committed to the success of the work community and both caring for the values of the others. Ideas flow freely as influence shifts from person to person. Any or all may propose or alter ideas, methods, problems, and solutions.

This is not counseling—unilateral action taken by the counselor toward the other person. Counciling-with followers, rather is finding out together what is right, proper, and needed. This shared approach is often discussed in terms of participatory or democratic approaches to management.

Respond to the following questions from the perspective of your present work situation.

1. When talking with coworkers, do I tell them things and encourage a sharing of information?

2. Do I encourage group discussions and facilitate group dynamics?

3. Do coworkers frequently exchange ideas with me?

4. Do I have the self-esteem to allow others to have good ideas and take the lead at times?

5. Am I able to synthesize group information and formulate decisions or next steps?

CHAPTER 14

Technique 11: Celebrating Success

Leaders engage in activities that do honor to the "personhood" and potential of their stakeholders while at the same time honoring the work community's— and their own—values. Of course, some of this recognition is demonstrated in traditional ways as leaders promote followers, assign them interesting work, provide them with both tangible and intangible incentives, and otherwise reward appropriate behavior.

Inner leaders, however, do not have control over the range of tangible rewards their top leader bosses have. Instead, they use intrinsic rewards—rewards that appeal not to their paychecks but to their psyches. Celebrating follower and work-community successes are ways inner leaders highlight community values and encourage these values as the measures of worker success.

DEFINING LEADERSHIP CELEBRATIONS

Inner leaders recognize that there are also rewards other than financial (Michlitsch, 2000) and that these intrinsic rewards are frequently more powerful in shaping behavior than material ones. They believe that simple recognition is a reward sought by many employees. They know that for most people money is not necessarily motivating because many see it as a right, whereas recognition is a gift. People want to feel important based on the work they do. They want to feel that what they do makes a difference and only formal recognition—often public recognition—can give them this feeling. Hence the need for reward celebrations of individual and group success (Chambers, 1999).

Frequent work-community gatherings, which have a primary objective to recognize and honor—celebrate—the individual performance of stakeholders, often result in increasing stakeholder performance, satisfaction, and commitment. These celebrations acknowledge work well done. They are a purposeful pause to acknowledge the work community's and individual member's success. Celebrations bind the followers in common cause of quality and service (Bolman and Deal, 1995). They recognize extraordinary community and individual performance. And they reflect the work values guiding community action. Celebrations dramatize the inner leader's commitment to the work community's values, its future potential and joint acceptance of that future likelihood by members.

Celebrations can take place at any time. Often they mark the end of a period of hard work on a project. They constitute rewards. Inner leaders reward their employees (in celebrations that deliver the best regards of top management) when groups or individuals meet established standards. Celebrations are held also when individuals or groups demonstrate exemplary behavior in creativity, imagination, or foresight. They mark employee activity in going beyond the call of duty. Rewards given at these celebrations are often simple fun and are related to the actual interests of the people involved. Of course, their success also depends on their being directly relevant to known follower behavior—behavior that is consistent with the leader's vision-values and culture and consonant with stated goals and methodologies.

Celebrations are community cultural ceremonies acknowledging shared work values and basic assumptions. They are events. These celebratory ceremonies display the ambient culture and honor it. They are usually memorable for members (Ott, 1989). Sometimes they are consciously elaborate, dramatic, planned sets of activities that combine various forms of cultural expression. But they need not be elaborate or formal affairs, only heartfelt. They often have both practical and symbolic results. While they may involve monetary bonuses or similar financial elements, those focusing on psychological "stroking" are equally useful (often more so) in encouraging desired performance and commitment to community values and performances.

Besides the use of celebrations to recognize and reward followers, inner leaders use them to help define the work group's culture and to manipulate it to serve their core value goals (Chambers, 1999). They are a significant cultural feature, one that defines and places in operational context the work values the inner leader has established for his or her work community. Celebrations provide an additional method—beyond policies, procedures, and processes, which tools may be beyond the inner leader's control—for leaders to inculcate work-community values, methods, and goals.

Award ceremonies serve a wide variety of purposes. One ancillary result is that they extol the symbols of the leader's work-community culture. They also maintain uniformity, assist in the initiation of new members into the community, and provide a sense of social involvement. They convey powerful symbolic messages about the value of the work, the methods used, and the importance of hard work. They provide connections and order—they bridge between order and chaos. They provide satisfaction, a sense of involvement and hope. Reward celebrations also communicate meaning from the inner leader to individual members and from one subunit to another and to their multiple external communities.

Dedicating time in the workday to celebrate current and past achievements can play an important part in accomplishing new challenges and realizing the future the leader has "created" for the group. Celebrating individual and community achievements is a powerful way inner leaders can praise people who improve, change, and accomplish set goals. Constantly imploring people to improve and get better quickly can become a negative drumbeat of "you're not good enough." Celebrations and other recognition ceremonies of follower performance are the tools inner leaders use regularly to honor their people and acknowledge what they do and have done well. They can also be used to further define and spotlight the leader's desired future for the work community.

Cheerleading

Inner leaders also enthusiastically support their people. They love, encourage, and inspire employees and other stakeholders to perform the work community's business in ways and for results these leaders set. A part of their work is to cheer on the workers as they do needed work. Cheerleading is the reverse of systematic control. It employs more personal, emotional, and psychological devices to nourish workplace cohesion, recognize accomplishment, and buoy up flagging morale.

As inner leaders "direct" their enthusiasm to some worker behavior rather than other, they can implant gradually their work values. For example, they can inspire strong service and quality work values in their followers. Or they can foster innovation as they encourage individual and work-community creativity. Inner leaders communicate their enthusiasm by their words, ideas, and deeds, and in so doing convey a sense of connection, excitement, and shared commitment to group goals or techniques.

Part of the inner leader's role is that of passionate booster of the work community, its mission, its services, and its stakeholders. Cheerleading can be defined as any personal action inner leaders take to encourage and enthuse others to attain the work community's vision purposes. Inner leaders are enthusiasts. They encourage stakeholders to accomplish leader-set vision-directed actions. They develop relationships, programs, events, and other activities that seek to single out and recognize excellent performance. These leaders are enthusiastic about their work, their workers, and the services they collectively supply. And they communicate that in their interactions with all stakeholders and with contacts in their larger communities of interest.

METHODS OF CREATING
LEADERSHIP CELEBRATIONS

Building community spirit involves leaders in activities that increase the bond between coworkers and between the worker and the work community. Part of this task is creating meaningful experiences for individuals, teams, and the whole work community. The intent is to inspire and recommit individual members to agreed-upon tasks, methods, and the leader's vision. If an idea (vision) is important, leaders must present it passionately if inspired action is to result. And they should celebrate any successes in reaching toward that vision. Two kinds of celebrations are discussed in this section: celebration ceremonies and cheerleading behavior. Together they encompass most activity inner leaders engage in to communicate their values via praise and recognition.

Celebrations come in many forms. They can be elaborate productions or informal get-togethers. Programs developed in the past may consist of easily duplicated certificates, suggestion reward systems, newsletter profiles, employee-of-the-month competitions, or formal or informal employee-initiated recognition of helpful colleagues. Some of the large number of success-recognition techniques are described in this chapter. Perhaps the best methods of celebrating individual and group success are those unique programs developed by inner leaders to meet the specific needs of the moment and unique work process peculiar to their work community's role in the larger corporation.

Conducting Reward Celebrations

A celebration is a technique inner leaders use to honor excellent—or at least, unusual and desired—performance (Chambers, 1999). It is taking time to reinforce wanted behavior or results and to acknowledge a job well done. Celebrations can take place at any time—in the middle of a project or at the end of one. Celebrations are held when individuals or the work community as a group demonstrates commendable behavior in hard work, creativity, imagination, foresight, or other values-enhancing effort. They mark activity that deserves celebration in that it goes beyond the call of duty.

Several characteristics of celebrations follow.

- The actual rewards given at these celebrations are often simple fun and are related to the actual interests of the people involved.
- Celebrations deliver the best regards of the leader.
- They can take place at any time.
- They constitute rewards and recognitions of outstanding individual—or group—performance measured against known, preset values.

Communitywide Reward Celebrations

Frequent work communitywide gatherings whose primary object is to recognize, honor, and celebrate community performance help create and maintain unit cohesion. Celebrations dramatize the leader's commitment to people and to work-community values. They are heartfelt expressions of appreciation. Ensuring that celebrations are directly relevant to specific actions that are in line with the vision, values, and culture of the work community also helps ensure their effectiveness. It is often the fun (Santovec, 2001) aspects of a celebration that make recognition ceremonies positive and motivating experiences. Fun, simple, and original rewards work best to motivate community members (Nelson, 1999). The goal is to make the rewards given clever and unique. The simpler and more creative the better. Informal—spontaneous, even—rewards are often very effective in bonding workers to work-community goals and methods.

Individual Recognitions

Celebrating success can also focus on individual performance. Inner leaders give followers a chance not just to do a job but to have some impact on the work community, its processes, and its products. When a follower does his or her work well, they reward them in a celebration that praises that performance. They know that recognizing extraordinary performance will engender more of that behavior in the individual and also in all other workers. They know that the most motivating incentives from their followers' point of view are based on recent performance. People want something for something—they want recognition for a job well done and they want to see a direct connection to work done and the resultant reward. And, inner leaders have learned that recognition means most when it comes from a leader whom the employee holds in high esteem.

As individuals perform in exemplary ways, some inner leaders create or develop ways to publicly acknowledge that behavior. One corporation created what came to be known as the Golden Twinky when an excited inner leader, seeking for something to acknowledge a coworker's completion of a particularly difficult and thorny task ended up handing the follower a twinky from his lunch with a cordial "Great job. Congratulations!" Over time, the Golden Twinky Award became one of the most prestigious honors bestowed on an inventive employee in that division (Nelson, 1999).

Michlitsch (2000) recommends multiple programs and events to celebrate success. He says leaders should reward employees for doing a good job, that is, for engaging in behavior that achieves the work community's mission and strategy. In doing this, inner leaders find out what motivates their employees, and then provide situations within which they can motivate themselves. The reward is sometimes money but often is things that do not cost anything except time, concern, and recognition. Knowing that you get what you reward, inner leaders make certain that they reward performance that is aligned with the community's values, vision, mission, and strategy (Michlitsch, 2000).

Suggestion Awards Systems

While thought of by many as an old-fashioned and almost meaningless human relations technique, innovative inner leaders use this generic idea to craft programs to recognize and reward creative ideas from followers. Such programs can be focused narrowly on the immediate work tasks of suggesters or broadly engage all followers in proposing ideas for performance improvement anywhere in the work community and the larger corporation. Rewards may be recognition only, be limited to token gifts, or be one-time bonuses or pay increments. In some corporations they are a significant percentage of first-year savings produced when the innovative idea is implemented.

Employee of the Month

Rewarding success does not have to cost much money or time. Developing criteria to identify outstanding performance by classes of worker and then measuring actual performance against those standards to highlight top performers is the basis of many recognition programs (Bowman, 1991). Some programs inner leaders initiate to honor a worker involve merely naming that person employee of the month—or week, or year, or other time period. Some inner leaders include a framed certificate attesting to that honor, provide a convenient free parking space, or otherwise give the winner visible special privileges.

Performance Certificates

Recognition for exceeding preset standards or personifying community values can also take the form of easily duplicated certificates honoring outstanding service. It also can entail filing an official commendation in the follower's personnel file to be considered in the future along with other data prior to decisions on raises, promotion, or selection for training or choice work assignments.

Personality Profiles

Profiling the employee in company newsletters or other bulletins or public relations documents also honors outstanding performance and adds to the honored individual's feelings of self-esteem.

Application of Bonus and Incentive Systems

While not always within the sole discretion of inner leaders, implementation of elaborate bonus and incentive awards programs is another recognition technique. Regardless of inner leaders' roles in creating and administering bonus and incentive plans, they use corporation-wide programs to foster their personal professional and work-community objectives as they make decisions about who will be included in bonus distributions and for how much the bonus will be for a given follower vis-à-vis other community members.

Group Bonus Plans

An innovative adaptation of bonus systems is one that focuses on work community as opposed to individual performance. Some inner leaders foster competitions among work units withing their sphere of leadership in which a unit endeavors to save more of its operating budget than other units. The problem with this plan normally is that such savings go back to the general fund and the saving unit reaps nothing but fleeting congratulations. Some inner leaders develop plans where a portion of the annual savings produced by a given unit is retained in its budget as an unallocated lump sum. That unit may keep that money in its budget and apply it to any other part of its work or use it to initiate other performance, quality, or cost-savings activities. Thus, the unit may use the bonus to buy technology, send people to needed training programs, or fund consultants to help propose new or improved systems, procedures, or products.

Cheerleading Techniques

The chief mechanisms for fostering enthusiastic commitment revolve around communications. Inner leaders broadly communicate their sense of excitement about the work community, its people, the work, their clients, and the situation in which they find opportunity to work together. Cheerleading may involve the leader in actions to bring work-community members together to celebrate their successes (any successes, not just their major ones). It often involves individual contacts in which the inner leader communicates personal gratitude to coworkers for their work, their commitment, their accomplishments, or for just being part of the team.

An Attitude of Praise

Inner leaders communicate an attitude of enthusiasm for the work and the workers (Lombardi, 2000). As inner leaders praise their followers for their values-directed work—whether it is truly outstanding work—they create trust, respect, and commitment within the organization. This kind of action helps build an attitude among work-community members that highlights achievement. Praise is a common virtue that is not as common today as it once was in normal human intercourse. If inner leaders cannot dispense monetary rewards in the same way that top leaders do, they can resort to courtesy, recognition, praise, and respect as incentives to others to behave in desired ways.

A Tradition of Excellence

Success is a matter of the mind as much as it is a matter of performance. Inner leaders use a variety of means to help followers think about success in the same way they do. They consciously project the precise picture of excellence that they have in mind for their work-community members. They embody in their actions and communications the qualities of mental intensity and commitment needed to fashion within their work community trust, respect, and commitment to the tasks and methods needed for success. And they are consistent over time in promulgating these values and behaviors. The result is that the community develops a tradition of excellence such that the members do not simply attain their goals, they maintain them over time. This is the real payoff from leading (Lombardi, 2000).

DISCUSSION ISSUES AND QUESTIONS

Issues

1. Inner leaders are enthusiasts. They encourage, buoy up, and cheer their followers.
2. Inner leaders engage in activities that honor the person and the potential of coworkers.
3. Inner leaders believe that simple recognition is a reward sought by many employees.
4. Money is not necessarily motivating because many see it as a "right," whereas recognition is a "gift."
5. People want to feel that what they do makes a difference, and recognition can give them this feeling.
6. Celebrations mark employee activity in going beyond the call of duty.
7. Rewards given at recognition celebrations are often simple fun and are related to the actual interests of the people involved.
8. Inner leaders encourage, enthuse, and inspire employees and others to perform the work community's business in ways and for results these leaders set.
9. As inner leaders direct their enthusiasm to some worker behaviors instead of others, they can inculcate their work and personal values in coworkers.

10. Part of the inner leader's role is that of passionate booster of the work community, its mission, its services, and its people.

11. Cheerleading can be defined as any personal action inner leaders take to encourage and enthuse others to attain the work community's vision purposes.

12. A celebration is a technique inner leader use to honor excellent—or at least, unusual—performance.

13. Celebrations dramatize the leader's commitment to people and to the work community.

14. It is often the fun aspects of a celebration that make recognition a positive experience.

15. Inner leaders cannot dispense monetary rewards in the same way that top leaders do, so they resort to courtesy, recognition, praise, and respect to induce others to behave in desired ways.

Questions

1. Do I sponsor frequent group gatherings whose primary objective is to recognize, honor, and celebrate individual stakeholder performance?

2. Do celebrations acknowledge both group and individual success?

3. Do these recognition celebrations bind followers to a common cause of quality and service and recognize both group and individual performance?

CREATING CELEBRATIONS LEADERSHIP LEARNING ACTIVITIES

The following activities may be useful to individual leaders to gain experience and comfort in recognizing follower performance.

Activity 1: Design Your Own Reward Program

Instructions. Of the many rewards, incentives, and recognitions available to the inner leader to encourage followers to perform congruently with the leader's vision, select one that seems appropriate to the organization employing you.

1. Design a new recognition celebration or other program—or adapt an existing program—and apply it specifically to your work community.

2. Specify as much detail as possible, including
   - The specific behavior (or behavior-sets) this reward celebration program is intended to encourage.
   - Any administrative procedures needed to implement it. You need not design specific procedures, forms, and the like; but be specific enough to give your

readers a sense of the scope and impact on existing administrative procedures this new program will have.

- Sketches of the layout of certificates or other frameable documents that display the honoree's accomplishments.

- Other information or policies that need to be developed and approved prior to implementation or during implementation and operating phases of this program.

3. Consider sharing your design plans with your leaders with the idea of implementing them.

Part IV

THE TECHNIQUES
OF INSPIRING
INNER LEADERSHIP

Inner leaders use psychological and ideological symbols to inspire others. To inspire is to stop questions or doubt and to impel people to change without thinking. There is an extrarational quality about inspiration. It goes beyond facts by putting into words people's dreams and hopes and giving them a sense of purpose (Bilchik, 2001). It is not motivation but another distinctive set of skills and attributes that goes beyond motivation's market-exchange theory—getting something for giving something—and engages the heart and mind as well.

Motivation theory is based on material rewards. It involves tangible benefits received in trade for designated performance. Sometimes the rewards dispensed are associated with the psychological well-being desires of followers such as recognition, affiliation, or status. Generally speaking, motivation can be described as an external exchange transaction between leader and follower where each gives something the other wants and receives something of value in return. However, the fact is that leaders are in the middle of the organization and do not normally control the range of resources under the CEO's control with which they can structure these material motivational exchanges. They have to rely more on the intangible technique of inspiration to secure follower compliance.

Inner leaders do not rely solely on authoritarian forms of leader–follower interaction, favoring indirection and subtlety and inspiration and logical argument. These leaders find they must use exposition and persuasion to convince others of the utility of their values, ideas, and goals and win them over to their point of view. Skill in persuasive communication is an important technique inner leaders use (Gareau, 1999). They also use humor to help their followers bond into a cohesive work community, one that values each member and that differentiates those included in the work community from all others (Santovec, 2001). Inner leaders use humor to direct follower attention to what they want them to think about and divert their attention from what they don't want. Humor is a powerful tool and is part of effective leadership (Avolio, Howell, and Sosik, 1999).

The three techniques highlighted in Part IV define tasks associated with animating, enlivening, invigorating, and infecting coworkers—in a word, inspiring them. Part IV techniques are not often included in discussions about leadership theory and practice. The three techniques in this part include being inspiring, learning to persuade others, and using humor.

CHAPTER 15

Technique 12: Being Inspiring

Inspiration is a key, if complex, tool in the hands of inner leaders (Bilchik, 2001). These leaders find opportunity to use the technique of inspiration frequently. While inspiration has always been either an actual or a potential tool in leadership, it is a relatively new concept in the literature. It is a powerful tool to reenergize followers and to bond them together in the joint enterprise. It is a tool that top leaders may also use, but often don't. The reason top leaders do not use inspiration is that it is frequently difficult to do. They can more easily employ motivation, a more physical, tangible method to secure follower compliance. Nevertheless, inspiration is a powerful weapon in the inner leader's arsenal (Fairholm, 1991).

DEFINING INSPIRATION

Simply put, inspiration is using words, ideas, information, and deeds to convey a sense of connection, excitement, and commitment to work-community goals or methods. When people feel inspired they want to act on that feeling. Inspiration is not motivation. It goes beyond motivation in appealing to a collective human need to be part of and engaged with others in lofty enterprise. Inspiring leaders strengthen coworkers, teach, and exhort them toward a common vision of what the work community is and can become. They tap something deep within the individual that strikes a responsive chord.

We now live in a world where interdependence, not dependence, is the mode (Lombardi, 2000). It is a world of uncertainty, not order; of negotiation, not edicts; of persuasion, not command. This kind of a world demands leadership, not management. The need is for leaders who will use their power to empower others. Today's corporations need leaders who can change workers' behaviors while staying in tune with their values. They need logic guided by intuition (Tesolin, 2000). The work communities in which people spend their time need someone to give voice to a vision of the future that exists now, if unstated, in the minds of followers. In short, they need inspiring inner leaders.

Inspiration is the name for that kind of influence that operates upon our minds so that we receive direction in extrarational ways (Roberts, 1907). Inspirational leaders have high self-confidence, dominance, and a conviction of moral rightness. They transfer these qualities to followers (see Bass, 1987; Peters and Waterman, 1982; Maccoby, 1981; Burns, 1978). Operationally, inspiration is defined by several emotional results (Burns, 1978).

These definitional elements of inspiration imply several ideas. First, inspiration involves a confirmation in the hearts of believers that the work community's common message (vision) is true. Second, it provides guidance for individual believers in their community relationships. Third, inspiration is a means to gain full understanding of an inspiring future vision. Fourth, via the inspirational messages, believers can have communion with other believers and form links to other like-minded people. Fifth, inspiration impels one to do good, toward excellence. Sixth, it carries with it a feeling of rightness. And finally, inspiration has a teaching component—it is a way to teach others.

Inspiration is what many mistakenly call motivation (Lombardi, 2000). They confuse the inspirational, emotional element in some leader behavior for motivation from without.

Traditionally, the task of getting others to comply has been called motivation, and an extensive theory and methodology have evolved encompassing the leader's tasks in causing directed change in others. Unfortunately, this theory and practice are largely wrong. The fact is that leaders cannot motivate followers—no person external to the individual can. Motives come from within the person; they are internal to each individual and directed by that individual. Leaders have little to do with creating motives. In short, all motivation is personal, done by the individual in response to his or her own values drives.

Another person—leader, manager, friend, or colleague—cannot motivate anyone. He or she does something else. When someone else, through his or her behavior, actions, or words, induces the individual to act, he or she can do so only via one or a combination of three approaches. He or she can create or alter an environment within which the individual can satisfy his or her own needs while (hopefully) also doing corporate work. Or he or she can do something to awaken a dormant motive or change the priority of someone's values motives to action. Or he or she can excite and inspire the other person to action to satisfy by that action his or her needs and, optimistically, the work community's.

CEOs and other managers, those in control of corporate resources, can induce follower action most easily by resort to approaches one or two. Inner leaders find that the third approach—inspiration—is most often the best approach available to them and that it is frequently a powerful inducement to stakeholder action. Inspiration, is an emotional appeal from one person to another. It is external excitation to action of another person, but it is not technically motivation because there is an element of coercion in motivation.

Assuming the accuracy of this reasoning, leaders cannot "motivate" others. All they can do is create a climate and the conditions within which others can find ways to self-motivate within parameters they set. Inner leaders can also interact with followers individually to help them see that some of their own motives, if satisfied through work community effort, can result in greater overall satisfaction than relying on their own current motives. That is, an inner leader can ask a follower to complete a difficult (or new, or creative) task, and through that effort the follower comes to realize that this work satisfies a new motive, and satisfying this need may be more rewarding to him or her than the one he or she currently spends effort in satisfying. Beyond this, motivation has little meaning as a leader technique.

Some of the inspiration techniques of inner leadership follow.

METHODS OF INSPIRATION

Chief executives are adept at ensuring that a corporation produces tangible things remarkably well. They are less adept at producing inspired people. Bosses control things, but they cannot "control" people into the commitment necessary to accept the risks of (for example) battle or any other significant social enterprise. This is in direct contrast to inner leaders whose purpose is to inspire volunteer followers to common action whether or not the leader is present to oversee behavior. These leaders are inspirational. They enliven and animate others and impel their people to act without thinking. They override sterile fact and put words to people's dreams and hopes. Inspiration gives our dreams purpose and direction (Lombardi, 2000). It articulates the felt needs, values, and visions of the work community and its individual members. It is fundamentally a power—empowering—activity.

Inspiration is a particular relationship between an individual leader and one or more others that enlivens both and provides them with new insight, new emotions, and new directions (Bilchik, 2001). Inspiration is not so much a quality in the leader (the inspirer) as it is a function of the needs of the inspired that the inner leader reflects and responds to. Inner leaders find useful insights, therefore, as they learn first something of the nature of followership. Several aspects of inspiration can be identified to help the inner leader operationalize this technique in his or her day-to-day work. Among them are the following. Inspiration

1. connects ideas to action.
2. is a highly emotional and personal experience.
3. promotes the development of people's talents.
4. enables others to feel and act as leaders.
5. helps people recognize the contributions of others.

6. stimulates others' thinking.
7. builds enthusiasm about projects and assignments.
8. is facilitated by the use of symbols.
9. appeals to collective work community history.
10. addresses people's psychological and emotional needs.
11. articulates people's dreams.
12. creates consensus.

Key Ideas in Inspiration

Developing the skills to inspire others is a matter of the leader's overall leadership philosophy. Inner leaders cannot compel compliance from their stakeholders because all followers are essentially volunteers. How they inspire followers to follow them is a critical technique inner leaders need to master. Inspiring others involves several tasks, the dimensions of which constitute the technique of inspirational leadership. Some of these techniques follow (Plas, 1996; Tesolin, 2000; Fairholm, 2001).

Provide a Sense of Purpose

Inspiration is activating the felt needs, values, and aspirations of the work community (Bilchik, 2001). The mechanism for inspiring a shared sense of purpose often is a common vision of what the work community is and can become. An inspiring vision includes three key elements:

1. *Purpose*: the fundamental set of reasons for the work community's existence.
2. *Mission*: an achievable focal point and goal aligning subgroup effort with the full work community.
3. *Focus on the future*: creating the future by doing or acting in the present with that future in mind.

A vision by its very nature implies a creative tension and a sense of anticipation—both essential aspects of any inspirational idea, situation, or individual persona. Inspirational leaders focus their stakeholders on the present, as well as what must happen to arrive at the desired future. Inspiration comes as inner leaders help followers see the vision as real for them today, while not yet having arrived at that future state of being (Ramsey, 1994).

Articulating Common Needs

The connection between the inner leader's vision and the personal psychological needs of followers is the essence of inspiration. Leaders are inspiring precisely because what they say impels another person to do something the leader wants and that also helps satisfy that person's personal needs. As inner leaders learn and then appropriately respond to their followers' needs, they trigger constructive psychological responses in members that facilitate commitment to the work community's tasks.

Many needs are present in any work community. Some needs are for affiliation. Others are for achievement or to exert power in relationships. All can be met through work-community involvement. Inner leaders find ways to help their followers understand these needs—and other needs—and help them develop expectations and find ways to assuage them through working in the work community.

Stopping Doubt

Inspiration appeals to the emotions of followers and causes them to come together in the common enterprise ("The Greatest Motivators of the Century," 1999). Inspirational messages are a way for the believer to have communion with other believers (Tesolin, 2000) and impel them toward excellence. They bring with them a feeling of rightness, correctness about what they do. They stop any feelings of doubt a follower may have about doing assigned work or holding suitable attitudes and values.

Articulating Follower Dreams

Inspiration consists of a confirmation in the hearts of followers that the common vision is true (Roberts, 1907). Inner leaders are inspiring when they take other persons beyond routine ways of thinking and behaving and lead them to higher level of interaction and focus (Fairholm, 1991, 2000a) consistent with their sense of spiritual integrity.

Helping Followers Act without Thinking

Inspirational messages are often found in the communications leaders make to followers. An obvious such message is the inner leader's vision statement. As followers accept the vision's goals, values, and ideals, this decision lets them act automatically in terms of it. They don't have to think through or rationalize each new situation any more. The vision clarifies the situation and dictates a course of action. An accepted inspiring message puts adherents in a kind of auto-pilot that makes future actions known, good, and simple. A vision states and dramatizes the purposes of the leader and reflects the system of beliefs that give the leader–follower relationship texture and coherence. Inspirational messages use distinctive language (Braham, 1999) to define roles, activities, challenges, and purposes. They are seldom, if ever, couched in explicit terms. Rather, they create patterns of meanings and consciousness reflected in the leader's relationship with followers. These messages raise the consciousness level of the stakeholder work community. They are a potent mechanism for directing and influencing others.

Using Symbols and Ideology

Leaders are symbol users. Bennis (1982) says that leadership becomes effective when individuals place symbolic value on the leader's expressed intentions. To inspire followers, the leader must appeal to them on a different level than mere physical drives. This appeal is often conveyed via symbols standing for the shared values and vision of the work community developed over time ("The Greatest Motivators," 1999).

Using Intuitive Faculties

Inspiration and intuition are connected in real ways. Intuition defines a way to receive knowledge and information without conscious, rational thought (Rowan, 1986). In using inspiration, inner leaders tap their own and the intuitive capacities of work community members. Inspiration is the almost intuitive appeal to innate follower values that inspires them to accept the leader and his or her vision and that gives the leader moral legitimacy (Tesolin, 2000). Tesolin says fostering intuition goes beyond intelligence. It lies in the ability of inner leaders to use their intuitive sense, which is closely aligned with common sense. Intelligence involves a wide range of people skills, including communication and creativity. On the other hand, intuition entails a deep level of self-knowledge and listening, irrespective of reality or social and cultural conditioning. Through intuition we learn what is right, how to live and work with integrity, and how to express our truest selves.

Using Emotional Appeal

Inspiration goes beyond facts by giving them an emotional connection to the leader, the work community, and the task.

Enlightening Followers

Both leaders and led share responsibility for communicating clearly (Townsend and Gebhardt, 1990) the joint activity. In inspiring followers, inner leaders make sure that followers know details both of the job and of their personal preferences. Inspiring leaders transfer understanding to their followers by example and by giving personal attention to each follower to make certain he or she knows his or her part in the overall work plan.

Serving Others

Hard work by itself is not as important any more (perhaps it never was) as is making a positive impact on results. Success is increasingly defined today as giving the customers and all stakeholders particular service, rather than producing a standard product at continuously lowered unit cost and forcing them to take it. Inspiring inner leaders reinvent their work communities (Naisbitt and Aburdene, 1985) and their workers and systems to make them service oriented. This service focus itself is inspiring and is the basis for much workplace inspiration.

Maintaining Open Communications

To be inspiring, inner leaders also must be able to clearly communicate with a growingly diverse group of stakeholders, each of whom desires unique services and attention. When information is not forthcoming, conscientious followers seek it out. Just as inner leaders need to keep their bosses informed, they need to communicate broadly with their followers useful information about both the internal and external job situation. Similarly, followers must keep their leader informed about details of their piece of the work. Often followers are better informed about issues such as the team's current capabilities for meeting customer demands than the inner leader (Townsend and Gebhardt, 1990). Effective leaders need such information, and good inner leaders have learned to ask for it if it is not offered. Effective inner leaders take steps to ensure that needed communications flow in all possible directions at all times. Ensuring this flow is a prime task.

Building Culture

Inspiration is more a function of the readiness of the work community member than of the leader. Creating a culture characterized by multiple layers of shared values is, therefore, essential. The culture is the physical and psychological place where the leader inspires followers. It defines the climate and conditions within which the leaders personal needs and particular personal needs of the core of followers can be juxtaposed in ways that let each satisfy the other. The culture provides a broad basis of consensus around core values, the vision guiding work community, and individual actions and the ways members can and should interact with one another. A central task inner leaders accept is to create the conditions in the work community surroundings that ease the task of inspiring followers to accept and act upon their (the leader's) vision, values, and strategic plans.

Building Individual Loyalty and Commitment

Loyalty, like other personal, intimate feelings, is caused by a myriad factors. Among the obvious contributing factors to developing or to reducing loyalty include changing social values respecting work. If workers are unwilling to prioritize work higher than other personal or family issues or they practice lifestyles that emphasize values other than work uses of their time, their loyalty quotient falls. The emergence of a highly independent society is also a critical factor in determining group and individual loyalty. Morale factors such as job eliminations, restructuring, downsizing, and mergers likewise impact the loyalty quotient, often negatively. Leader indifference, breaking of commitments, arbitrary actions, lack of opportunity to earn promotions or grow on the job, and poor supervision are also conditioning factors. Loyalty suffers when their leaders show favoritism, are discriminatory, fail to recognize outstanding follower performance, or are authoritarian. Factors like low pay, unfair salary programs, and seniority-based raises, of course, also affect loyalty or disloyalty.

Fostering Trust

Experience and observation suggest that inspiration is delimited by the nature and extent of member trust. Unfortunately, none of the traditional theories of culture and trust clearly defines trust as an essential element in the cultural surround. (One exception is Fairholm, 1994.) Yet trust is central in understanding the pull of culture on individual member actions. The culture created allows members to behave with varying levels of trust that certain actions or events will produce expected results. This kind of trust culture is a component of inspiration. One culture may allow for more trust than another, but without the constraints on member behavior to trust each other imposed by cultural features neither leaders nor any member could exercise inspiration at all.

Setting Values

Understanding the techniques of inspiration in leadership in today's world requires examination of shared values. Leadership, at its heart, is a value-laden activity. People may need to be ordered and directed, but they must be inspired also. Creating and promulgating a unique set of values that support the inner leader's agenda is, therefore, a major task underlying his or her success in inspiring follower to desired action (Crosby, 1996). Leadership models that forgo values because values contaminate the objective process fail to understand the true function of leadership.

Foster Change

Inspirational leaders inspire stakeholders to accept, even seek, change (Lombardi, 2000). They do this as they engage in actions to replace traditional controls and substitute an inspired vision, leading by example and being involved, visible leaders. An inspired vision is one that challenges, excites, one that captures followers' hearts and spirit, as well as their minds (Bolman and Deal, 1995).

Visioning

The inspirational actions or words of the inner leader are inspiring precisely because they clarify and animate what followers already know in their hearts. The reason we describe the leader's vision as a vision is that leaders put into words the hopes and dreams of followers that are already in their hearts (Conger, 1994). If the inner leader's vision does not persuasively articulate the latent dreams shared by all or most followers, the leader's vision cannot be compelling. Visions become inspiring because of this and because leaders have somehow touched powerful values, emotions, and desires shared by members of the work community. Leaders interpret the community vision in unique ways consistent with both the group's tasks and its history. As they do this, if the leader's vision appeals to follower needs, the vision statement becomes inspirational.

DISCUSSION ISSUES AND QUESTIONS

Issues

1. Motivation is based on material rewards and involves physical—material—benefits received in trade for designated performance.

2. The only true motivation is self-motivation. Others cannot motivate anyone. They do something else. They inspire.

3. Inspiration, based on shared ideas or ideals, is based on the leader's character, values, ideals, vision, and similar intangibles.

4. Inspiration is using words, ideas, and deeds to convey a sense of connection, excitement, and shared commitment to work-community goals or methods.

5. Inspiring others asks leaders to use more-than-rational means to persuade followers.

Questions

1. Do I encourage teamwork, inspire cooperation, mentor, and otherwise shape member behavior to agreed-upon goals often via one-on-one relationships?

2. Am I inspiring?

3. Do I take steps to confirm in coworkers' hearts guidance about work-community values, a full understanding of the work community's vision, and ways to communicate with other like-minded workers?

4. Do I convey a feeling of rightness about our joint work?

INSPIRATIONAL LEADERSHIP LEARNING
ACTIVITIES

Activity 1: Self-Assessment—Inspiration Quotient

Instructions. Indicate the degree to which you think the following statements are true or false by circling the appropriate number. For example, if a statement is always true, you should circle the 5 next to that statement.

5 = Always true

4 = Generally true

3 = Somewhat true, but with exceptions

2 = Somewhat false, but with exceptions

1 = Generally false

0 = Certainly always false

5 4 3 2 1 0   1. In social situations I have the ability to alter my behavior if I feel that something else is called for.

5 4 3 2 1 0   2. I am often able to read people's true emotions correctly through their eyes.

5 4 3 2 1 0   3. I have the ability to control the way I come across to people, depending on the impression I wish to give them.

5 4 3 2 1 0   4. In conversations, I am sensitive to even the slightest change in the facial expression of the person I'm conversing with.

5 4 3 2 1 0   5. My powers of intuition are quite good when it comes to understanding others' emotions and motives.

5 4 3 2 1 0   6. I can usually tell when others consider a joke in bad taste, even though they may laugh convincingly.

5 4 3 2 1 0   7. When I feel that the image I am portraying isn't working, I can readily change it to something that does.

5 4 3 2 1 0   8. I can usually tell when I've said something inappropriate by reading the listener's eyes.

5 4 3 2 1 0   9. I have trouble changing my behavior to suit different people and different situations.

5 4 3 2 1 0 10. I have found that I can adjust my behavior to meet the requirements of any situation I find myself in.

5 4 3 2 1 0 11. If someone is lying to me, I usually know it at once from the person's manner of expression.

5 4 3 2 1 0 12. Even when it might be to my advantage, I have difficulty putting up a good front.

5 4 3 2 1 0   13. Once I know what the situation calls for, it's easy for me to regulate my actions accordingly.

Scoring key: To obtain your score, add up the numbers circled, except reverse the scores for questions 9 and 12. On those, a circled 5 becomes 0, 4 becomes 1, and so forth. Inspirational leaders are defined as those with score of approximately 53 or higher.

Activity 2: Inspiring Ideas about Inspiration

Instructions. Inspiration is a word most commonly used in religion and the arts to describe a wave of emotional stimulation. Its use in leadership is less common.

1. Review the following quotations.

   A leader inspires his staff to believe in themselves and their ability to succeed long before they recognize their own potential.

   Sherman Hamilton

   Leaders get followers to reach beyond themselves. The task of the leader is to get his people from where they are to where they have not been.

   Henry Kissinger

   True leadership must be for the benefit of the followers, not for the enrichment of the leaders. In combat, officers eat last.

   Lao-tzu

   The institutional leader is primarily an expert in the promotion and protection of values.

   Philip Selznick

   Leadership is the ability to decide what is to be done and then to get others to want to do it.

   Dwight D. Eisenhower

   The extraordinary appeal of Mao Tse-tung is hard to identify. Some may suggest that it lies less in the man and more in the nature of the Chinese society, for the Chinese do seem compelled to make all their leaders into imperial figures.

   Lucian W. Pye

   Churchill had learned the great truth that to move other people, the leader must first move himself.

   Sir Robert Menzies

2. Study these quotations and assess their implications for being an inspiring leader. What can you learn about how to inspire others by applying these statements to your practice of leadership?

3. Write an explanatory essay that summarizes your conclusions.

CHAPTER 16

Technique 13: Persuading Others

Leadership remains, as it always was, basically concerned with communications. Transferring information—facts, values, ideas, and their meanings—is the heart of the leader's task. Recent technological improvements, largely in the computer and telecommunications fields, have made possible important new developments in the way leaders—indeed, all people—move information. The effective use of information transfer techniques is critical. Even more critical to effective inner leadership is the need to control the type and content of its communications to followers so that the leader's desires are realized in subsequent follower actions.

Several techniques are presently associated with the idea of attaining the inner leader's desired performance. Among them are electronic mail, cellular telephone technologies, image processing, teleconferencing, fibre optics, and the Internet. A detailed discussion of features of each of these techniques is not pertinent to this discussion. Nevertheless, these technologies represent new, faster, more generally accessible channels of communication delivery that will continue to enhance and extend the scope of influence of both leaders and led.

These newer electronic techniques also represent alternative sources of information available to followers, sources that may make inner leadership both easier and more difficult. These new ways to communicate multiply the inner leaders communications options and the speed at which knowledge can be transferred. For example, e-mail has opened multiple channels of communication and information flow. As a result, work-community structural boundaries have become fuzzier and corporate culture looser, less formal, and less important to work communities in the inner levels of the corporation.

At the same time, as followers use these nonleader channels to get needed information, the influence of inner leaders is lessened, since a traditional source of leaders' influence has been as prime conduits for external information needed by work-community members. E-mail focuses on the message, not the person communicating the message or his or her position in the hierarchy. It also breaks down barriers of gender or status in the work community. It takes away many normal formal social structural constraints.

While some of these factors move toward better communications systems, others may complicate, and even reduce, accountability for the communications between the leader and stakeholders. Nevertheless, these and the other communications techniques portend significant change in the manner and locus of leadership practice now and in the years to come. They do not change the purpose of most of the communications between inner leaders and their followers: to get them to think and act in ways the leader wants them to think and act.

DEFINING PERSUASIVE COMMUNICATION
IN LEADERSHIP

Leaders are preeminent communicators (Bennis and Nanus, 1985). They are symbol users, whether it is words, songs, artifacts, speech, or something else. Leaders communicate meaning. Inner leaders make use of a specific kind of communication: persuasion. Mostly, they set and then communicate work-community requirements via persuasion, not orders, instructions, or policy statements. Leadership by command is an outdated conception of the leader's task. The days when any leader could order employees to do the work and it got done are over if, indeed, this ever was the case. In fact, leadership based on and through the authority held by the incumbent is not leadership at all. It describes a management, not a leadership, concept. The interior world of the corporation today is one of interdependence, not dependence; of uncertainty, not order; of negotiation, not fiat; of persuasion, not command. This kind of a world demands leaders, not managers. And leadership success demands leaders who can persuade others, who can influence them to act and sway their opinions without resorting to traditional authoritarian force or compulsion (Gareau,1999).

Much more effective in transferring standards and values is the technique of persuasion by logical argument. Leaders set the values context of the work community and convince stakeholders to accept the values as their own (Klenke, 1996). In doing this, they appeal to stakeholders at their inner, spiritual level. They couch desired values in task terms or in people terms or in a balance of each. In either case, the vision defining the work community and the attitudes about relationships with coworkers held in common defines the core of shared values that makes leadership possible.

The key is to persuade followers to follow the leader's lead. Gardner (1990) sees leadership as simply a process of persuasion and example. Through their communications skills leaders cause work-community action that is in accord with their purposes and, eventually, the shared purposes of all. This definition, common to many theorists, implies a developmental role and makes the process explicitly one of communicating to persuade (see also Bedell, 2001; Brumback, 1999; Gareau, 1999; Throgmorton, Mandelbaum, and Garcia, 2000).

The Leadership Task of Persuasion

Persuasive communication implies an interaction between leader and follower that involves engaging the minds of both. Persuasion, as a form of communication, is different from other forms. It implies equality, caring, and respect for the ideas and logic of those to be persuaded. Leaders in the middle establish and communicate standards via persuasion. Persuasion is much more effective in conveying standards and values given contemporary culture. It relies on the relatively bias-free use of logical argument. Inner leaders set work-community standards, teach them, and live them; and then they persuade others to live them by the example of their word and deed.

Persuasion is a common technique inner leaders use. It is an aspect of the leader's capacity to use power, the intent of which is to convince others to do what the leader wants them to do. Persuasion is a generic name for a variety of communications skills and techniques that have as their purpose altering another person or group to the leader's point of view. Persuasive communication may be directed to get followers to know something the leader wants them to know. Or it may provoke desired follower behavior or change followers' attitudes or values. This technique of inner leadership relies on another value system—rational discussion—and another range of resources—ideas, values, and ideology—than those mentioned to this point.

The act of leading in the middle of the corporation involves the leader in communication to change the values, the knowledge base, the logic, and thus the behavior of stakeholders to conform to the leader's vision objectives. Sharing that vision is accomplished in numerous contacts with work-community members as a group and in both formal and informal individual contacts with them. The intent of these multiple communications is to get followers to always act authentically within the constraints of group values.

Inner leaders practice persuasive communications techniques toward every stakeholder. They use persuasion upward toward their bosses, downward toward their subordinates, and laterally toward their peers, nondirect-line colleagues, customers, advisors, and other experts whether inside the corporation or not (Bedell, 2001). In the corporate interior perhaps more than in any relationship in which inner leaders participate, the need for sensitive persuasion to build collaborative relations is acute. The targets of the inner leader's persuasive communications may also be other inner leaders who are motivated by many of the same values yet seek similar goals. Most often these others are not obligated to cooperate; they will do so only if they receive cooperation in facilitating their own goals. That is, they have to be convinced that doing it the leader's way is also good for them.

In a sense, all interior interpersonal relationships are situations in which persuasion is the preferred communication technique. Inner leaders are constantly moving from a guiding position to a follower one and vice versa. At times they persuade others to do something they want them to do—to follow orders, to get them something, to laugh at their jokes, or to understand and respect their ideas and values. At other times they are persuaded to behave as a stakeholder desires them to. The operative aspect of the process of persuasion is in the personal relationship between one leader and one follower reiterated in a series of one-on-one relationships throughout the work community. Communicating to persuade is central to any interaction between coequal, independent, and interdependent people. It is a cornerstone of inner leadership behavior as practiced throughout history.

METHODS OF PERSUADING OTHERS

Persuasion can be effective in situations where both parties care about the result in similar ways. Persuasion is an egalitarian technique that leaves intact the free choice of the person persuaded. Persuasion is effective, requires little expenditure of resources, and (given a skillful inner leader), involves little risk. It is nothing more than logical argument—successful argument. It is a relationship in which one person independently weighs and accepts the ideas, instructions, and values of another who elaborates his position to the first. In this technique, the decision to accept the leader's argument is essentially unconstrained by considerations of penalty or reward (except via the logical results of this "desired" behavior).

When inner leaders use argument, they suspend use of force or the authority of position. Persuasion is a form of give and take in which both parties interact in relative equality. It partakes of the following characteristics, which also constitute steps in the persuasion process.

Persuasion Is Characterized by Sharing

The individuals in a given communications situation typically begin with different views, information, ideas, values, biases, and the like. Interactive dialogue convinces one of the other's point of view and therefore causes that person to take action that that person would not otherwise have taken. The members of a given work community almost always differ in their talents, experiences, information, intelligence, and logical capacities. As they interact, they engage in relationships that employ the techniques of persuasion, negotiation, and selling others on their ideas. The context of persuasive communications is in the collaborative unit characterized by shared values, information, and goals. The skills are those of logic, argument, and negotiation.

Persuasion Is Successful as Inner Leaders Develop Rhetoric

Persuasion depends on capacities and abilities inner leaders have or control that give them an advantage in rhetoric. In a word, persuasion is the art of expressive speech. It is oratory. The middle-level leader must be more eloquent, convincing, and verbal than others to use it successfully in interpersonal situations. Properly directed, persuasion is an effective technique leaders master as they prepare to lead. It is one of the most effective and reliable leadership techniques in existence precisely because it is so common in social interaction. Almost every communication exchange involves both parties in trying to persuade the other to laugh, to cry, to like them, or in any other way to get the other to do what they want as a result of their words.

Persuasion Asks Inner Leaders to Think

Persuasion is a discipline of the mind. It asks leaders to reason, analyze, and examine ideas, information, situations, and possibilities. It asks them to integrate sometimes seemingly disparate information into an integrated whole that is internally consistent and reflective of the core vision and values guiding the work community. Inner leaders are successful in building a work community when they can induce members to endorse, accept, and then incorporate the leader's vision and values into their own personalities. This task requires that leaders know their followers, know the work processes and the end results sought, and merge all into an intellectually coherent unity.

Persuasion Allows a Free Flow of Information

Part of the technique of persuasion is skill in the techniques of creating communications patterns between the inner leader and each work community member that encourages the free flow of discussion between them. Inner leaders share their core values, but they also share information about the joint tasks and encourage followers to do the same. Sharing data and information can take several forms:

- Meetings—both formal and informal
- Informal conversations with individuals
- Written reports
- Electronic and printed newsletters
- E-mail
- Internal corporate Internet Web sites (sometimes called "intra-net")

- Statistical summaries
- Bulletin boards
- News releases

Inner leaders adopt an open, sharing, egalitarian mind-set about information, one of the most valuable resources under their control. Sharing work-related data freely, however, is not the normal pattern of communications in many corporations. Rather, the norm is to hold data and release it only on a "need-to-know" basis. The pattern for many top leaders is to provide information to coworkers only if their task assignments specifically require a piece of information or other data. Psychologically, it is safer to keep information to yourself—especially negative information.

On the other hand, inner leaders share information about the history of the corporation, current status and practices, and future plans and alternative scenarios of action. They also couch these data in language that attracts others, excites their emotions, and arouses feelings of commitment to the work community. All information about the corporation—its work programs, methods, people, and plans—is potentially useful, even critical, to individual member success. Perhaps the most critical is future information. Inner leaders share their ideas about what the future of the corporation and its workers might be through their vision and all other statements they make.

On that measure alone, the vision statement becomes a vital element in leadership and a tool for persuading others to adopt it as their own. Indeed, keeping information about what future outcomes the leader envisions for the work community effectively thwarts any other efforts the leader makes to secure follower commitment to work-community effort, as this action effectively denies followers direction and purpose.

Persuasion Involves Designing Communications Systems

Communicating to persuade others engages the leader in a complex interactive communication process. Besides learning to be expert logicians and debaters, inner leaders understand and practice sophisticated techniques of interpersonal communication (Bedell, 2001). They are experts in selecting the message, coding it appropriately, determining the mode of transmission, and assessing the fidelity of the information to be received by followers. Indeed, they are expert in all aspects of this core human process.

Persuasive Communications Includes Feedback Loops

Feedback mechanisms insure that leaders' desired messages are in fact received by followers. Feedback loops must be established and must be continually in play in any persuasive communication event. Feedback is an aspect of any communication that lets inner leaders learn how fully and authentically their messages have been received and understood by the receivers of those messages. Feedback mechanisms include active listening, requiring reports from receivers, observing resultant behavior, attitudes, body language, the manner of speaking, and a myriad of detailed actions falling into one or the other of these processes.

Summary

Persuasion is an interactive process that can enliven, animate, and invigorate followers and inspire them to achieve the leader's vision. Both people in this communication exchange are active participants. Each is free to influence the other as he or she sees fit and as his or her skills permit. Inner leaders' success, therefore, is the result of the quality of their ideas and their skill in persuading others to their point of view. While feedback is important in any communication exchange, it is essential in persuasion. The leader cannot know what his hearers are receiving unless direct steps are taken to find out what they think was said. Argument is futile—maybe, not even argument—unless both parties understand the logic of the other person. Only then can they set in motion further debate to make their case.

DISCUSSION ISSUES AND QUESTIONS

Issues

1. Leaders are symbol users who communicate meaning through interaction that involves engaging the minds of both.
2. Leadership is simply a process of persuasion and example.
3. Persuasion is argument—successful argument.
4. Persuasion is an egalitarian technique that honors the free choice of the person persuaded.
5. Persuasion implies equality, caring, and respect for the ideas and logic of the other person.

Questions

1. How does sharing information affect me in my inner leader role? My followers?
2. What would a decision to share information freely ask me to do differently?
3. What kinds of information should I share with followers that they do not now receive? Be specific.
4. What new techniques would I need to learn?

5. What new mind set must I adopt?

6. What feedback mechanisms are in place in my work community?

7. Do I encourage feedback by my personal responses? How? Be specific.

8. Do I give feedback to my follows?

PERSUASIVE COMMUNICATION ACTIVITIES

Learning to be an inner leader engages the individual in a variety of behaviors intended to persuade others to his or her point of view. The following may be useful to leaders to assess and increase their experience in learning to persuade followers.

Activity 1: Self-Assessment—Persuasion

Introduction. One of the key elements of exemplary inner leadership is the leader's persuasive credibility. Having credibility allows a leader to undertake the task of persuading others of necessary changes with sincerity and with followers' trust. Following are the elements of persuasive credibility.

1. Rate yourself on each of the items using the following scale:

1	2	3	4
Always	Never	Occasionally	Often

_____ 1. I state my position clearly.

_____ 2. My coworkers and subordinates always know where I stand.

_____ 3. I listen to other people's opinions carefully and respectfully.

_____ 4. I accept disagreement from my coworkers and followers.

_____ 5. I try to integrate my point of view with those of others.

_____ 6. I encourage and practice constructive feedback.

_____ 7. I encourage and practice cooperation.

_____ 8. I build consensus out of differing views.

_____ 9. I develop my coworkers' and subordinates' skills.

_____ 10. I provide frequent positive feedback and encouragement.

_____ 11. I hold myself and others accountable for actions.

_____ 12. I practice what I preach.

              Total: _____

Scoring key: Add up your rating for all twelve items. The maximum score is 48. A higher score indicates demonstrations of behaviors that build persuasive credibility.

2. Are there any items for which you have a low score? If yes, those are areas that you need to target in order to build your persuasive credibility. List items with a low score.

3. What can you do about them? Concentrate on clear and specific behaviors.

4. Develop short-term and long-term goals.

5. When will you know that you have improved?

6. How will you measure yourself?

Activity 2: Case Study—A Problem in Listening? Or What?

In the Midland Toy Company two of the sessions in the ten-session leadership development program are concerned with the topic of communication and its importance in leadership success. Near the end of the first session, Jim Brown, head of the maintenance section, volunteered the comment that even though he found the topic to be interesting and agreed that it was important, something vital was missing in the corporation's training program. "As a unit head, my problem is that people just don't know how to listen," he said. "With a lot of my people after I spend a great deal of effort instructing them as to exactly what to do, they're just as likely to be doing something entirely different when I check on their progress later. What we should do is set up a course in good listening and have all our employees take it."

1. What do you think the real problem is that Mr. Brown is discussing?

2. Do you agree with Jim that communication can be improved by having people develop better listening skills?

3. Do you agree that such a course would be helpful in your work community? Why or why not?

4. In any communication situation, who has ultimate responsibility for communication success or failure? Why?

5. Is Jim Brown a good persuader? What role does persuasion have in this kind of communication process?

6. Do you think Mr. Brown is effective as a communicator? How might he be better?

CHAPTER 17

Technique 14: Using Humor

For many people a best friend is someone to whom they can reveal their true selves, including their absurd selves, their humorous aspects. Given the centrality of their work for many Americans, they are seeking this kind of relationship on the job. Effective inner leaders use humor as part of their effort to inspire and direct followers to some ideas, activities, and approaches and away from others. Santovec (2001) says workplace humor is driven by leaders who set the environment within which humor is used, define the parameters of its use, and more than other members of the work community apply it in work-related interactions.

Humor is a useful, if little recognized, measure of status in the group. It helps define a member's place in the work community, who that member is as an individual, and how the community defines itself. Abramis (1992) says that humor is an essential part of "humanness." He suggests that if a work community is humorless, if humor is suppressed, the likelihood is that other essential characteristics required to do business are also suppressed, and the members' humanness is restricted. When people can laugh at themselves and each other they feel better about themselves and others and are more connected, bonded.

DEFINING HUMOR IN LEADERSHIP

Human beings are alone among all creatures in their ability to laugh. It is a core characteristic that helps define the human being. Humor is a way people express their true, intimate, core selves, including their vulnerable, foolish, irrational, ridiculous sides. Humor harks back to the individual's childlike nature, that part of self that remains unchanged from childhood, perhaps the person's most accurate and authentic expression of self (Abramis, 1992).

A sense of humor is a characteristic frequently associated with leadership, especially that kind of leadership that prioritizes growth, involvement, and personal concern for followers—in other words, with inner leadership (Avolio, Howell, and Sosik, 1999). Abramis (1992) reports that suppression of humor results in suppression of creativity and reduction in follower mental health. Both of these factors are essential to the healthy work community and are key in the mix that defines the inner leader (Terry, 1995). As inner leaders use humor and encourage its use by community members, both experience higher job satisfaction, more job involvement, and more committed followers. Many work communities attribute higher levels of employee commitment, cohesiveness, and performance to their leaders' use of humor (Avolio, Howell, and Sosik, 1999).

Humor has both direct and indirect effects on individual and unit performance. The use of humor directly enhances followers' motivation to change. Using humor in work communities has been associated with improving morale among workers. It helps create a more practically functional work culture and enhances work community cohesiveness. Inner leader use of humor inspires both member and community creativity and increases individual motivation (Avolio, Howell, and Sosik, 1999).

Avolio, Howell, and Sosik (1999) report on numerous studies that relate the use of humor with higher levels of productivity and with unconventional and innovative thinking. Humor points out discrepancies in logic and beliefs and can stimulate innovative thinking. It allows people to stand back from a problem and take a new and unique perspective to address it. It clarifies differences between individuals in terms of their needs and aspirations and builds greater cohesion, unit identification, and commitment to others in the work community.

A sense of humor comes out of the individual leader's sense of his or her authentic self. Humor reaches that part of human beings that is not physical, a part many call spirit or soul which others refer to as personality. Using humor helps overcome self-doubt and helps lead to success and prosperity. What has just been said for leaders also applies to those led. The way to assure that inner leaders meet common needs is for both leader and led to add humor to their interrelationship dynamic.

Humor conveys important cultural messages. It identifies the "ins" from the "outs" in the work community. That is, it determines who is part of the core group and who is external to it. Humor helps determine domination and submission relationships. Who uses humor and who cannot, who can make light of whom, what humor is about, all show the status of the user of humor. It is a key part of culture creation and maintenance. Deal and Kennedy (1988) include use of humor as among the potential cultural norms that help the work-community change process. They suggest that leaders can ease change in a work-community culture by using humor along with collegiality, openness, high expectations, appreciation, caring, and recognition of important matters.

Humor socializes; it conveys membership. It showcases cultural values. Humor is symbolic. It has an "as if" function. Humor lets us assume something stands for something else in the situation. It integrates otherwise disparate work communities and helps sustain and establish solidarity. It is a face-saving tool. And humor is a way to show arbitrariness in a situation. All in all, humor is a little used but powerful tool leaders can use to gain and maintain control over a situation or work community, to socialize new members, and to gain and continue desired results.

Humor moderates the relationship between the inner leader's style and work unit performance. When humor is properly used, it can amplify the inner leader's action and performance (Avolio, Howell, and Sosik, 1999). It helps cope with stress. It also is a helpful tool work-community members use in dealing efficiently with their interpersonal problems. Humor mitigates the impact of tension in leaders, relieving their own and that of their followers. Humor has value in helping make positive circumstances understandable and acceptable. It also is a tool to assist inner leaders in making negative life events more endurable and moderating the level of negative mood disturbance. Santovec (2001) reports that her research suggests that workers feel that a workplace including an element of humor is a benefit.

METHODS OF USING HUMOR

While some CEOs use humor as part of their leadership style, most top executives have little need to use it to get their orders obeyed. CEOs rely on more objective means. Inner leaders, however, often find humor to be a powerful informal tool in influencing work community members to their expectations. They use it to socialize followers into a cohesive work community distinct from all others. It helps to break down barriers between people and makes a work community more participative and responsive.

Humor can be either a help or a hindrance. For example, off-color humor and humor that alienates coworkers is not acceptable. Racial, ethnic, or sexist jokes create the potential for discrimination, disaffection, and isolation. They also risk litigation. Making an employee the brunt of a joke can result in retaliatory action by the target of the inappropriate joke. This type of behavior can pull apart even the strongest of work communities. Inner leaders know that one person's humor is another person's lawsuit, because what may be funny at home is frequently not appropriate for the workplace.

Nevertheless, workplace humor can reinforce positive behavior. And adding humor doesn't cost a lot. Most of the humor found in the workplace happens spontaneously (Santovec, 2001). Inner leaders foster humor in the appropriate context of the environment. Appropriate workplace humor is healthy. Self-effacing humor, where the leader is the object of his or her own joke, works well (Santovec, 2001). It shows the work community is not afraid to laugh at its own mistakes or ridiculous situations (McLaughlin, 2001).

Uses for Humor by Inner Leaders

Following are some areas where the use of humor by inner leaders is effective:

1. Humor is a useful tool inner leaders use in helping to close the communication gap between them and their followers by providing an alternative channel of communication. Using humor lets inner leaders acquire information that might not otherwise be volunteered from members of the work community. The inner leader's use of humor makes work-community confusion more bearable and draws attention to areas in need of the leader's attention. Effective use of humor stimulates a shift in viewpoint that allows people to stand back from a problem and take a new and unique perspective to address it.

2. Humor is a way to show arbitrariness in a situation. It lets inner leaders assume something stands for something else in the situation. Humor can mute strong emotions or reinforce them. Humor can express skepticism. It can contribute to desired goals of flexibility and adaptability. It integrates otherwise disparate work communities and helps leaders gain or retain desired attitudes. Pointing out discrepancies in logic and beliefs can stimulate innovative thinking (Avolio, Howell, and Sosik, 1999) and result in creative and innovative change.

3. Humor is a determinant of inclusiveness and exclusiveness and their negative impact on performance. Humor enhances work community solidarity. It conveys membership. Appropriate use of humor builds greater identification, cohesion, and commitment in groups. Who uses humor and who cannot, who can make light of whom, what humor is about—all show the status of the user. The inner leader's use of humor also can enhance trust, facilitate change, and encourage acceptance of his or her vision (Barsoux, 1996). Appreciating the various functions of spontaneous humor helps middle-level leaders communicate and lead productivity programs more effectively.

4. Humor is an effective tool to denigrate some ideas and to reinforce others that are more compatible with the leader's vision values. Humorous actions inner leaders take can result in the proposals, ideas, or values of another person to be rejected in favor of the leader's own by getting work community members to laugh at, ridicule, or scorn the other person's proposals. If respect is lost, so is much of one's power. Without respect, dominance cannot be maintained. Getting others to laugh at or ridicule in any way the proposals of others is another way to exercise power in the situation. While risky and most often used early on in discussions with colleagues, the effective mid-level leader can reduce others' "trial balloons" to irrelevance by the effective use of humor.

5. Using humor is a way to promote greater flexibility and innovation, qualities that enhance cooperation and commitment. Research results suggest that

experience in a given work community educates leaders to use humor in constructive ways. This experience helps leaders view the nature of the extant culture and that of the culture they want to create while also being aware of potentially negative impacts certain kinds of humor may have on individual worker performance (Avolio, Howell, and Sosik, 1999). Based on this knowledge, inner leaders may need to vary their approach to humor to conform to followers' expectations to have a positive impact on culture creation and modification to enhance both individual and group performance. Different styles of humor may be more or less effective on desired levels of commitment depending on the composition of a work community (e.g., ethnicity, gender, experience levels, etc.), its history of interactions, its stage of development, and the circumstances in which it is operating. Seeing these situational factors from the perspective of humor is yet another skill inner leaders cultivate.

6. Humor reduces negative feelings followers may have about their leaders, their vision, policies, or interrelationships practices and their orientation to productivity, quality, and flexibility. The relationship between leader action, humor, and performance is complex. By using humor, inner leaders may be able to reduce the negative effects typically associated with a lack of top leader direct involvement with workers in the middle and lower echelons of the corporation. Some of the positive effects of humor may mitigate the effects of the avoidance behaviors associated with leadership. Humor may create a climate that allows individuals to feel better about the unit, even though they are dissatisfied in some ways with their leader. Humor is a way to effectively create a positive atmosphere within a work community and thus stimulate higher levels of collective productivity. On the other hand, the use of humor may have been seen as a distraction from the leaders' attending to their followers' individual concerns (Avolio, Howell, and Sosik, 1999).

7. Humor can help inner leaders induce followers to accept personal and professional developmental assignments without taking offense. When work-community members are encouraged or told outright to attend a skills development or communication or other training session, they immediately think they are poor performers and get defensive (McLaughlin, 2001). Humor can help reduce these feelings and move members to accept the training or other changes. Almost any productivity or performance improvement program or training can come alive with comedy—providing the comedy used is appropriate. Humor allows people to make mistakes and say the wrong things (McLaughlin, 2001). Even getting downsized can be dealt with humorously once the initial shock subsides.

8. Humor helps inner leaders influence followers to accept problem-solving roles. Humor is a way to help followers to let go of the feelings and psychological blocks sometimes created when they are faced with the heavy responsibility of making choices affecting the work community. Because laughing allows community members to be more receptive to positive messages, it is a helpful step into problem-solving tasks. The power of multiple competing ideas,

activities, and goals typical of many work communities today can measurably reduce followers' attention spans. Using humor, inner leaders can keep them involved long enough to let them deal appropriately with the issues, information, and alternatives incidental to any significant decision. There are, of course, alternative ways to get followers to decide, but most people respond more fully when they laugh (McLaughlin, 2001).

9. Humor can reduce the tension attendant on increasing diversity in the work community. Rather than delivering the typical heavy presentation, it is sometime healthier to joke about diversity. Humor loosens the tension present when diverse work community members are placed in a work community of relative strangers. Humor lets them put aside differences to complete a task. It changes the energy in the room, keeps people interested, and helps them deal with important subjects. Humor helps diffuse the stress of the situation. Using humor in diverse groups is a risk technique. It is vastly more difficult to construct a humorous statement acceptable to multiple people holding multiple values than it is with a homogeneous group. The leader's task in these situations is to insure that the humor used is not offensive to any community member but, rather, furthers the task of integration and cultural homogeneity at least around needed work tasks.

10. Humor adds another incentive for members to join or stay in the community. Employees stay in a job not just for the money. Many factors in addition to salary influence retention, such as a desire for stimulating work. The opportunity to grow and learn through the work done also encourages workers to stay in the work community. They also stay because they enjoy working with their supervisors and coworkers (Carson, 2001). Incorporating humor into the workplace adds another reason for long tenure. It stimulates more of these positive workplace characteristics and qualities. Laughter in the workplace is a sign that the inner leader's followers are connecting with other community members (Santovec, 2001). Humor contributes to creating a more positive organizational culture .

11. Given today's complex and high-stress work environment, humor can do much to reduce time lost due to illness and other stress-related problems. High stress leads to anger, anxiety, or depression, all of which cost money as unhappy, underproductive employees lose time, file workers' compensation claims, and raise the general turnover rates. While some stress actually helps increase productivity, high stress can lead to burnout. Studies have shown that laughing exercises the lungs, increases oxygen in the bloodstream, and stimulates endorphins, the brain's natural painkiller. A good laugh will temporarily lower blood pressure (Santovec, 2001). Research finds a strong correlation between a positive outlook and an improved immune system. Thus, a fun-filled workplace can translate into less absenteeism, lower health insurance rates, and less stressed employees (Santovec, 2001).

12. Humor facilitates improving morale among workers (Santovec, 2001). Santovic also reports that humor is a strong, low-cost way of keeping and

motivating employees. Correctly used, humor relieves stress, helps resolve conflicts, reduces turnover, improves communication, and promotes teamwork. Inner leaders who can remember a punch line to a joke or sharing a laugh over an absurd situation build relationships and enhance collaboration.

13. The use of humor has been described as motivating divergent, unconventional, creative, and innovative thinking. Avolio, Howell, and Sosik (1999) contend that the use of humor stimulates a shift in perspective that allows the inner leader to stand back from a problem and to take a new and unique perspective from which to address it. It highlights discrepancies in logic and beliefs to stimulate analytical and creative thinking. Humor can help employees step into key problem-solving roles and allow them to make mistakes and say the wrong thing without long-term detrimental consequences (McLaughlin, 2001).

According to proponents, creating fun is a tool inner leaders use regularly (Santovec, 2001). Learning through humor makes almost any leader–follower situation come alive, providing the comedy used is appropriate.

Suggestions for Using Humor in Leadership

While the type and kind of humor inner leaders use is idiosyncratic, some guidelines about the use of this technique can be deduced from observation and from the experience of others. The following principles might simplify application of this technique by emerging inner leaders.

First, humor is distinctive for each inner leader and, critically, it is unique also to each work community member. Leaders need to be intimately conscious of the background, values, and (at least the work) experiences of each community member because humor is in the eye of the hearer, not the teller of a joke or funny story. In short, what is funny to one person may be insulting or a social slur to another.

Second, self-deprecating humor has a better chance of being funny to your hearers. "Everything," said Will Rogers, "is funny so long as it is happening to somebody else." Inner leaders may expect success more often as they focus the humor on themselves and away from their followers.

Third, a person's character is at least partially revealed by what he or she laughs at. Inner leaders can use humor to ascertain the character of their work community and individual members and to shape that character. What individuals laugh at, how they respond generally to a joke, whether or not they reciprocate, all these things tell inner leaders something about the individual member that can help them better understand and subsequently help their work community.

Fourth, humor can be used to reduce tension and stress. Routinely any work community goes through moments of tension and stress that can be eased by a well crafted joke, story or anecdote. Successful inner leaders have learned to gage the temper of their followers and match humor to the tense situation. While it is not an easy task, it often means the difference between leadership and disaster. (Abramis, 1992)

Forming a Humor Committee

One inexpensive way of deliberately injecting humor in the workplace is to create a specific committee for the purpose (Santovec, 2001). Santovec describes a mid-level unit leader who formed a committee and gave it a budget to coordinate many of its humor-producing events. Eighteen to twenty representatives from various branches meet monthly to organize different activities. The committee's goal is to encourage the staff to play while working. The committee plans at least one event, and often more, each month. It tries to establish a humorous environment for the employees.

DISCUSSION ISSUES AND QUESTIONS

Issues

1. When people can laugh at themselves and each other, they feel better about themselves and others and are more bonded.

2. People seek others with whom they can reveal their true selves, including their absurd—humorous—side.

3. Effective inner leaders use humor as part of their effort to inspire and direct followers toward some ideas, activities, and approaches and away from others.

4. Inner leaders set the environment within which humor is used, define the parameters of its use, and more than any other member of the work community apply it in work-related interactions.

5. Humor helps define the place in the work community of individual members and who they are both as individuals and as a community.

6. If a work community is humorless and suppresses humor, the likelihood is that other essential characteristics that are required to do business are also suppressed, and the members' humanness is restricted.

7. Humor helps define the human being. Humor is a way people express their true, intimate core selves, including their vulnerable, foolish, irrational, ridiculous sides.

8. The use of humor directly enhances followers' motivation to change, has been associated with improving morale among workers, helps create a more practically functional work culture, and enhances work-community cohesiveness.

9. Inner leader uses of humor inspire both member and work-community creativity and increase individual motivation.

10. Humor points out discrepancies in logic and beliefs to stimulate innovative thinking. It allows people to stand back from a problem and to take a new and unique perspective to address it.

11. Humor reaches that part of human beings that is not physical, a part that many call spirit or soul.

12. Using humor helps overcome self-doubt and will help lead to success and prosperity. What has just been said for leaders also applies to those led.

13. Humor identifies the "ins" from the "outs" in the work community, that is, it determines who is part of the core group and who is extraneous to it. Humor conveys membership.

14. Humor is symbolic, it lets us assume something stands for something else in the situation.

15. Humor is a face-saving tool.

16. Humor moderates the relationship between the inner leader's style and work-unit performance.

17. Humor has value in helping make complex circumstances understandable and acceptable.

18. Workers feel that a workplace including an element of humor is a benefit.

Questions

1. Do I use humor as part of my leadership style? Why? Why not?

2. How have your past uses of humor influenced the expectations of your work-community members so that they can work cooperatively?

3. What kinds of humorous situations or stories have you found most effective in your work community? List some acceptable and unacceptable topics or foci of your humor.

4. What works best for you: self-effacing humor or humor that is directed (positively) toward a member of your work community or that is directed to a member of a competing community? Why?

LEARNING ACTIVITIES USING HUMOR

Activity: A Humorous Story

Instructions. Relate a situation in which you used humor effectively to accomplish a planned objective for your work community.

1. Include details of the ambient situation so the reader can understand the factors incident to this use of humor.

2. Describe the characters involved in enough detail so readers can see their values perspectives.

3. Relate in some detail the story itself.

4. Analyze the event:

- Why was it humorous?
- Were any people offended? Why?
- What was the net impact of the story from your perspective? From the perspective of others involved?

5. Assess this use of humor from a leadership perspective.

   - Will you use this or similar humorous stories again? Why? Why not?
   - What can you say about humor as an effective leadership tool?

PART V

THE TECHNIQUES OF INNER LEADERSHIP POWER USE

Inner leaders are influential power users. Power—the ability to get others to do what the leader wants them to do, whether the others want to do so or not—is strongly reminiscent of the definition of inner leadership itself. The results of power use and of leadership are the same: to get others to behave in desired ways. It is the essential inner leader task, since power is the extra element in interpersonal relations that lets the leader prevail upon others and secure their compliance. The thing that separates the inner leader's use of power from its use by top leaders is that these leaders get followers to willingly comply with their wishes rather than to merely obey orders.

Power use is part of the interpersonal interaction in any group (Fairholm, 1993). Inner leaders use power as a means to achieve some desired future action through the work of others. Power has utility for the inner leader, most often as an intermediary tool, to achieve some personal desired end value. What has been said about the leader's use of power is equally applicable to every follower. It is a component of any social interaction; and, while little is discussed in the professional leadership literature, it is a useful tool to describe social interaction and measure member success.

Inner leaders engage in specific efforts to increase their own situational power. They also expend energy to empower their followers to act independently within the constraints of the common vison. Skill in personal power use and in engendering its directed use by others involves the inner leader in intense interpersonal relationships with followers, the central nature of which is influencing them to do what the leader wants done. It involves both learning the parameters of power, teaching that technology to followers, and creating opportunities for its synergistic use in accomplishing agreed-upon goals.

The successful employment of the techniques of power use demands inner leaders acquire expertise in areas not routinely used by top leaders. These techniques circumscribe a part of the inner leader's work environment, an environment pregnant with power, competition, conflict, and opposition and yet redolent with potential satisfactions not attained in many other activities. These techniques include using power, empowering others, teaching and coaching stakeholders, and encouraging followers' self-governance.

CHAPTER 18

Technique 15: Using Power

Few concepts are more indispensable to understanding leader behavior in work communities than applied power use. Whether we treat power use as the aim of leaders or as instrumental to other, higher goals, it is a necessary part of leadership. It is central to any interaction with people. Power use is a cornerstone of both inner leadership theory and its practice. It is the heart of leadership behavior. Learning to comfortably use power in the work communities in which they have membership is central to every other inner leader task.

DEFINING POWER

All organized interaction is political—a competition between members for status, material acquisition, or ideological advantage. The vernacular term for this is office politics or organizational power politics (Fairholm, 1993). All members in any work community engage in power politics as part of their routine relationships (Serven, 2002). It is indispensable to personal and group effectiveness and survival. Member and group success, regardless of the community, is dependent on the appropriateness of the particular power techniques used in the interrelationship. Inner leaders continually engage in power use. Their task is an influential one that make use of a range of applied power-use techniques.

The idea of using one's personal power in social contexts has emotional overtones and carries both positive and negative ethical connotations. Some see power as "manipulation," "coercion," "control," or "force." For these people, power use is "Machiavellian." Certainly, power can be manipulative. It is in play in behaviors such as "brown nosing," "yesing" the boss, and similar ingratiating action. In fact, "Machiavellian" has come to epitomize the worst in manipulative, exploitative, self-serving power use. But that is not all that power is.

A more balanced perspective sees power as ethically neutral. The ethics of power lies not in power use per se but in the motives and values of the user. As with any other tool, we can use power for "good," that is, for socially developmental purposes, or for "bad," for personal aggrandizement. User goals and objective results achieved, not power application itself, are the ethical criteria (McClelland, 1976). A leader can use power without destructive result to either self or others. Results attained depend on the motives and skill of the particular leader. The inner leader's power effects also are conditioned by the skill in power use of all others involved in a particular power exchange.

Power is, of course, central to leadership, planning, directing, controlling, and performance evaluation. Leaders use power to secure their goals; control scarce resources, negotiate agreements among individuals, or take autonomous action to try to achieve their personal outcomes. It is to influence these processes that most inner leaders use their power, and it is in this context that power use has its most telling impact on the inner leader's personal and work-community success. Conventional top leadership techniques like participative management, decision making, or system change and conflict management are no longer enough to fully explain action in the various subunits of the corporation. An applied power perspective provides better analytical tools and new skills and competencies, as well as the motivation to alter ineffective patterns of individual and collective behavior. Judicious use of power increases the inner leader's ability singly and as a part of a unified work community to respond to a constantly changing environment.

Power is a relative concept. An inner leader may be relatively powerful in one circumstance and not so powerful in another. The energy expended in any given power-use situation is a function of its importance, the presence or absence of needed resources, and the leader's skill in using appropriate power tactics or techniques. Described as we have done so, power is a ubiquitous part of all work-community life. It is at the center of the inner leader's attention and not only assists him or her in ensuring work-community success but ensures his or her own professional achievement as well.

METHODS OF USING POWER

Inner leaders do not arise simply as a result of a grant by others of the powers of command claimed and exercised by them. They acquire power only when they appeal to followers by stimulating their emotions and offering suggestions to them that they see as helpful in attaining the followers' personal and professional goals. This explanation of the inner leader's source of power is counter to the authority basis for top leader power. The inner leader's role in using follower emotions and personal motives to insure commitment to work-community purposes is also distinct from traditional top leadership theory.

Effective use of power asks inner leaders to master specific skills that implement the subtleties of this leadership technique within their work community. Mastering the techniques of power use in the interior regions of the corporation centers on developing skill in intimate interaction by the inner leader who is in a kind of competition with stakeholders over who gets control and use of needed and scarce resources. These power-use skills take the form of a variety of tasks centering in the intimate one-on-one relationships constituting the conventions of inner leadership relationships.

Power Use Techniques

Inner leaders prepare themselves to exercise power within their work communities in many ways (see also Fairholm, 1993).

Creating (or Making Use of Existing) Power Situations

Inner leaders are aware of the power component in every interpersonal interaction in which they engage. In fact, all members of the work community are continually negotiating for power to gain their desires. It is a ubiquitous and legitimate part of work—all—life. All members of the work community are regularly in situations where they compete for advantage so they can get their own way in the face of competing action by others. Inner leaders understand that the component parts of a power relationship (a situation in which power is and ought to be used to gain success) are normally present in most work relationships. The components of such a power situation include interdependence, differing goals, and competition to see who will achieve desired goals in a situation of scarcity where if one participant gains his or her goals the others do not. It is a situation where at least one participant in the relationship attaches enough importance to the situation, goals, or approach to be willing to expend energy in the relationship. Unless all these factors are present, operational power use need not be called upon to get one's way. But the fact is that almost every interpersonal situation in a work community can be defined in terms of these characteristics.

Understanding the Classic Power-Use Model

Understanding the theory of power use is a crucial aspect of the inner leader's success in using this technique. The characteristics of any group where power politics is a part of a relationship include the following: The relationship must involve a decision situation characterized by choice among competing alternatives. Power use depends on a social situation where action by one party impacts the behavior or choices of the others and where a condition of scarcity of resources critical in achieving the work community's or an individual's purposes is present. Inner leaders use power in situations where participants are free to act to achieve desired results. Power arises from the leader's ability to take needed action to achieve desired results or to withhold action. It is a dynamic, interactive process.

Using Power to Increase Power

Using power increases one's cache of power. Failure to exercise it can result in its loss. This characteristic of power use places inner leaders in a complex interactive and dynamic power relationship with everyone with whom they interact, one purpose of which is to gain and maintain their relative power positions in the work community.

Facilitating Power Use by Creating Conditions That Foster It

Inner leaders insure the presence of the following factors in their work culture as these factors increase their relative power in the work community and further the potential for its productive use.

Discretion. Inner leaders structure the work community to maximize discretion.

Centrality. They manipulate relationships to insure that they are at the center of activity.

Exchange. Inner leader create situations where both parties have something to give and some expectation of potential attractive results from their decision to engage in communal relations.

Status vis-à-vis superiors. Inner leaders endeavor to have multiple intimate contacts and influence with people superior to them in the hierarchy.

Conformance to work-community norms. They take actions to insure that followers see them as the personification of work-community norms. They model desired behavior.

Legitimacy. Inner leaders insure that followers see them as having legitimate authority.

Association. Inner leaders associate in friendly ways with members of the work community and with other like-minded people.

Personal status. Inner leaders try to present themselves in ways that induce followers to hold them in high esteem.

Personal characteristics. They also try to get others to think of them as possessing personal attributes like integrity, commitment, high energy use, interest, skill, and personal and professional attractiveness.

Accommodating to the Limits of Power Use

Power use is constrained by a variety of factors in both the situation and the character of participants. Effective inner leaders understand and accommodate to these limitations. For example, they are constrained by whether they see power per se as an end or as only instrumental to other ends. Their character and physical appearance may also impact their effective use of power. Position held in the hierarchy may help or hurt their capacity to use power, as also their socioeconomic status, the size of the work community, or the nature of the tasks dealt with.

Overcoming Resistance to the Inner Leader's Power Use

The act of applying power can, and often does, produce a countervailing power use by the inner leader's coworkers, the intent of which is to (1) destroy or limit the inner leader's power, (2) to wrest from the inner leader sources of power held, or (3) to disengage from relationship with the leader. Of course, resistance sometimes results from the followers' inability to respond appropriately. Or followers may fail to respond to power use because they do not have the requisite skills, time, materials, or information needed to effect desired outcomes. Resistance also can result from an unwillingness to comply. In any case, the resistance is genuine, and the impact on the inner leader is similar. Leaders must increase the force or scope of their power use or give up. Inner leaders understand that using power is a risk relationship that can produce resistance and failure if improperly applied.

Power Is Both an Offensive and a Defensive Tool

Inner leaders use power to realize desired behavior, attitudes, or attributes in others or in their work community. They use power when the situation requires a choice. Using power speeds up work-community member action and hastens goal accomplishment. And power use increases the assertiveness quotient of the inner leader.

Controlling as Many Sources of Power as Possible

The essence of power is control over needed and scarce resources. The more needed and scarce the resource, the more useful it is as a basis for achieving the holder's desires from others who require that "commodity." The more scarce resources an inner leader controls, the more powerful that leader is in the eyes of followers. Resources include anything physical or psychological inner leaders own, control, or exclusively can make available to others and valuable to them in meeting their perceived needs. To be useful from a leadership perspective, the target of the leader's power action must see the resources as available only (or most economically) from the inner leader. In effect, inner leaders have power when others perceive them as having desired resources in some kind of monopoly. Examples of power sources include

Controlling rewards. The inner leader's capability to provide benefits to followers allows him or her to control follower behavior and achieve desired results to the extent of the followers' need for that tangible or intangible reward.

Criticality. Control over vital information, time, expertise, or other resources needed by the work community or any member gives inner leaders power over those in need.

Alliances. Inner leaders multiply their power as they collaborate with groups of independently powerful people and thus increase their potency to attain a sufficient critical power mass to achieve desired results.

A perception of legitimacy. As recipients believe their inner leaders have a legitimate right to command, whether those leaders have actual authority or not, leaders can exercise power toward those persons or groups. Legitimacy comes from a perceived delegation from the community or higher corporate—or other—entity. Acceptance of that delegation comes as affected individuals accept the inner leader's actions as appropriate.

Identification with powerful others. Affiliation with other people whom their followers perceive as important can augment inner leaders' power. Such identification can be actual or merely perceived, or it can be symbolic. Inner leaders can acquire or increase their power by adhering to the ideals, norms, or goals stakeholders value in their heros (Covey, 2001). Perceived identification with ideas, values, methods, or goals of famous, wise, attractive, or powerful people adds to the inner leader's perceived power in the same way that direct association does.

Expertise. The leader's own expertise becomes an important base of power as the targets of the leader's power use come to depend on his or her expertise in needed skill areas. Being perceived as expert lets inner leaders exert power beyond their official role in the work community in any direction—up, down, and laterally.

Use of power. The act of using power tends to increase one's power.

Personal difference. As inner leaders make themselves different from their colleagues (positively, but also negatively—say, as a curmudgeon), they are more likely to have and exercise power.

Centrality. Physical location in the center of activity, in the middle of work operations, or close in proximity to powerful people. A central location adds to the development and effective use of inner leaders' power and the likelihood that they will be in the circle of powerful cliques and have access to other powerful people in the hierarchy.

Becoming Expert in Many Power Techniques

Inner leaders have learned to use several kinds of power such as these:

Reward power. Founded on the inner leader's ability to provide benefits to another.

Information power. Based on unique data needed by others.

Coercive power. Based on the leader's ability to punish noncompliance.

Expert power. Built on the unique skill or knowledge that the inner leader has.

Referent power. Fashioned on desires others have to be identified with the inner leader.

Legitimate power. Based on a perceived grant of power from an external and recognized source.

Wielding Power in Relationships with Top Leaders

Inner leaders continually engage in power politics with those people who are superior to them in the formal corporate structure. Several specific tactics of power use with superiors are listed below. This listing follows Fairholm's (1993) work and relies largely on aspects of personal character rather than prerogatives of position.

Proactivity. Using proactive power is nothing more than using power first and seeking permission afterward. It is often seen as a *fait accompli*, a situation in which the inner leader presents the boss with a completed decision or action and seeks support and endorsement after the fact.

Using outside experts. Inner leaders at times use authorities not connected with their immediate work community to convince others that their proposed decisions or alternatives are the correct ones. They frequently select an expert who is known to favor a given approach, philosophy, or technique so they can ensure that the perspective they favor will be reflected in the recommendations ultimately given.

Displaying charisma. Charisma—personal magnetism—is based on an almost visceral connection between the powerful and the relatively powerless. It involves inner leaders in any of a wide variety of behaviors and demeanor intended to elicit follower compliance because of their attraction to the character of the leader in some ways.

Rationalization. Anything an inner leader does to consciously engineer reality, to justify decision results or specific points of view, can be included in the rationalization power technique. The rationalization tactic uses language or symbols to construct a particularized view of reality that legitimizes the inner leader power user's decisions. Rationalization involves persuasion, structuring reality, appeal to the emotions, and the use of humor.

Using ambiguity. Inner leaders use or create situations of multiple, chaotic interactions where understood norms of human interaction are broken down and new standards have not been solidified to gain their desires. These ambiguous situations allow the leader to assume power and authority for accomplishment in ways and to degrees not possible in a highly structured, controlled, and predictable environment.

Building a favorable image. Building a favorable image refers to attempts inner leaders make to create or change the perceptions others have of their personalities, skills, capacities, values, or attitudes to enhance their power among colleagues including their bosses.

Exerting Power in Relationships with Peers

A peer relationship is one between persons who do not have a clear, unambiguous hierarchal relationship defining their association. Peer relationships require a nonhierarchal formal or informal relationship. Because of this structural relationship parameter, inner leader power behavior is not commonly characterized by force or authority forms of power. When working with their peers, inner leaders exert power through the following kinds of power use tactics:

Allocating resources. Inner leaders often allocate needed resources to others in their work community in exchange for their compliance. Examples of use of this power tactic range from giving or withholding needed or desired space, material, information, financial resources, skills, association, cooperation, or work assignments to allowing a competitor to participate in decision or policy activity or have access to other powerful, influential, or attractive people. These and similar resources are routinely used to aid the inner leader in gaining compliance from peers.

Quid pro quo. Inner leaders spend much of their power-related time in exchange relationships with peers where one person has comparably more of a desired resource and is willing to trade it for specified peer behavior or support or access to another scarce resource. This tactic involves any of a wide variety of efforts to negotiate tradeoffs with others to secure desired results from peers using both material and nonmaterial resources as negotiating "chips."

Forming coalitions. Coalition building involves leaders in allying themselves with certain members of the work community, and sometimes with persons outside the work community, to add to their perceived influence. Examples of this power tactic include creating informal work groups or associations of people who belong to professional associations or other work-community clusters of like-minded people. However, such coalitions are fragile. Typically, they are specifically formed for each power issue.

Coopting opposition members. Using a kind of coalition building, inner leaders sometimes attempt to add potentially powerful individuals from opposing forces whose support would aid in goal attainment or whose opposition would hamper goal realization to their decision councils. Coopting a rival causes the coopted person to become linked in the public mind with the position and rationale of his or her former opponent. Often persons thus coopted begin to defend the position (or at least not oppose it as vigorously) in public forums.

Incurring obligation. This tactic involves inner leaders in developing a sense of obligation in others to induce them to do what they (the leaders) want. Obligation is incurred when the inner leader provides another person with specific and needed actions or rewards which then places the recipient under debt to him or her. Friendship, too, can be a form of debt. Self-sacrifice may seem altruistic and moral, but it can also be capitalized on as an obligation and thus become a power behavior. Obligation can also be incurred through praise.

Using surrogates. This tactic describes situations in which the inner leader makes use of a third party (or parties) through which to exercise power. Leaders sometimes use other people to mask their use of power and seek to gain compliance by having their proposals for action presented by a popular individual who "fronts" for them.

Controlling the agenda. Inner leaders also use the simple expedient of controlling meeting agendas to attain their desires over possible opposition from peers. Selecting agenda items and even controlling their placement on an agenda insures that the issues discussed are those the inner leader wants to discuss and has prepared for. Obviously, placing an item on the agenda when the leader is ready increases the likelihood that arguments proffered will, at the least, receive a hearing. Withholding an item until the inner leader is prepared or placing it on the agenda when others are not expecting it and, therefore, are not prepared to deal with it also enhances this leader's relative power position.

Brinkmanship. Any effort directed toward disturbing the equilibrium of the work community as a prelude to other action the inner leader might take to control peer choice is brinkmanship. The key element for success lies in proper timing in introducing the inner leader's preferred action to ameliorate the crisis that he or she has allowed to develop. This is a risky technique but an often-used one.

Building a favorable image. As noted, this power tactic is also often used in inner leaders' relationships with top leaders. Many mid-level leaders also find it helpful in achieving their goals in peer relationships. A carefully cultivated reputation can attract other peers to the inner leader's point of view or dissuade them from opposing it. Building an image of expertise, of having special knowledge, status, wisdom, prestige, presence, or specialization, allows inner leaders to influence peers' behavior and aids them in personal goal attainment. Sometimes building a reputation for hard-headedness, confrontation, or other nominally negative personality achieves a similar result.

POWER ISSUES AND QUESTIONS

Issues

1. Leaders are influential power users in the work community and with its members.

2. Power is the ability to get others to do what the power user wants them to do whether the others want to or not.

3. Power use is a cornerstone of current inner leadership theory and practice and the essence of leader behavior in the interior regions of the corporation.

4. Inner leaders use power instrumentally as an aid to achieving their intended results in the work community.

5. The ethics of power lies not in power itself but in the motives and values of the user.

6. Power use is critical in understanding normal work-community life since both inner leaders and their coworkers use power to secure their goals, control scarce resources, negotiate agreement, or take independent action to try to achieve their personal goals.

7. Power is a relative concept—the inner leader may be relatively powerful in one circumstance and not so powerful in another.

8. Using power tends to increase power; failure to exercise it can result in its loss.

9. Effective leaders know that power use has limits and have learned to accommodate their use of power accordingly.

10. Inner leaders learn to use and become expert in as many power tactics as they can.

11. Inner leaders use power in relationships with both peers and superiors in the formal work community structure.

Questions

1. Do the hierarchies you create focus on maintaining and keeping power? Sharing and distributing power? Provide specific examples.

2. What obstacles do you face in using power in your relationships with coworkers in the middle of the corporation?

3. Do you make use of all the techniques of power usage in your relationships with your superiors? With your peers?

4. Which power techniques do you use most? Which are most consistently successful for you? Why?

5. Can you provide examples of each of the sources of power referenced in this chapter from your present work situation? Are some sources of power more useful than others? Explain.

6. What is the risk to you as a leader of providing stakeholders with as much power as possible? Does this action risk loss of power for you? Explain.

7. Do you recognize that you can give more of your power to your coworkers and still retain all your power? How does power multiply when the leader shares power with others?

POWER USE ACTIVITIES

The following activities may help the reader understand their power potential better and add to their skill in its effective use.

Activity 1: Influence Lineup

Instructions. Neither the literature nor practicing inner leaders talk much about their use of power or that of others working with them in their work communities. Experience, however, suggests that most people most of the time are aware of their power and its relationship to the power of all others in the work community. This activity will help readers get in touch with their relative power in their work (or other) community. (If you and your work community colleagues do this activity as a group, proceed as indicated below. If this is not feasible, mentally align your work community—including yourself—along a line from most powerful to least powerful.)

1. Begin by marking one end of a line as the spot for the most powerful person in your work community.

2. Have each member stand in line according to how you see yourselves— as most powerful to least powerful. The most powerful person will be at the "power end" of the line.

3. After the line has stabilized, ask if anyone wants to move himself to a different location from where he or she is now. Allow members to realign themselves along the line.

4. Discuss the self-perceptions and perceptions of others.

   • How does your power as perceived by other members compare with how you see it?

   • Were there disagreements among members about who is the most powerful?

   • Does the work community have certain biases about power, such as the richest person being seen as the most powerful? (Or the smartest, of higher ranking member, etc.?)

   • Why do you think it was relatively easy (or difficult) for you to do this?

Activity 2: Your Power Personality

Instructions. The way in which someone handles power and influence has a direct bearing on his or her functioning in the work community. The questions below are aimed at helping you clarify your power behavior in work communities. How aware are you of the power you have over others in the work community? How do you usually express your power in the work community? How do you react to being influenced by other members? To help answer these personal questions complete the following questionnaire.

1. Rank the following six items from most important to you "1" to least important to you "6".

   When other work community members try to influence my behavior, I am likely to do the things they want me to do because:

   _____ I admire them for their personal qualities, and I want to act in a way that merits their respect and admiration.

   _____ I respect their ability and good judgment about things with which they are more experienced than I am.

   _____ They can give special help and benefits to those who cooperate with them.

   _____ They can apply pressure or penalize those who do not cooperate with them.

   _____ They have a legitimate right, considering their position, to expect that their suggestions will be carried out.

_____ They have information I need in order to accomplish my goals, and therefore I listen carefully and use what they have to say.

2. Circle your most accurate response to the following questions.

When I participate in a work community task, I am completely conscious of how much power I have and how I can use it to make sure my needs and wants are met.

Never   1   2   3   4   5   Always

When it comes time to set work-community priorities, I seek out other work-community members who have compatible goals and try to form coalitions to increase my power and therefore the likelihood of my influencing the priorities in the way I want.

Never   1   2   3   4   5   Always

I am quite comfortable dealing with power. I like influencing other work-community members, and I enjoy being able to build enough power to get what I want from the work community.

Never   1   2   3   4   5   Always

3. The way in which I would describe my power-oriented behavior in a work community is

_____

_____

_____

Answer key: The possible responses to question 1 correspond to the six traditional kinds of power identified by French and Raven (1959). They are, in order of the responses: charismatic, expert, reward, coercive, legitimate, and information power. Your response to question 1 suggests your preferred kind(s) of power use.

Responses to other questions further elaborate your preferred power personality. As colleagues also complete this questionnaire, you can compare your responses with those of others in your group and define a work-community power personality.

Activity 3: Power IQ

Instructions. There is little discussion of power in classrooms, boardrooms, offices, or shop floors. As a result, many people are unaware of the power they routinely use and the importance of their personal power in getting their personal agendas realized on the job.

Getting in touch with your power IQ, therefore, is a necessary first step to its effective use. Complete the following list of questions as fully as you can. Honest responses will shed light on your present power uses and your feelings abut using power and having it used toward you. They may provide guidance as to next steps in increasing your skill in power use.

1. List a few appropriate uses of power.

   What are the factors that make them seem appropriate?

   If you decided to install a new work system and one of your division heads continued to oppose it in direct and indirect ways, how might you use power to get what you want?

2. List a few inappropriate uses of power.

   What are the factors that make them seem inappropriate?

3. Recall a time, at work or at home, when you used power on someone else to get him or her to do something he or she didn't want to do.

   How did you go about using the power you had?

   How did the other person respond to this use of power?

   If you were in the same situation now, would you chose to act differently? Why? How?

4. Recall a time, at work or at home, when you had power used on you to get you to do something your didn't particularly want to do.

   How did the person go about using his or her power?

   How did you respond to this use of power?

   If you were in the same situation now, would you respond differently? Why? How?

CHAPTER 19

Technique 16: Empowerment

Today's work communities are in a place in time that has changed drastically from that of former work communities. Today's inner leaders are in relationships with people who are essentially volunteers. Their coworkers refuse to be treated the way they once were treated. As a group, today's followers are better educated and far more independent, aware, and wanting. Pfeffer (1977) confirms that workers today want to achieve control over their environment and take action to realize this desire.

DEFINING EMPOWERMENT

People are empowered when they individually accomplish collaborative and participative work with their leader and coworkers. Empowerment appeals to the human values of independence, self-reliance, and individualism. It allows people to self-actualize on the job via interesting, challenging work and responsible assignments. People want to make a difference; and when inner leaders empower them to do so, they support their deep psychological needs. Empowered people are more self-confident, self-controlled, and self-motivated. In the act of empowerment, inner leaders gain willing followers.

In its simplest definition, empowerment means "to enable." It is freeing followers to act independently, controlled only on the basis of their results, not activity, events, or methods. The leader's actions to empower also involve sensitizing coworkers to their power and training them in its full use. Empowerment endows followers with the power required to perform a given act or set of actions. It is granting others the practical autonomy to step out and contribute directly to job requirements. It does not mean the leader gives away his or her power; rather it involves adding to the power of coworkers. Empowering others is developmental of the leader's human assets. No one is powerless. Empowerment is sensitizing coworkers to that fact and liberating them to respond accordingly.

Conger and Kanungo (1988) define empowerment in motivational terms. They say it means to enable rather than simply to delegate. Bennis (1982) says it involves helping people feel useful, assisting them in learning about their work and that of coworkers, and involving them in work-community planning and decision making. Empowerment helps make work exciting for followers. Witham and Glover (1987) conclude that empowered employees are more committed. Absent a sense of empowerment, workers respond by withdrawing their full talent, energy, or commitment.

In developing, rewarding, and enabling those around them, leaders are allowing the human assets with which they work to appreciate in value. The leader's actions to empower also involve sensitizing coworkers to their power and training them in its full use. All leaders have the power to empower others (Reuss, 1987). Only inner leaders see empowering followers as essential to their success. Henry Miller said that the only way in which someone can lead us is to restore to their work colleagues a belief in their own capacity for self-guidance. That is empowerment.

Elements of Empowerment

Several ideas underlie empowerment. First, people achieve more when they feel the job is worth doing and is challenging enough to arouse their interests. Second, people need to be able to see how their work contributes to the final result. Third, people work harder and more consistently when they feel the result is morally worthwhile and valuable. Fourth, people work harder when there is mutual respect and concern for one another as human beings and mutual integrity among the work-community members. These ideas are appropriate for the chief executive of the work community as well as the lowest worker. Unfortunately, since most CEOs can use other techniques to get workers to do what they want, they do not empower their employees as much as inner leaders do.

Inner leaders empower people because empowered people work harder. They are more committed and attentive to their work when they can function independently and are allowed (encouraged, even) to make use of more of their talents, capacities, and creative selves. Enriching the job assigned to them so it is fuller, more demanding, more complex, and asks more of the total capacities of the follower is attractive to many workers. It increases personal motivation when leaders assign workers tasks that include some control over their work environment and discretion as to when and how work is done.

People who feel their leaders have concern for their personal, individual development and maturation as human beings are more committed to that leader. They will follow a leader whom they feel is concerned for them as individuals, quite apart from what they can do for the work community. Empowered, committed people are also more creative and innovative in their work. They produce more new ways to do the work that challenge past methods. Empowered people focus on their capacities and those of their coworkers. Empowered workers are more open to change, more supportive of change, and more involved in determining the direction of change in the work community. Empowered leaders are hypothesized to be innovative, upward influencing, inspirational, and less focused on monitoring to maintain the status quo (Spreitzer, De Janasz, and Quinn, 1999).

There is some risk inherent in empowerment of others. It requires the leader to trust in the essential goodness of followers. Leaders need to trust their followers, their talent, commitment, and capacity to do work independently and in different ways than the leader would use. This is a different mind-set than traditional leadership models. It requires leaders to be teachers of others as they communicate understanding of and commitment to a common vision of the work community's future. This kind of trust, preceded by effective, appropriate training and values displacement, assures cooperative action even when the leader is not physically present.

METHODS OF PRACTICING
EMPOWERING LEADERSHIP

The move to empower employees redefines both the work community and its members' lives. Although powerful roadblocks to change still exist, successful inner leaders act on the belief that broad participation by all stakeholders is the most compelling strategy for designing and implementing lasting change in organizations. It is increasingly clear that participation improves organizations. It empowers people in all parts of work life. Research shows workplace participation results in greater political participation (Plas, 1996).

Increased participation in the workplace will better align both leader and led with the inner leader's vision of freedom and democracy, helping to create the genuine democracy that nurtures human progress and increases bottom-line results Enabling others involves the inner leader in creating situations where work community members can self-motivate. The techniques may be as simple as providing as much information as possible to as many stakeholders as possible about what they and others are doing and need to do. When leaders enable their followers, they allow them room to take risks without mindless controls. This helps workers find a place in the work community where they can make full use of their strengths for the benefit of themselves and the work community. It is following Peter Drucker's (1988) advice to emphasize the strengths of employees in job assignments.

Empowerment is intellectually connected with leadership theory ideas like teaming and community building. Use of team, or other participative action structures, implies empowerment, although few theorists identify it explicitly. Empowerment is also part of transformational leadership theory. The underlying idea behind this concept of leadership is to choose purposes and visions based on follower strengths and interests and create a structure supporting them. Transformational leadership implies changing the individual, as well as the work community. It is self-actualizing. Transformational leadership enables both leaders and followers to reach higher levels of accomplishment and motivation. It releases human potential for the collective pursuit of the common goals. Consequently, it is empowering. McGregor's (1960) Theory Y is another intellectual foundation of empowerment. People who fundamentally believe that others are good, want to work, and accept responsibility will give those others the opportunity to use these capacities. That behavior is empowering.

Empowerment engages the inner leader in the kinds of actions described in the following sections.

Goal Setting

Empowerment begins with goals. Inner leaders clearly relate work-community and individual follower goals. The fundamental mechanism is the vision statement, a concise amalgam of the basic purpose for which the work community exists. An effective vision relates directly to both individual and work-community ideas of purpose and articulates the value of joint effort. Properly stated and widely communicated, the vision statement triggers followers' interest. They must see in adherence to its challenge a way to exercise their various talents. It must challenge them to want to become involved in planning, policy, and process decisions and in other ways they can individually contribute in recognizable ways.

Empowerment requires the inner leader to set the vision, communicate it broadly, and inform coworkers about the work community, its purposes, processes, accomplishments, and shortcomings. Thus, leaders become facilitators of the work of others. In effect, they go to work for the follower. They provide necessary authority and the physical, operational, and psychological resources and services the follower needs to be effective. Inner leaders must also be prepared to have the work done in ways different from the ways they would use. It is possible that the work will be done better. It is conceivable, at least in the beginning, that it will be done worse. It will almost always be done differently. Acceptance of the need for flexibility in method and even in results is part of the preparation of the leader for empowerment of his or her followers.

Challenging Followers

Empowerment works when followers see that adhering to its challenge is a way to mature their various talents. Empowerment challenges followers to want to become involved. It is accomplished via participative efforts between leader and worker. It asks leaders to use innate values of independence, self-reliance, and individualism to challenge workers to sacrifice for the leader and for the work community as a way to self-actualize on the job.

Delegating to Followers

Key in empowering others is delegation of job assignments and decisions to the lowest possible level and allowing room for coworkers to take risks without undue controls or tight accountability. This kind of delegation by inner leaders helps workers find their niche—the place in the work community where their strengths can be best used to the benefit of workers, the inner leader, the work community, and the larger corporation itself. Empowering inner leaders create job situations where workers can be self-motivated, not intimidated. They provide as much information as possible to as many people as possible about what they and others are doing and their degree of success. They do not suppress data about the work. Effective inner leaders take the time and effort to recognize individual differences and use them constructively (Truskie, 1999) through delegation that focuses on individual member strengths.

Focusing on Workers

Empowerment focuses primarily on the members of the work community (Plas, 1996). Effective inner leaders actively encourage their coworkers to acknowledge their true feelings and values and their personal goals and aspirations to help them learn who they are and then use that knowledge in joint work activity. This expression of their authentic selves can occur only in an environment where workers feel secure—a community accepting of divergent views and opinions, one in which the inner leader really cares about them.

Encouraging Participation

To enable individual workers and ask for real participation, inner leaders must first take advantage of the power of the individual by transforming it to create an environment where individuals can work together—exploiting their differences to the benefit of the work community and themselves (Plas, 1996). This can be done only in a work community where mutual cooperation and interdependence are built into the structure of work assignments.

The psychological foundations of this kind of participatory leadership are rooted in the counseling philosophies of psychologists such as Carl Rogers

(1964) and Abraham Maslow (1962). Several guidelines direct the inner leader's empowering efforts. To empower followers to full participation is to give them meaningful work to do and to recognize their accomplishments as often as possible. Perhaps the most beneficial contribution of participatory inner leadership is its fundamental role in making workers into an effective community.

Specifying Follower Roles

Plas (1996) argues that values like individualism that undergird contemporary diversity ideas can subvert attempts to implement successful community strategies. She recommends that work communities be structured—like a sports team—with a specific role for each member. This role specialization enables each member to make unique contributions and permits the personal recognition needed to satisfy the individualist spirit that typifies most Americans. When each work community member has a unique role to play, the emphasis shifts from the group to the individual.

Encouraging Self-Reliance

The essence of cooperative action is member empowerment. Work communities led by inner leaders have to rely on the willingness and capacity for members to manage themselves for their professional and work goals to be met because a large part of work-community life involves members making decisions on their own (Kulwiec, 2001). Self-reliant work communities represent a major paradigm shift from classical hierarchal organizational structures.

A key part of empowerment is building and implementing self-reliance in the workers. Inner leaders form work-community structures and operating systems that facilitate workers' taking personal responsibility for seeing that the work that needs doing gets done. Such self-reliant work structures include the overarching culture that provides grounding for all that is done and all relationships systems used. These cultures honor independence in thought and action. Inner leaders create these structures and ensure that that kind of development and growth happens. These leaders also ensure that they change as the needs of coworkers and the purposes of the larger community change.

Centered in a vitalizing vision, self-reliant cultural systems allow workers maximum independence of action within the context of an interdependent system of values, rules of behavior, and standards for measuring success. Leaders concerned with fostering follower self-reliance engage in actions to encourage followers to get involved in the work community's work and use the work community's accepted behavior patterns—patterns that involve independent action.

Kulwiec (2001) says such work units set target performance goals and track progress toward those goals. The areas tracked for improvement might include such activities as safety, quality, cooperation, productivity, and scheduling, as well as continuous improvement. Although independent work performance is an important criterion, each individual is also responsible for his or her own performance to the inner leader and to colleagues.

Other Empowerment Techniques

A review of the literature reveals other ways to empower members of work communities to help the inner leader attain his or her goals for the community. They include the following:

1. Letting members talk to anybody in the firm to resolve problems and get the job done.
2. Ask members for their contributions and ideas.
3. Give work-community members full control of their own operations.
4. Involve members in selecting all new recruits.
5. Get members to train their colleagues.
6. Adopt individual member-set objectives at every level.
7. Adopt self-assessment appraisals.
8. Give each community member responsibility for assets and areas of the common work.

DISCUSSION ISSUES AND QUESTIONS

Issues

1. Inner leaders routinely engage in empowering techniques that support deeply held needs of people to be involved.
2. In doing this, inner leaders pursue two purposes: to attain mutually desirable goals and to help followers develop into mature professionals.
3. People want to make a difference; and if leaders let them and teach them to do it, they gain willing followers.
4. The inner leader's task is to allow the human "assets" with which they work to appreciate in value.
5. Empowerment appeals to the human values of independence, self-reliance, and individualism.
6. Empowerment means "to enable." It releases the power in others through collaboration.
7. Empowerment produces results of greater follower achievement, self-satisfaction, and hard work.
8. The risk inherent in empowerment is that it asks the leader to trust in the essential goodness of followers.

9. Empowerment is facilitated by building and using structures that encourage self-reliance.

10. Empowerment is intellectually connected with several ideas such as teaming, participation, delegation, transformation, developing follower strengths, visioning, self-actualizing, and increased productivity.

11. Empowering leaders exercise control on the basis of results, not activity, events, or methods.

Questions

1. Do I make specific efforts to increase independent action of employees, expand their decision-making capacities, and more fully use their unique abilities in task accomplishment?

2. Do I relate to coworkers with the understanding that self-directed action supports deep psychological needs of people in work communities?

3. Do I treat coworkers as if they want to make a difference?

4. Do I recognize that coworkers will follow my lead if I let them and teach them to do the work-community's work?

5. Do I recognize the independence of my coworkers, or do I consistently try to tell them what to do?

6. Have I established a culture that encourages new ideas and independent thought that enhances the work community's vision?

7. Do I help others interpret their actions based on the work community's values and vision?

8. Do I encourage and enthuse coworkers to accomplish vision-directed work?

9. Am I comfortable with the ambiguity and uncertainty that may come from an autonomous workforce?

10. Do I encourage coworkers to take personal responsibility for the success of the work community?

EMPOWERMENT LEARNING ACTIVITIES

Learning to be an inner leader engages the individual leader in behaviors like the following that may be useful to leaders to gain experience and comfort in caring for followers.

Activity 1: Blocks to Empowerment

Introduction. This activity is designed to help participants recognize the readiness of the work community and its members to accept empowerment and recognize the potential blocks to its implementation.

1. Complete the following questionnaire by checking the appropriate box either yes or no. For each question, think about the current state of your work community or department and tell us what it is.

Yes No

_____ _____ 1. Is your work community undergoing major change and transition?

_____ _____ 2. Is your work community a startup or new venture?

_____ _____ 3. Is your work community facing increasing competitive pressures?

_____ _____ 4. Is your work community a hierarchical bureaucracy?

_____ _____ 5. Is the predominant leadership in your work community authoritarian and top down?

_____ _____ 6. Is there a great deal of negativism like rehashing and focus on failures?

_____ _____ 7. Are employees provided with reasons for the work community's decisions and actions?

_____ _____ 8. Are performance expectations and goals clearly stated?

_____ _____ 9. Are goals realistic and achievable?

_____ _____ 10. Are rewards clearly tied to performance or the accomplishment of work-community goals and mission?

_____ _____ 11. Are rewards based on competence and accomplishments?

_____ _____ 12. Is innovation encouraged and rewarded?

_____ _____ 13. Are there many opportunities for participation?

_____ _____ 14. Are most tasks routine and repetitive?

_____ _____ 15. Are resources generally appropriate for performing the tasks?

_____ _____ 16. Are opportunities for interaction with senior management limited?

Scoring key: For items 1 through 6 and 14 and 16, give a score of 1 if you have marked Yes, 0 if you have checked No. For items 7 through 13 and item 15, give a score of 0 to Yes responses and 1 to No.

Analysis. The maximum possible score is 16. The closer you have rated your work community to that maximum score, the less ready it is for implementation of empowerment. An analysis of individual items can point to specific blocks to the implementation of empowerment.

2. What are the key blocks to empowerment in your workplace?

3. What is the role of the inner leader in empowering the team? List as many tasks as you can.

CHAPTER 20

Technique 17: Teaching and Coaching Stakeholders

Inner leaders are teachers of their followers as much as anything else. To be effective, these leaders develop the techniques of effective teaching. Their role is to communicate with, inform, and ultimately persuade followers to cooperative joint action. This role involves leaders in teaching stakeholder colleagues (employees, clients, constituents, citizen-customers, others) the principles, values, and techniques of excellent performance. The teaching method most often used is coaching. Coaching is based on observing workers, exciting them, teaching them individually, encouraging them, and creating situations that give each worker the opportunity to take independent action in accomplishing work-community goals. Coaching lets inner leaders give followers continuing support so they can act for the work community. Coaching includes providing valuable feedback crucial to personal motivation and performance improvement.

DEFINING COACHING LEADERSHIP

Inner leadership is essentially coaching—the ability to associate with others in ways that enable them to act. Coaching is based on exciting workers, dealing with them individually, encouraging them, and creating situations within which, after preparation, they can take independent action in accomplishing joint goals. Coaches do not coordinate the work of their players (workers); they train, inspire, and perfect their full capacity to play their part (do their segment of the work). A result of good coaching is that recipients are enabled to act for the common good.

Coaching is one-on-one interaction with followers to teach, train, and aid in the development of their personal skills, values, and capacities. Coaches encourage teamwork, inspire cooperation, mentor, and otherwise shape member behavior, often one member at a time.

Simple observation confirms more formal evidence (see Chapter 7 and the rest of this book) that the essence of leading is the development of those with whom leaders work. This can best be done face to face (Kulwiec, 2001). Coaching is personalized leadership that pulls together people with diverse backgrounds, talents, experiences, and interests and treats them as full partners. It is a process of building on their strengths. At its heart, coaching involves caring enough about followers to take the time to build personal relationships with them. It is finding a reason every day to meet with them to underscore that both leader and follower are really linked in the common endeavor. It is the power of personal attention that communicates only one way: physical presence (Fairholm, 1993).

Coaching is value-shaping. Coaches change behavior (skills), but their most important task is to change the attitudes and values of members to conform to those of the work community. It involves the principle of supportive relationships Rensis Likert (1961) described. Supportive relationships are those that ensure a maximum chance that in all relationships members—given their values, desires, background, and expectations—will view the relationship as positive. The coaching relationship is one that supports, builds, and maintains the individual's sense of personal worth and importance. Much coaching comes from example. As leader-coaches reflect work community values in their actions, individual members come to understand them, accept them, and behave accordingly. Coach-leaders also voice work-community values, consistently communicate them, and reflect them in both oral and written contacts with stakeholders.

Coaching is a new conception of the role of the leader. Few writers suggest what is the observable fact about many executives: that leaders are primarily teachers of their followers. Few writers relate leadership with teaching. Henry Leavenson (1968) is an exception. Inner leaders often act in a coaching relationship with their followers. There is a significant implication in this activity.

Leader coaches are good role models. They are supportive—not overpowering. Leadership is about really paying attention to the people—believing in them, caring about them, involving them. Some of the most vital aspects of coaching are the same as the definitional aspects of the values model of leadership. Thus, coaches and excellent leaders listen to understand. They are visible, set limits, shape values, stretch their followers, accept difference, and capitalize on them. And they let their followers' specialties be seen, perfected, and recognized.

Coaching is the essence of leading, that is, developing all those with whom the leader works. Coaching pulls together people with diverse backgrounds, talents, experiences, and interests and treats them as full partners (Lombardi,

2000). Coaches spend time—sometimes lavish time—on followers. Coaching is a real-time effort, taking place in the instant of interactivity. It is not a cerebral but an action technique. Coaching takes place where the action is, at the time of the action. You have to be out of your office to coach. It is relating the individual to the rest of the work community in productive ways. The best coaches spend as much time strengthening the work community's capacity to operationalize shared values as they do developing individual member ability to do needed work. The best coaching result is getting people personally involved with how the leader does his or her own job. It is showing followers that what they do moves the work community a little further toward their goals and at the same time moves the work community closer to its goals.

METHODS OF COACHING

Coaching is a leadership style based on exciting workers, teaching them, and encouraging them to personal and team (work-community) excellence. Coaching involves leaders in five activities or roles. The paragraphs following apply these roles to effective inner leadership.

Educator

For inner leaders, educating the members of their work community includes drilling followers in the basics of their work. Both coaching and leading are about letting individuals know that they belong and that they can contribute. Coach-leaders educate their stakeholders to feel a part of the work community, to take ownership of the collective work methods and sought-after results, and otherwise to commit fully to its work. Full access to information about how things are going in the work community and with each individual member is an essential part of this education process. Coach-leaders make their assignments and expectations clear, simple, and concrete and communicate them broadly and often.

Coaching asks inner leaders to provide needed skills and knowledge to individual followers and make opportunities for them to exercise them. Feedback on progress is a part of this education process. It provides information that is at the follower's level of understanding. Many times it is quantifiable, outcome oriented, and operational (observable). Coach-leaders give feedback that is clear, timely, accurate, and about significant behaviors, nor irrelevancies. Coach-leaders voice their work community's values, consistently communicate them, and reflect them in both oral and written contacts with all stakeholders. This is also a part of a process of feeding back to followers data about their progress toward full acceptance of community standards and values. Good inner leaders give feedback—good feedback. Good coach-leaders accept the fact that members will make mistakes along the way. They make use of these "learning moments" as they present themselves to reenforce group values and behaviors.

Just as much teaching comes from example, so too do inner leaders model desired follower behavior. As leader-coaches reflect group values in their actions, individual members see those actions and learn appropriate attitudes and behavior and come to accept them and behave accordingly.

Also part of this educating coach-leader component is experimentation. In many respects interesting, inspiring work is often a perception in the imagination, not an intrinsic characteristic of the work itself. As inner leaders get followers to bring to their work an inquiring mind, a readiness to experiment in applying vision-centered principles, and an openness to inspiration and to the ideas of followers, they find their followers will accept the challenge and grow and mature both as coworkers and as coleaders of the joint enterprise.

Wise inner leaders learn that followers cannot rely on others for their strength. To do so is to build weakness. People can receive help from others while learning new skills. But when they rely too much on someone else for expertise, information, or vision, they subordinate their development to convenience and as a result suffer loss of strength. Inner leaders create situations within which followers can test their budding knowledge and skill in controlled (by the leader) situations until they gain the confidence to practice their new knowledge and skill in routine work-community tasks.

Sponsor

Inner leaders sponsor work-community members as they experiment with taking charge of their work lives and of the tasks of maturing and developing their skills and acquiring useful bases of information about their work situations. In this role, leaders become advocates of their followers, supporting them in relationships with other leaders and sponsoring them for increasingly important work assignments and positions. Coach-leaders act as advocates for individual followers as their maturing competence prepares them for increased responsibilities and more varied and comprehensive work assignments.

Sponsoring followers includes granting them guided autonomy as they grow in their work skills. It also places responsibility on the leader for the actions of each member. Sponsoring a follower has an element of risk attached. When leaders champion their followers' skills, knowledge, and abilities and recommend them for advancement, they place their own reputations on the line. Subsequent follower success redounds to the leader's benefit. By the same token, follower failure hurts the sponsoring leader's reputation.

Counselor

Counseling is the vital, but delicate, role of providing feedback about progress and contribution. People have a right to know where they stand. Timely, complete, compassionate explanation and evaluation of their conduct and contribution to the success of the work community is constructive. It lets people discover where they are helping most. It also helps them understand where they can contribute further (or differently) in the future. Counseling also involves meeting with coworkers who are behaving in ways that do not help. Confronting low performance is difficult. The alternative—ignoring the situation—is worse. Unaddressed low performance can destroy an otherwise effective community.

In their one-on-one counseling contacts with followers is the opportunity to be of specific service to them to aid in their personal change. Change is accomplished only by the individual. Inner leaders act as catalysts, not always decision makers, in this personal change process. The follower sets the pace. The individual follower is the only person who can surely change himself or herself. Externals (like leaders) cannot. They can only help followers to see a better way and counsel them to follow that way. Leaders function to facilitate change in their associates' lives through application of principles of counseling liberally peppered with affection and sacrifice.

The purpose of counseling is to have the counseled person experience a change of attitude and action. Counseling sessions should result in the change, development, and progress of the person counseled. Inner leaders facilitate this change. Indeed, this is a prime purpose of any counseling session—to get the counseled person to change. Inner leaders must be willing to sacrifice—to forgo personal convenience and invest time—for their followers. They create an atmosphere of concern that is conducive to learning and sharing of confidences. Inner leaders are willing listeners. They actively listen to the thoughts and emotions as well as words of followers. And they need to share with them their own feelings about their personal, intimate selves, and about the place of the work community's values and vision in their lives.

The counseling contact is personal, intimate, and open. Leaders express their true feelings. Finding the right words is essential; it is part of the art and creativity of inner leadership. The following precepts constitute some of the main principles supporting counseling.

Be compassionate.

Be nonblaming.

Be nonjudgmental.

Be committed to the message delivered.

Be patient, sincere, and temperate in demeanor.

Counseling followers makes it possible for the leader to know their followers as individuals and to understand their level of professional and other maturity, the extent of their commitment, and their personal and professional goals and values. This understanding is essential to the proper delegation of duties to the individual. Armed with this knowledge, the leader can select a set of responsibilities to fit the current and evolving needs of each follower and relate their amelioration to work needed by the work community.

Counseling gives inner leaders an unparalleled opportunity to develop closeness and unity with their followers. The counseling contact is a way for the leader and the follower to relate in mutually helpful ways. This closeness carries over into other aspects of their work and social relationship. More understanding of the goals of the work community and of individual motives followers strive for through their work in the organization is obtainable in these counseling contacts. Silence and distance do not bring safety or protection and peace. Forgoing counseling and the resultant opportunities for change is foolhardy.

Comforter

Leadership is also a task of securing and maintaining a safe workplace, an important part of which includes insuring that the workplace is emotionally safe and comfortable. In addition to their roles as educator, sponsor and supporter, and counselor, inner leaders also accept the responsibility to console team members as they are overwhelmed by the pressures of the job. Leading others involves leaders in the intimate personal lives of their coworkers. As interpersonal relationships—or personal, family, or social issues—arise, inner leaders are often called on to assist in their resolution, to provide moral support, and to soothe emotions. As a general statement, leadership is a task of strengthening followers' capacities to be successful in professional work tasks and related interpersonal relationships. As performance in either is less than desired, the leader's job is to resolve the problem, which often involves sustaining and nurturing their coworkers. Similar interaction is appropriate when the worker's performance is above the standard. Such people often need nurturing too to help them sustain their high performance over time.

Comforting followers is an inner-leadership task that depends on the leader's capacity to authentically care for his or her followers. One of the principles of inner leadership has to do with how leaders associate with their followers. Inner leadership is based on love—love for the members served and love for those who serve with the leader in his or her leadership cluster of work community members. Leading through authentic caring—love—is the only approach to the conduct of the work community's work today that will be fully successful. It is the only real basis of leadership that guarantees continued success. As leaders strive to grow and to comfort others in their quest for personal growth and professional maturation, they are guided by a need to be close enough to the psyches of their followers to know when and how to offer comfort and support.

Coach

Like coaching a sports team, leading the workers who inhabit the middle ranges of the corporation depends for success on a base of values including motivating team players, encouraging teamwork, inspiring cooperation, mentoring others, and shaping behavior. These are all-important skills for today's inner leaders. Like coaches, inner leaders need to be able to inspire and empower others to develop goals and achieve their personal and group objectives as efficiently and effectively as possible. Outstanding leaders (coaches) also project a vision of the mission to be accomplished and elicit the commitment and dedication needed to achieve this vision (Lombardi, 2000). These, like the other elements of coaching, are power techniques: Their aim is to get others to do what the inner leader wants.

The Coaching Process

Leading in the middle regions of the corporation presents many challenges to the leader, perhaps more than leading from the top of the organization chart. Inner leaders work intimately with their colleagues—bosses, peers, subordinates, suppliers, and customers. This role asks them to intimately understand human nature. They learn to understand how people see the world, how they process information, and their preferred approach to problem solving (Badaracco and Ellsworth, 1989). For example, some followers see the world as black or white, right or wrong. For them, all knowledge is known, and right and wrong answers exist for everything. They see knowledge as merely a collection of information that they can learn. Typically, they look to the leader for needed knowledge. They see the leader as the authority and the source of truth. The follower's role is to receive the knowledge and demonstrate having learned the right answers.

Others see the world in diametrically opposite terms. Nothing is known, and there are no right or wrong answers. Since there is no certainty, all individuals can "do their own thing." Anyone's opinion can be just as valid or invalid as all others. The inner leader's role is to model the way they want their followers to think and to ascertain the mind-set of followers and to couch training and instruction in terms to suit the individual follower's mind-set.

Given these considerations, understanding followers is a complex and difficult task. Fortunately, leaders have several simple tools that go a long way toward making their jobs doable. Prime among these tools is the uncomplicated task of getting out where the work is being done, seeing firsthand what is happening, and then forming adaptive strategies to improve what is going on. A method for doing this is called Management by Walking (or Wandering) Around (MBWA).

Presented formally to the world in the 1980s by Tom Peters and Nancy Austin (1985), MBWA puts leaders in touch with their people and the work community's work, as well as customers and their concerns. It balances "book" knowledge with operational knowledge. Walking around is getting out of the office and seeing firsthand what the work of the work community and the problems of its workers are. It lets the leader collect firsthand data on operations, interests, problems, ideas, and frustrations of the workforce—indeed, of any stakeholder. The purpose is to tap often neglected information sources and understandings of what is going on, what is needed, and how to go about closing the gap. It is staying in regular, informal contact with coworkers and clients at their work stations, not just in formal meetings.

Besides keeping the leader informed and up to date, frequent on-site visits provides leaders the opportunity to transmit their values in a most effective way, via face-to-face contacts. This is a flexible technique that allows leaders to be where the action is and to be involved in the action. Practiced by many leaders, MBWA is fluid and adaptable. Being where the action is facilitates informal, open communications between leaders and their followers. It helps them learn the key actors and cultivate the right people in the stakeholder pool best suited to tap into developing needs, problems, and solutions, as well as opportunities for growth. It is getting and staying in regular contact with employees and customers. It is forming informal relationships with those closest to the work, not necessarily most senior in the hierarchy.

The heart of the coaching technique is mind-set (Lombardi, 2000). Its success is contingent upon how much the leader commits to the idea of hands-on interaction as a tool to distribute influence (power) throughout the work community. Leaders must constantly be on guard against the pitfall of thinking they have the answers and therefore forgetting to listen naively to their followers.

DISCUSSION ISSUES AND QUESTIONS

Issues

1. To be effective, the inner leader must develop the techniques of effective teaching: communicating to inform and persuade followers to cooperative, joint action.

2. The teaching method most often used is coaching or one-on-one interaction with employees to teach, train, and aid in development of their individual skills, values, and capacities.

3. Coaching is a supportive relationship, one that ensures a maximum chance that in all relationships members, given their values, desires, backgrounds, and expectations, will view the relationship as positive.

4. To coach is to facilitate, or to make easy.

5. Coaching involves leaders in five roles: educator, sponsor, counselor, comforter, and coach.

6. Leaders learn to understand how people see the world, how they process information, and their preferred approach to problem solving and then use that information in their leadership.

7. In coaching followers, leaders are in face-to-face relationships with followers who are in the middle of work activity so they can see what followers do, how they think, and what their problems are.

Questions

1. Have I given sufficient time to understanding the people and the relationships in my office?

2. Do I understand the peculiarities of my followers?

3. Do I use individual follower's skills, knowledge, and other assets to their best advantage?

4. Am I willing to invest the time to develop professional, quality, face-to-face, and other relationships with my coworkers?

5. Have I developed enough people skills to effectively relate with others?

COACHING LEARNING ACTIVITIES

Activity 1: Coaching

Instructions. Coaching includes teaching followers to both accept and apply the vision and values connotations of the work community into the work they do (Fairholm, 1991). In a leadership context, teaching or coaching focuses on helping followers to understand the vision and its values context, to accept as their own these values and the implications of the vision, and to apply the principles inherent in the vision as they perform their organizational work. The result is that the work community becomes more explicit and the order, productivity, and unity that emerge become a practical extension of a shared values context. If leaders do not teach their values and vision, other values and a different vision will guide the organization and work against the leaders' purposes.

1. Respond to the following questions:

   Do I understand my role as a coach in the work community?

   Have I developed the skills to relay information and values in a way that adults can understand and adopt?

   Do I take the time and the many opportunities I have to teach the vision and the values of the office?

   Do I encourage teaching among my coworkers?

2. Develop an action plan to increase your skill as a coach-leader.

Activity 2: Coaching Checklist

Instructions. Coaching for improved work performance includes getting agreement that a problem exists and on what the problem is, generating solutions, agreeing to a plan of action, implementing it, and following up after the solution has been implemented to ensure it worked.

1. Review the following statements that may help you improve your coaching skills:

   Good coaching begins with separating the behavior from the person, and that, in turn, means identifying causes rather than the effects. Listening to the member's point of view may be helpful in seeing the real issues.

   Sometimes, performance problems exist because the individual worker thinks his or her performance is acceptable. Sometimes, although the worker may know that performance is lacking, the deficiency itself is considered acceptable. These perceptions often result from too little feedback.

   One reason members don't perform up to the inner leader's expectations is that they don't know what the expectations are and consequently don't know that a problem exists.

   Even when members know what is expected of them, they may not know what they are supposed to do or when to do it.

   Outside factors can have a direct effect on a performance. Among these factors are equipment failure, late or incorrect reports or data, conflicting instructions, too many bosses, and lack of materials or supplies.

   Unsatisfactory performance may occur because good performance is punished. An example of negative consequence is the technician who has to complete another person's work because he or she finished his or her own tasks early.

   Similarly, the technician who has part of his or her work taken away is rewarded for not getting his or her own work accomplished.

2. Develop a coaching plan for your firm that considers these statements. Include in the plan as many work situations and coworkers as you can. In preparing this plan, consider issues like the following: (Of course, not all of these may apply to your situation today. Use those—and other issues— you see as pertinent to your current situation.)

   Orientation and training of a new employee.

   Teaching a new job skill.

   Need to explain standards of the work unit.

   Need to explain cultural norms and political realities of the organization.

   Corrections to performance are required.

   Goals or business conditions change.

   New members are added to the work community.

   Work-community members facing new work experiences.

   A member who needs help setting priorities.

   Follow up to a training session.

   Members who display low or moderate performance.

   A members who needs reinforcement for good performance.

A member wants to become a peak performer.

Formal or informal performance reviews.

A member needs preparation to meet his or her future career goals.

A member needs preparation for more challenging work assignment.

A member needs self-confidence developed.

Power or control battles are affecting the work community's cohesiveness.

Others?

3. Consider sharing your plan with others in your firm.

CHAPTER 21

Technique 18: Follower Self-Governance

Inner leaders have a goal of producing high performance. They also have the duty to create of their followers highly developed, self-led leaders who can exercise the necessary power to function more or less independently within the constraints of the values and vision set by the leader. The various traditional leadership theories each argued that their brand of leadership would result in enhanced productivity. They sought improved follower performance measured in physical (tangible) goal terms. The follower remains in each of these models subservient to the leader. These models essentially cast workers as tools to help achieve the leader's personal or institutional goals—in past theory they are targets of power rather than wielders of power in the work community.

DEFINING SELF-GOVERNANCE

The inner-leadership model is unique in its emphasis on improving the individual follower's capacity for self-directed action to accomplish shared goals. Both the context and specific methods of this power technique move the follower toward this result, along with performance improvement. Inner leader success is attaining both results. Failing this, leaders must alter or improve either the corporate culture or the techniques they employ in a given situation.

This double objective activates all facets of the leader's job. The open, self-guiding culture fostered by in-the-middle leaders aids in the realization of this outcome. The vision they create includes this outcome. So must the skills and techniques they use. All action by the leader needs to communicate this objective (along with all others) to followers. Inner leadership is changing lives—the leader's own and those of his work colleagues. The job is to create a climate and the conditions that foster follower autonomy and development. The direction of the follower life-change sought is toward a more empowered follower. It is a task of changing followers to help them be independent, free, and self-governing.

The Nature of Success

Inner leaders redefine success. As they share governance, this action has a tremendous impact on both workers and leaders. As the work done changes, leader and led change, as do their measures of success. Success, defined as being "in-charge," is the traditional norm and is as dependent on factors outside the individual's control—luck, the whims of others, office politics, and so on—as it is on personal capacity. Accepting this conventional definition of success is to lose much of the potential influence inner leaders may have over their destiny and the future they envision for themselves and for their followers and the work community they lead. Effective inner leaders resist allowing the terms of their success to be determined by others—by anything outside themselves.

Nonetheless, the traditional definition of success is a seductive lure. Our society is preoccupied with winning and personal prominence, and these can become accepted and expected outcomes of the leader's work. Certainly, they have come to be central in the conventional textbook definitions of leadership success. Once inner leaders accept the concept of shared governance, the definition of success necessarily changes. Instead of being successfully in charge, inner leaders come to think about success as a personal, intimate, feeling of satisfaction in seeing themselves, as well as their colleagues in the work community, put to use more of their whole selves at work.

Perceptive inner leaders define success not just in terms of being famous or anything else that comes from external sources. For them, success is defined by the scope of (1) workplace parameters they can influence and (2) "developed" followers. Thus, success is attained as inner leaders nurture followers' talents and let them practice those talents in a variety of satisfying ways and in different venues (Heenan and Bennis, 1999). It can be found in providing a designated service to a stakeholder or in a personal talent they strengthen. Success is also defined as achieving peace of mind and satisfaction—even fun—in seeing protegées fulfilling designated responsibilities.

Leading self-governing work communities requires a kind of leadership orientation particularly adapted to leadership in the middle: stewardship (Block, 1993). Block and others have effectively refocused attention on the nature of the relationship between leader and follower to one that can be conveniently encapsulated in the ideas of service and stewardship. Block defined stewardship as holding something in trust for another. Inner leaders are trustees (stewards) as they see their organization as a shared community and each stakeholder as a coequal leader.

METHODS OF PREPARING FOLLOWERS
TO GOVERN THEMSELVES

Helping followers learn to accept shared governance is often hard. It asks inner leaders to change themselves and get followers also to change on several levels: attitude, skills, and philosophy. Each is critical to this kind of collaborative leadership. Conceivably, learning to accept the philosophy of shared governance is the most important phase of initial follower preparation to lead in the middle. Tradition suggests that leaders alone guide and focus the work community. This may be true in theory—not practice—for top leaders, but inner leaders are guided by an alternative value system, one that shares power—even the power to lead. They accept that a values foundation highlighting follower growth and development of their full capacities is implicit in this leadership model.

Inner leaders learn to master the skills of self-development. They learn to control their natural urges to accept that leadership gives them license to do what they want and instead come to understand that leadership is an opportunity to serve their followers—all stakeholders—and that their greatest satisfactions—and professional success—come when they submit themselves to the maturing capacities of their followers. Thus, a prime task in learning to lead self-governing followers is how to develop the leader's own time and skills appropriately. Another skill requires leaders to know their followers as they know themselves. As they do this, they come to trust in their followers' abilities. These leaders recognize that their own professional maturation is a lifelong learning process that includes among other things learning to sacrifice, serve, and sometimes follow their followers.

Both theory and practice suggest that only persons who possess certain tendencies practice this kind of joint leadership. Key among these is personal maturity (Metzger, 1987). Leaders are people of exceptional maturity. They accept experiences for what they are. The challenge of sharing leadership asks them to learn to know their personal role-fit within the work community, a significant part of which is that leaders are teachers of their followers. Learning to lead in a shared governance situation involves leaders in increasing their skills in goal-directed action to enlarge their followers. It is a task of continual personal and follower learning and growth.

This technique of inner leadership asks leaders to be horizon thinkers—to encourage future-oriented thinking in increasingly self-governing followers. And it is helping followers to participate in defining and shaping their joint future. Inner leaders pay attention to what is important about tasks and values, both now and for the future, and encourage this kind of leadership behavior in followers.

Defining the Scope of Sharing

Sharing their authority and responsibility for corporate governance and stakeholder development asks leaders in the middle of the corporate hierarchy to become expert in a variety of skills and techniques not often covered in traditional top leader development programs. Facilitating this technique of shared governance is the fact that inner leaders occupy positions within the corporate system where their strengths can both produce corporate results and assist them in improvement of their own personal goals and capacities—and make this happen for their followers as well. Inner leaders are engaged in a quest for follower development toward self-governance that includes at least the kinds of activity described in the following sections.

Correcting Bad Habits

One essential self-governance technique is that of helping to rectify followers' unfavorable habits—the things they do or fail to do that inhibit their effectiveness and performance (Bennis and Townsend, 1995). Inner leaders try to get followers to waste as little effort as possible on unproductive values, attitudes, and actions. They assess followers' personal traits, determine those that have potential of helping secure community goals and those that have low potential. Then they work on the helpful, but unperfected, traits and largely ignore those with low potential for assisting them in attaining their goals. Their energy, resources, and time go instead to maximizing follower competencies.

Using Their Talents Wisely

Inner leaders try to help followers position themselves where they can make the greatest contribution. This entails intimate understanding of follower capacities. It also requires leaders to time follower changes and learn how and when to encourage change in the way they work—even the work they do. Inner leaders teach followers how to place themselves where they can make the greatest contribution.

Practicing Self-Control

Most people have to learn to manage themselves (Drucker, 1988). Effective inner leaders have already done so, and they try to help followers do likewise. Self-managed people are relatively rare in work communities. They are so unusual, in fact, that both their talents and their accomplishments are often considered to be outside the boundaries of customary human conduct. For leaders who seek to share leadership with their followers, helping them discipline their work lives may be an even more important issue than assessing their personal and professional assets.

To be able to govern themselves, followers also have to deal with their personal sets of values. This is not merely a question of ethics. Ethics are only part of a person's value system. To work in a situation where the value system is unacceptable or incompatible with his or her own condemns that follower both to frustration and to underperformance. To be effective in the corporation, followers' personal values must be (or come to be) compatible with the work community's values. Otherwise, followers will not only be frustrated but also will not produce needed results. The inner leader's task is to facilitate values displacement and thus encourage ethical follower responses.

Developing Personal Self-Confidence

Self-confidence is a sense of personal identity (Deal and Kennedy, 1988) that includes the ideas of esteem and control. Developing that confidence takes directed personal effort. For inner leaders, the task is to encourage followers to develop self-confidence, to be centered, to have the ability to sustain balance, even in the midst of action. Being centered means not being subject to passing whims or sudden excitements. Centered followers know where they stand and what they stand for. They have a sense of stability and a confident sense of self. Warren Bennis (1999) says there is no greater teacher about self than responsibility. Good leaders learn that when followers are aware of their true feelings about working with others they are most effective. Thus, they develop sources of feedback.

Being Goal-Directed

The essence of success in any kind of leadership is having all involved direct their energies toward common goals and high personal performance. This requires some system of control and accountability. The primary mechanism inner leaders use for assuring goal-implementation and application, however, is not in the authority mechanism that top leaders typically use but in the attitude and behavior of the inner leader. Inner leaders focus their need and capacities upon future outcomes that are also consistent with those of their followers. The task of conforming work-community values and actions with the leader's horizon goals is a critical, if simple, process of defining goals and prioritizing values that support goal-accomplishment. While simple, it is not always an easy task. Nor is it always easy to induce followers to think and behave similarly.

Developing Follower Skills

Program success depends on the skill and knowledge of workers, especially if the leader intends for them to share governance of the common work. A key responsibility of inner leadership, therefore, is in ensuring that all followers are aware of and competent in doing needed work. This is a task of informing and training all work-community members in their duties and, in doing their work, to use their personal and corporate resources effectively to bring about preset goals. This information transfer is accomplished in the normal ways and particularly in the behavior of leaders as they model desired behavior. On the principle that you cannot teach what you do not know, leaders have to portray desired behavior before they can expect followers to behave that way. They reflect common values, methods, and outcomes in everything they do and say, both formally and in informal settings. For inner leaders, staff development becomes a mutual process of growth and change toward independent action.

Thinking Strategically

Leaders pay attention not so much to what is important today as to what will be significant tomorrow. They seek to discern the future through research, planning, and taking actions today that are intended to create a future that corresponds with their present goals and aspirations. In reality, nothing can be done today to affect the past. Understanding this, inner leaders spend their time on preparing their followers to ensure the work community functions effectively in the future, a place where they will spend the rest of their productive work lives.

Techniques Supporting Self-Governance

In the past, most work-community members were told what to do, and their energies were dictated either by the work itself or by a supervisor. Today, most workers are knowledge workers—people who perform work using words and numbers and producing products consisting of words and numbers. And these tasks are typically unique and cannot be easily proscribed by another person. The question for leaders today is how can they help followers ensure that their work helps them become better persons, better workers, better corporate citizens? How can leaders make it meaningful to them on their own terms? Inner leaders understand the need to have a follower perspective and take steps to help followers be fully functioning, self-directed contributors to the common good while also helping themselves realize their personal aims.

The following sections may further elucidate the inner leader's task in the twenty-first century.

Stimulating Leadership Behavior

Leading in the middle of the corporation asks leaders to prepare their followers to share in that leadership. Leaders take every opportunity to let followers take the lead in parts of the work community's functions. Thus, followers may be asked to head a task force or committee. They may substitute for the leader in his or her absence. Followers' advice may be solicited about possible plans, decisions that need to be made, or alternative programs under consideration. Each helps the follower develop the skill to lead.

It is sometimes stressful to the inner leader to do this. There 1s a risk inherent in letting someone else perform tasks and take responsibility for functions the inner leader normally assumes. The leader's most difficult task sometimes is to train followers to lead and then sit back and let them lead. There is a risk that the work will not be done, or it will not be done as well as the leader would have done it. Sometimes, even more frightening, inner leaders risk that the work will be done better than they could have done it. Preparing followers for self-governance is mostly a task of preparing the leader's mind to accept that the work will be done but be done differently—maybe better—than it otherwise would have been done.

Empowerment

Getting followers to accept their goals and values is not so much an exercise of the inner leader's personal power as it is of follower empowerment (Bennis and Nanus, 1985; Adair, 1986). The idea of increasing the self-control and self-direction of coworkers is a substantial part of self-governing community-building. McGregor (1960) asked leaders to discover and make use of the unrealized potential in workers by letting them act independently. Burns (1978) suggests that we can lift people out of mediocrity to fulfill their better selves through transforming them (and empowerment idea). Bennis and Nanus (1985) say empowering followers also enhances and strengthens them. Inner leaders recognize this and change their behavior to share power with coworkers. Empowerment works because it supports deep psychological needs of people in work communities. People want to make a difference; and if the leader lets them and teaches them to do it, they become committed and productive followers.

Providing Participative Structures

The degree of sharing possible in a work community is dependent on the needs and preparedness of each follower. Formal decision committees and councils are helpful tools inner leaders use in this connection. They provide a necessary structural framework for dissemination of authority and responsibility throughout the work force. New structural enhancements and procedures and processes can also be introduced into the work community to formalize shared responsibilities. These can take the form of task forces, standing committees, or operating councils of workers and leaders. Such joint councils take responsibility for discussing obligations, developing policies, operating processes, and supervising job tasks. They form a distinct self-governance culture that supports both leader and led. An example of such a structure is stewardship.

Practicing Stewardship

The idea of stewardship depends for success on a special kind of organizational restructure aiding self-governance. Introducing stewardship ideas is, in fact, to propose a revolution in leader–follower relationship. Stewardship is not a single guiding principle but a compound of empowerment and partnership, as well as stewardship. Stewardship brings accountability while partnership balances responsibility among participants (Moxley, 2000). It is a sharing of the governance system so that each member holds control and responsibility in trust for the work community as a team. It is a relationship system (Crosby, 1996) based on mutual accountability. Stewardship operates at the whole-person—spiritual—level of existence and interrelationship.

Stewardship systems ask inner leaders to identify and articulate shared values and empowerment principles and to share leadership. Stewardship formats drive the work community beyond the bottom line, positively affecting both work and work-life satisfaction. In doing this, inner leaders capture the spirit, values, and principles of the work community and individual members.

Several elements of the idea of the leader as steward are discernable. Inner leaders use stewardship principles to unite them with stakeholders in the common enterprise. They free stakeholders to accept a personal stewardship responsibility toward those principles and to their vision. They force followers to be accountable to the group vision and to each other (Covey, 1997). They help followers take ownership of the common work. And they foster interdependence.

At its core, shared governance is a long-term, transformational approach to life and work. It is a way of behaving that has the potential for creating fundamental and positive change in followers (Spears, 1998). Stewardship emphasizes the trust that exists between the inner leader and independent stakeholders so together they can blend long-term socioeconomic, human, and environmental growth (Petrick, Scherer, Brodzinski, Quinn, and Ainina, 1999). Stewardship structures are based on the assumption that a successful corporation links individual knowledge workers in a manner that elicits a level of corporate commitment (or creativity, or loyalty, or integrity, etc.) that is greater than the sum of each individual's creativity.

Application of Self-Governance at Work

Service to stakeholders has always been part of the underlying infrastructure of inner leadership. However, few researchers have integrated service values into the technique of self-governing leadership structures. Nor have they done much to instruct the novice leader in the mechanics of this task. Yet inner leaders rely on a set of leadership competencies useful in selecting, developing, and guiding them and all stakeholders as they set up a self-governing structure in their work community where each member is, or may become, a coleader over parts of the total enterprise (Dunn, 2000).

According to Dunn, the following are among those most obvious in this connection. Inner leaders establish standards for follower performance, including descriptions of acceptable and proficient performance. They also translate their expectations of their followers into a framework of task competencies and skill-sets necessary to accomplish the followers' specific part of overall corporate goals. Then they release power to individual followers as they internalize these expectations as demonstrated in their action. They also ensure that building these competencies is incorporated into individual development planning for the work community via training. Inner leaders also reinforce desired behaviors and encourage sharing of successes. They facilitate follower actions to learn and implement these skills at every opportunity, including rewarding excellent performance. They institute awards, bonuses, and other rewards to recognize proficiency in and commitment to work community competencies and skills.

DISCUSSION ISSUES AND QUESTIONS

Issues

1. Inner leadership is changing lives, the leader's own and that of his or her work colleagues to facilitate follower self-governance.

2. Learning to lead in a shared governance situation involves leaders in increasing follower skills in goal-directed action. It is a task of continual follower learning and growth.

3. Inner leaders know that their role is an opportunity to serve their followers and that their greatest satisfaction comes when they submit themselves to the evolving capacities of their followers.

4. Inner leaders encourage followers to pay attention to what is important about tasks and values both now and for the future.

5. Shared governance in the work community changes the definition of leader success. Instead of being successfully in charge, inner leaders see success as a personal feeling of satisfaction in seeing their colleagues exercise more of their whole talents at work.

6. At its core, shared governance is a long-term, transformational approach to life and work, a way of behaving that has the potential for creating fundamental and positive change.

7. Leading self-governing work communities requires a kind of leadership orientation particularly adapted to leadership in the middle, one that prioritizes the idea of service and stewardship.

8. Stewardship emphasizes the trust that exists between the inner leader and independent stakeholders so together they can blend long-term socioeconomic, human, and environmental growth.

Questions

1. Do I take every opportunity to delegate to followers to the maximum degree of their competence? Why? Why not?
2. What is there in the act of delegation that might redound to my detriment and undermine my place in the firm? Are these unfounded fears or potential risks to my status? Explain.
3. Do I accept the fact that I may not have all the answers to work-related questions and may increase both my personal and the work community's success potential by involving my coworkers in key decisions, plans, and programs? Briefly describe a recent situation where you did (did not do) this.
4. Do I see my employees as extensions of my ideas, skills, capacities, and expertise; or do I see them as almost coequal partners with me in doing the work community's work?

SELF-GOVERNANCE LEARNING ACTIVITIES

Activity 1: Delegation for Self-Governance

Introduction. A key to self-governance is the leader's ability to delegate parts of the leadership tasks to followers. The task is more a psychological exercise than the procedural one.

1. Using the following scale rate yourself to indicate how much you agree with the following items:

1	2	3	4	5
Strongly disagree	Somewhat disagree	Neither agree nor disagree	Somewhat agree	Strongly agree

_____ 1. I can do most jobs better and faster than my coworkers.

_____ 2. Most of my tasks cannot be delegated to my coworkers.

_____ 3. Most of my coworkers do not have the appropriate skill levels to do the tasks that I could delegate to them.

_____ 4. I feel uncomfortable delegating many of my tasks to my coworkers.

_____ 5. I am responsible for my coworkers' mistakes, so I might as well do the task myself.

_____ 6. If my coworkers do too many of my tasks, I may not be needed any longer.

_____ 7. Explaining things to coworkers and training them often takes too much time.

_____ 8. My coworkers already have too much work to do; they can't handle any more.

_____ 9. If my coworkers do the tasks, I will lose touch and be out of the loop.

_____ 10. I need to know all the details of a task before I can delegate to my coworkers.

_____ Total

Scoring key. Your total score should be between 10 and 50. The higher your score, the less inclined you are to encourage self-governance, since you agree with many of the common excuses used by managers to not delegate tasks to their coworkers.

2. If feasible, compare your raw score with that of others of your colleagues.

3. What conclusions can you draw from this comparison about your capacity to promote self-governance within your work community?

4. What are some of the most important elements of delegation for self-governance?

Activity 2: Images of Self-Governance Leadership

Introduction. One way to clarify our assumptions about shared governance leadership is to use images to describe our ideal leader. Through the use of pictures, diagrams, or other physical representations, we can visualize this concept as a way to help us understand our views of the role of leaders in self-governing work communities. Making a pictorial image also helps us solidify our expectations and image of leadership generally and self-governance leadership in particular. These images reflect our personal theories of self-governing leadership. For example, viewing leaders as facilitators presents a very different image from viewing them as parents. Thinking of our role as an inner leader as being "in charge" conjures up ideas far different than thinking of our leadership in service terms.

1. Choose an image to represent your ideal self-governing leader. List the characteristics of that image.

2. Using any available art form, draw a picture or diagram of your preferred image of a leader.

3. Think about the image you have just drawn. Share your image with others as a way to clarify its implication about your view of self-governing leadership.

4. Discuss implications of various images on

   Your leadership style.

   The impact on your work community culture and structure.

   Your compatibility with current or past leaders in your work community.

   Potential shortcomings of each image.

Part VI

THE TECHNIQUES OF
TRUST LEADERSHIP

Inner leadership is a function of people in interdependent, voluntary, and trusting relationship (Crosby, 1996). Effective inner leadership can only take place within a community where both leaders and followers are free to trust the purposes, actions, and intent of others enough to risk themselves in joint relationship. This is and has always been a characteristic of leadership. Still, today many theorists, responding to a specious social and emotional appeal to inclusiveness, propound individual difference, independence, and diversity over cooperative interdependence. This is a formula for failure. Leaders can only lead volunteers who have freely chosen to share their values, vision, methods, and techniques.

Leaders in the middle of the corporation can only lead people who are in harmony with the values and purposes of their work community and its leader. Indeed, community is founded on the root word, unity, not difference, on harmony, not diversity. There is little hope that blind acceptance of coworkers with multiple and diverse internally competing value systems will produce stable, effective, and responsive, economic, governmental, or social organization. Of course, leaders should employ workers from as broad a pool of potential colleagues as possible—it is not only the law but good business and morally demanded. But the leadership challenge in the new millennium is to quickly shape these diverse workers into a work community characterized by shared vision, values, methods, and attitudes—the only venue where colleagues can trust each other enough to work collaboratively.

Either in-the-middle leaders foster freedom of choice broadly in the work community, or, over time, members will estrange themselves. The workplace created by the inner leader simply cannot sustain either human existence or individual liberty for long outside the interdependent communities to which they belong (Etzioni, 1993). The techniques of trust leadership are key inner leadership techniques. These techniques set inner leaders apart from top leaders or managers. The three techniques described in Part VI sum up a growing list of knowledge, skills, and techniques that facilitate cooperative group action. They include learning to trust others, creating community, and developing stewardship structures.

CHAPTER 22

Technique 19:
Learning to Trust Others

Today, active, dynamic leadership is scarce in society and its institutions. The reason is that today's workplace is characterized by diverse people and a pervasive mind-set that values individual differences as the basis of forming work communities. This situation and this mind-set tend to pull the organization apart rather than integrate it. And a unified, harmonious culture is essential to any leadership, especially inner leadership. If inner leaders are to be successful in realizing their personal and professional goals, they need to do something to integrate diverse workers into a functioning community defined as a cluster of interdependent coworkers who share values, methods, behaviors, and goals and who trust each other enough to work together.

Given the need for a harmonious culture, the task is to build a trust culture within which leader and led jointly agree to link their efforts in achieving mutually valued goals using agreed-upon processes. This task is complicated by the fact that the leader–follower relationship in the middle of the organization is essentially voluntary. Inner leadership is a problem of integrating workers into a functioning community of shared interests that can meet the needs of both. The task is as much a matter of community culture creation as it is of the inner leader adopting a style of leadership that prioritizes interactive trust. In fact, both are essential to success.

DEFINING TRUST

Part of the present confusion about leadership versus management is that analysts have seen leadership in system, control, and structure terms. The conventional wisdom is that to control individuals, leaders need only to change formal structures or work systems. This model denigrates individual workers and treats them as interchangeable parts, cogs in the corporate machine. Workers are asked to change as the organization's leader sees a need, whether they want to, are ready for, or even are capable of the proposed change. Inner leaders use a more effective model, one that suggests that to change we must change people's attitudes first and let them in turn change system and structure. Shaping a culture in which members can trust each other enough to work together in this way lets inner leaders create a mental and physical context within which they can lead effectively (Klenke, 1996).

The Impact of Trust on Culture and Leadership

Trust is a critical element in defining inner leaders, as well as the cultures they create that sustain effective leadership (Vanfleet and Yukl, 1989). Trust also is prerequisite to any attempt by leaders to transform (change) their work community's culture (Sashkin, 1986). Top leaders can function without trust—using coercive authority power. But inner leadership of volunteer followers is successful only in a context of mutual trust based on shared vision, ideals, and values.

The process of gaining trust relies first on having or securing some accurate, real (true) knowledge of the person, thing, or situation trusted. As inner leaders exercise trust in a follower (or a program or event) in the absence of direct knolwledge, that action empowers the follower to change to become what the leader trusts him or her to be. Each successful attempt reenforces that trust. Successive positive experiences with another person cumulate until the leader comes fully to trust that person to be and do what he or she at first only hoped he or she would be and do.

A part of the inner leader's willingness to trust depends on the work community's culture—created by the leader. That is, the ambient work culture affects the inner leader's willingness to trust, and the level of willingness to trust helps define the culture. Without the constraints imposed by the cultural surround, leaders could not exercise trust at all.

The inner leader–created work community's culture defines trust relationships, their quality and extent. And, the leader's actions apply it in everything he or she does or says. In fact all aspects of the working relationship are based on the quality of the mid-level leader's trust—of superiors, peers, subordinates, and all stakeholders. The problem today is not a lack of leaders but a lack of trusting environments within which leadership in the complex realms of the middle of the corporation is possible and without which it is impossible.

Creating a compatible culture in the middle of the organization becomes, therefore, a central task of inner leadership.

Interpreting Trust

We can define trust as reliance on the integrity or authenticity of people or things. It is a logical, thoughtful hope in their reality, their authenticity; in a word, in their truth. The idea of trust implies both an expectation and a personal obligation for both parties to the relationship to be authentic, trustworthy, reliable. It places obligation on both the truster and the object of that trust. It is a risk relationship but a necessary one. It implies proactivity, takes time, and becomes a unifying and coalescing idea essential to any working relationship. Inner leaders base their trust on a given level of truth, not falsity. The trust relationship includes an expectation and a personal obligation to be authentic, trustworthy, reliable, which is provable by ensuing experience. Seen in this light, it is a value supporting the culture that helps define how and in what degree members value others.

Trust is a risk relationship, but a necessary one (And, 1972). When we trust another person we agree to accept as true what we can now only assume is true. In theory, we do not need to trust in situations of absolute knowledge of the truth of a given person, action, or event. In these cases there is no risk, we *know*. Such absolute knowledge, however, is rarely present. Hence the need for cultures that support trust.

METHODS OF PRACTICING TRUST LEADERSHIP

Trust has long been considered a factor in leadership. However, recent research suggests that in addition to a desirable leadership trait trust can be an important strategic competitive advantage. This research proposes that leaders who develop relationships based on trust can improve their work community's performance. Trust, they say, must be deserved. Leaders who trust too much may not only be fooled but also may damage their work communities. Those inner leaders who do not trust enough can become isolated and create a detrimental work environment. Optimal trust is based on prudent relationships and is shaped by a variety of factors, such as the trustworthiness of the leader and extant social norms (Fairholm, 1994).

Being able to develop trusting relationships is particularly important when inner leaders and their work-community members have interdependent relationships with other stakeholders, such as their suppliers, industry partners, and customers. Such interdependencies are increasingly common in today's work communities. When corporations are committed to such relationships, they must seek operating inner leaders who are willing to trust and are themselves trustworthy and credible.

Becoming Trustworthy

Inner leaders cannot demand trust from others. It must be earned. And that takes time. While leaders can ask others for their trust, they cannot enforce that demand simply because they have the authority to hire and fire. Trust is a gift, given freely by others because it is based in their confidence in their leaders, their respect, even their admiration for them.

Developing trust relationships, like creating cultures, shares common elements since trust is an inextricable part of any culture. As they strive to be both trusting and trustworthy, inner leaders need to master several specific techniques to become experts in the technique of trust. Learning to trust asks inner leaders to first become trustworthy. Not until their followers see that a leader's words and deeds are true (authentic) will they offer their trust. As this part of the trust relationship develops, leaders can take actions that communicates their trust of followers, the other half of the trust relationship.

Inner leaders prepare themselves to be expert in the trust technique by mastering the following elements of the trust relationship.

Leading

Several factors that condition the process of developing trust have been noted by a variety of writers. For example, Bennis and Nanus (1985) say leading so followers can predict the leader's actions or behavior builds trust. Most writers agree that leading on the basis of consistent and persistent open communication is essential in the trust-development process. Sinatar (1988) suggests that leader–follower cooperation is another key to developing trust. He also says that a gentle manner is important and that congruent leader actions, where both word and deed convey the same message, is essential. And, Greenleaf (1977) says a leader's record of service to followers is critical in defining the leader's trust relationship with followers.

Predictability

To the degree that the leader is predictable, to that degree he or she builds trustworthiness. Erratic and or irregular behavior limits trust. Followers appear to trust their leaders only as they can confidently predict what they will do in a given situation. Trust and predictability also imply truth. People trust when they are confident that the relationship will produce a true result—that they will get what they expect.

Acceptance of Self and Others

Trust is part of open social relationships. Inner leaders convey their trustworthiness as they are willing to be open about themselves and others. Such leaders are willing to communicate their strengths and, just as important, their weaknesses. As they communicate their true selves, they encourage followers to behave similarly. Work-community decision making is therefore easier, and determination of joint aims and methods of accomplishing them is facilitated. Mutual acceptance also encourages intrapersonal and interpersonal control, the need to participate in work-community action, and appreciation of difference in others.

Assumptions

Inner leaders' assumptions about life dictate their professional actions (Barns, 1981). Barnes identified three assumptions that guide people's trust behavior and that of their leaders. The first assumption is that important issues fall into two opposing camps exemplified by either–or thinking. The second is the idea that hard data and facts are better than soft ideas. And finally, there is the assumption that the world in general is an unsafe place. These assumptions tend to lead us away from full trust of others' actions, words, or statements. When inner leaders act opposite to these three assumptions, they increase the level of follower trust in them.

Authentic Caring

When followers see the inner leader's behavior as both consistent and caring, they can develop positive assumptions about the relationship; and this kind of relationship is the basis of the expectation that accompanies trust. When followers have a perception that their leaders authentically care for them (Gibb, 1978), see the leader as open, and feel that he or she is personally interested in them, they are inclined to trust him or her. While caring is a risk relationship, inner leaders' willingness to demonstrate caring enhances their inherent trustworthiness. Fairholm (1991) says trust protects and heightens the dignity of followers. Caring leader behavior communicates inner leaders' desire to serve, that is, their willingness to minister to the needs followers have. As this behavior becomes a routine part of the leader's relationships with a follower, the work community changes and becomes more supportive of interpersonal trust.

Ethical Considerations

The idea of ethics is imbedded in the idea of culture, custom, and character (Sims, 1992). Ethical behavior is that behavior work-community members accept as right and good as opposed to wrong, bad, or evil. In the work community it is sometimes institutionalized in a document codifying the work community's values and norms. It is also reflected in the institutional structures, interpersonal relationships, and sanction systems. Most often, and most influential, the community's ethical foundation is a function of the values implicitly revealed in its leader. The inner leader's actions, decisions, and comments more than anything else determine the level of follower trust in him or her.

Ethical leadership is a task of setting and enforcing one ethical standard as opposed to all other possible standards, some of which also may be good. It asks the leader to articulate a clear, compelling, and useful set of values to guide the action of individuals in the work community. Once attained, a given leader's trustworthiness must be continually maintained, improved, and reenergized. Any substantive change in trust risks a change in the ethical climate as well. Inner leaders ensure that their ethical values foundation keeps pace with changes in the work community. As people with differing ethical standards come into the work force, the leader's challenge is to build a new ethics that is founded in the past and is responsive to the future.

Individual Character

We can also view a leader's trustworthiness as either a characteristic of the individual, a factor in the situation, or both (Klimoski and Karol, 1976). For Klimoski and Karol, trust is a way of life. They view trust as an expectancy held by individuals that they can rely upon the word, promise, or statement of another person. In their view, trust is a hallmark of a healthy work community (Terry, 1995). The level of trust the leader creates by his or her actions in the work community affects member willingness to solve problems creatively. It also affects the degree of defensiveness present in the workplace (Gibb, 1961). Meadow, Parnes, and Reese (1959) suggest that a trusted leader affects the degree of problem-solving effectiveness of the work community. For them, a worker who does not trust others will distort, conceal, or disguise feelings or opinions that he or she believes will increase his or her exposure in the work community. They also correlate high leader trustworthiness levels with honesty. Trustworthiness is critical in the middle of the work community where the leader desires spontaneous behavior and where frankness is essential.

Learning to Trust Others

Developing trustworthiness is difficult. Developing a capacity to trust others is equally difficult. It is not that the techniques are complicated, they are not. The problem is one of mental willingness to risk trusting others. Handy (1976) says to trust another asks the inner leader to take a chance on the other person. Trust is a risk relationship that increases the inner leader's vulnerability. And's (1972) work, including a survey of 4,200 supervisors, suggests that high trust relationships stimulate higher performance. Handy revived Rogers's (1964) assertion that we can causally link trust to increased originality and emotional stability.

Trust or distrust is cumulative—the more the inner leader trusts others the more trusting the overall relationship. Alternatively, the more leaders distrust others, the more distrust is present in the work community. Breaking this cycle is difficult and can involve the leader in either of two sets of relationship actions. In the first, the follower strives to gain the leader's trust. This is hard for the follower to do. It requires maturity, strength, and perseverance. The second approach is for leaders to give their trust. This also takes strength.

Trusting behavior is that which shows a willingness to be vulnerable to another person (Rossiter and Pearch, 1975). The mental state that allows the inner leader to trust another person is reflected in an attitude of faith or confidence in that person. This faith is such that the leader believes the other person will behave in ways that will not produce negative results. Thus, to trust another person is to have an unquestioned belief in and reliance on someone or something. Confidence implies trust based on good reasons, evidence, or experience. Trust is a condition that asks inner leaders to be willing to share their intimate feelings.

The level of trust is contingent on several situational factors. One involves settings in which the trusted person's behavior affects the leader in nontrivial ways. Willingness to trust others also develops in situations where the leader can predict with some accuracy a given behavior or result from his or her actions. In trust situations, inner leaders need to be able to predict with some degree of confidence the trusted one's response. A final condition of the trust situation that Rossiter and Pearch (1975) describe has to do with alternative options. Trust is possible when the trusting persons can do more than trust. That is, they can increase or decrease their vulnerability to the other.

Trusting others also flows from self-trust. Effective inner leaders have confidence in their own ability, integrity, and ethical fidelity. This kind of self-trust comes as a result of several characteristics leaders exhibit. Among them, the most important are knowledge, responsibility, and faith. Knowledge refers to the stored truth leaders gain resulting from their cumulative learning and experience. Responsibility defines the inner leader's acceptance of accountability for self and for his or her work and other actions. Faith is confidence in the correctness, the appropriateness of a course of action, and the ability to attain desired goals.

Self-trust lets leaders trust others, It helps insure loyalty, cooperation, efficiency, and satisfaction. The inner leader's willingness to change, which is also important in learning to trust others, is dependent largely on the trust levels present in their relationships with other communities—besides the immediate work community. Feelings of trust develop initially by the way in which two people interact. These feelings become established only after a series of incidents that prove the intrinsic level of trust in the relationships. Established work community values also influence the development of feelings conducive to trusting others. However, it is only though direct interaction that inner leaders develop a deep conviction that others are worthy of their trust.

There are several critical personal characteristics inner leaders develop to facilitate their capacity to trust others.

Integrity

People of integrity are honest, authentic, and dependable. Their motives are known. They are open and willing to expose details of self with others and share how the other person's behavior is affecting them. They are feeling, communicate truthfully and authentically about who they are and what they think is important. They are also discreet, never violating a confidence. Inner leaders develop these characteristics in sufficient strength to let them trust the words and action of others. Their task is also seeing these qualities in followers when they may not always be obvious.

Patience

It takes time—a long time—to learn to truly trust someone else. While inner leaders may volunteer their trust on first meeting, a fully trusting relationship has to mature out of the matrix of shared experiences. Trusting others is not a one-time event. It rarely sprouts full-blown at the instant of the leader's first contact with a follower. It is the result of a process of interaction that matures over time. This element of a trust relationship makes development of patience a critical virtue for inner leaders.

Altruism

Trust is, in part at least, a present from one person to another. Inner leaders trust others because they care or out of a desire to help others. Leaders give their trust to others. It cannot be taken. And leaders can withdraw it also on their decision, not that of the other persons. Bestowing trust is a volitional act, not a constrained one. It is a gift, an act of service, an endowment, an offering even.

Vulnerability

Trust consists of (1) action that increases the inner leader's vulnerability to another, (2) whose behavior is under his or her control, and (3) in situations where the penalty the leader suffers if the follower abuses his or her vulnerability is greater than the benefit the leader might gain if the followers does not abuse that vulnerability. Trusting others is a risk relationship, and the risk increases as inner leaders increase their level and scope of trust in other persons or things.

Action

Inner leaders build trust or tear it down by the cumulative actions they take and the words they speak. And their trust of others is based on the developing record of authenticated interaction built up in their relations with followers.

Building trust is an active process, not a passive one. Actions more than reputation ensure both leaders' trustworthiness and their willingness to trust others.

Friendship

Friendship is a composite of relationships such as shared values and experiences, compatibility, pleasure in associations with another person and comfort in his or her company. These and similar feelings contribute to the presence of trust and its depth and scope. Logic, as well as anecdotal evidence, confirms that friends trust each other more than enemies do. Rogers (1964) suggest that friendship relations contribute to the helping relationship that is founded in large part on mutual trust. Trusting leaders find friends among their coworkers and base their relationships, at least in part, on friendship.

Personal Competence

Trusting leaders place confidence in their followers' abilities, expertise, and skills. They have confidence in their followers' competence to work with them and one another. Inner leaders value their followers' overall sense of the task and their common sense, expertise, experiences, and inventiveness.

Judgment

The followers' capacity to make decisions that are perceived to be right, correct, and appropriate by inner leaders increases their trust quotient with them. Sound ethical and moral professional judgment is affected by a wide variety of factors, only some of which the leader can impact. The following is illustrative of the kinds of concerns making up the inner leader's action agenda in helping followers become worthy of trust: ethical decisions, personal self-interest, work-community goals, friendships, the norms of the larger society, personal morality, and applicable laws, rules, and regulations (Sims, 1992).

DISCUSSION ISSUES AND QUESTIONS

Issues

1. Leadership is a process of building a harmonious cultural surround within which leader and led trust each other enough to link efforts in achieving mutually valued goals using agreed-upon processes.
2. Effective inner leadership can take place only within a context where both leaders and followers can be free to trust the purposes, actions, and intent of others.
3. Shaping such a culture lets inner leaders create a mental and physical context within which they can in fact lead.

4. We can define trust as reliance on the integrity or authenticity of others. It is a logical, thoughtful hope in their reality, their authenticity, and their truth.

5. Trust places obligations on both the truster and the person trusted.

6. Trust is a risk relationship, but a necessary one. When we trust another person, we agree to accept as true what we can now only assume is true.

7. Leaders cannot demand trust of another or in themselves. It must be earned and developed, and it takes time.

8. Inner leaders communicate their trustworthiness as they are open about themselves and others.

9. When followers have a perception that their leaders authentically care for them, see them as open, and feel that they are personally interested in them, they are inclined to trust them.

10. Developing trustworthiness is difficult. Developing a capacity to trust others is equally difficult.

11. Inner leaders come to trust those whom they think have moral character.

12. While inner leaders may volunteer their trust on first meeting, a fully trusting relationship has to mature out of the matrix of shared experiences.

13. Trust is, in part at least, a gift from one person to another.

14. The followers' capacity to make decisions that are perceived to be right, correct, and appropriate by inner leaders increases their trust quotient with them.

Questions

1. Do I really grasp the power of trust to keep relationships and work communities together?

2. How is trust important in keeping my work unit together? Compare it with other factors like formal communications systems, fear, and the like.

3. Am I trustworthy?

4. Am I a willing to trust others?

5. Am I willing to take the risk to let others take control of the work because I trust the intentions and talents of my coworkers?

6. Do I really grasp the power of trust to keep relationships and work communities together?

7. Is trust the glue that keeps my work unit together, or is some other concept at work (i.e., fear, transactional exchanges, etc.). Elaborate on this idea.

8. Do I trust my coworkers enough to let them follow simple guidelines rather than strict and detailed rules?

TRUST LEADERSHIP LEARNING ACTIVITIES

Activity 1: Current Status—A Feedback Activity on Trust

Instructions. The Trust Status Inventory allows you to examine your current feelings toward other work community members. Completing this inventory lets you examine unexpressed feelings of trust or distrust within your ongoing work community and to clarify the reasons for these feelings. It may also help you increase your own feelings of trust within the community and promote self-disclosure and risk taking. Assessing these feelings can provide a basis for subsequent assessment of your trust levels in any work community.

1. Complete all the following questions. You may want to share with colleagues any of your answers after completing this inventory.

Trust Status Inventory

Name: _____ Date _____

1. How did you feel as you joined this work community?
2. How do you feel right now?
3. Which person in this work community do you feel the most positive about right now? Describe what makes you feel good about that person.
4. Toward whom in this work community do you react most negatively right now? Describe what that person does that produces this negative feeling.
5. What prevents you from being more open and honest in this work community?
6. Which person in this work community do you perceive as feeling the most positive toward you right now? Why do you feel that this person feels positive about you?
7. Which person in this work community do you perceive as feeling the most negative about you right now? Why do you feel that this person experiences negative feelings toward you?

2. Rate each of your work community members on a 5-point scale according to how much trust you feel toward him or her. Use "1" to indicate "very little" and "5" to indicate "very much."

Name	Rating
1. _____	_____
2. _____	_____
3. _____	_____
4. _____	_____

5. _____ _____

6. _____ _____

7. _____ _____

8. _____ _____

9. _____ _____

10. _____ _____

11. _____ _____

12. _____ _____

Total Score _____

$$\text{Average Score} = \left(\frac{\text{Total Score}}{N} \right) \underline{\hspace{2cm}}$$

3. For those individuals to whom you have given low trust ratings, list several ways in which

1. You can change your behavior to increase your feelings of trust toward them.

2. They might behave to allow you to feel more trust toward them.

Note: You may begin by answering questions 3 and 6 to identify behaviors that contribute to feelings of trust. Questions 4, 5, and 7 may be examined subsequently to identify behaviors associated with distrust.

Activity 2: Dimensions of Trust—A Symbolic Expression

Instructions. Although most individuals will acknowledge the need for trust in relationships, it is often difficult to relate the term to the feelings involved in the expression of trust. The following activity may help you internalize your own perceptions about what elements and feelings are involved in trust and explore these ideas thoroughly with others.

1. Using a variety of drawing materials, draw a picture that symbolically represents trust concepts as you perceive them. (Use any drawing materials easily available to make your drawing.)

2. Further, prepare some statement about your trust model.

3. Be expressive and creative in both your drawing and your statement so that what you indicate will aid both you and others you may share it with in understanding the dimensions of trust on which you are focusing.

Activity 3: Conditions That Lead to Conflict or Trust

Instructions. In this activity, you will be able to locate the conditions in any work community that help or hinder the free exercise of trust and identify those conditions that apply to your specific work community. By completing this activity, you should be able to assess the trust level in your work community and exercise greater intracommunity dedication to trust others and cooperate more fully in work-community work tasks.

Note: This activity is best done by the reader in conjunction with a small group of coworkers. Of course, it can be done alone, but consensus-building is hampered.

1. Make a list of all of the conditions in any work community that maximize creativity, individuality, and trust.
2. Make a list of all the conditions in any work community that minimize trust and maximize dependency.
3. Underline those statements in each of the above lists that describe conditions that presently exist in your own work community.
4. Analyze your two personalized lists.
    1. Identify the conditions contributing to conflict in your workplace.
    2. Identify those conditions in your work community essential to a trusting culture.
    3. List any insights into your own work (work community) you have gained.

Activity 4: Trust as an Indispensable Factor in Inner Leadership

Instructions. Both theory and practice confirms that trust is a necessary ingredient in any interpersonal relationship. It is therefore of vital interest to the student of leadership.

1. Read the following brief statement about current research about trust in organized work communities.

    The qualities that describe the cultural context within which leadership takes place are as significant as the personal qualities of the leader. The leadership context is a climate of mutual, cooperative interaction where leader and led are united on values terms and trust each other enough to risk self in participation in joint activity. In such cultures both leaders and followers can be free to work together because they trust the purposes, actions, and intent of others.

    Trust is central to inner leadership in work communities because followers are people who choose to follow leaders. No collaborative work can be done over time without some measure of interpersonal trust. The culture the leader creates produces a trust environment where the leader can be assured that certain actions will produce certain results. It may also constrain willingness to trust. A given culture may allow some to trust one group more or less than another; but without the constraints imposed by the ambient culture, nobody couldt exercise trust at all.

    We can define trust as reliance on the integrity, or authenticity, of a person or similar qualities or attributes of someone (or something) in the absence of absolute knowledge or proof. In essence, we base our trust on faith in another person.

Nevertheless, in the final analysis, the information we use to base our trusting behaviors must eventually prove accurate, or we withdraw our trust. Trust becomes both an expectation and a personal obligation to be authentic, trustworthy, reliable, which is provable by ensuing experience.

It may not be an overstatement to suggest that trust is the foundation upon which cooperative action between individuals and work communities, the firm, even the nation, is built. It is only when work-community members trust one another that we can say that leadership is a part of the work-community dynamic. You must consider the degree of interactive trust in your work community as you develop your leadership style. You must also spend time in creating the kind of harmonious culture that lets trust relationships develop and flourish because the specific features of the ambient culture conditions what you (all leaders) do and how you do it.

Seen this way, your prime leader task is to create a culture supportive of your desired values. As your followers internalize these cultural values, they develop a devotion to the institution that cannot come in any other way. They come to trust your leadership, the vision, and the common tasks. The job is not simple. It is fraught with difficulty and pitfalls. Given this reality, your leadership role is to create and institutionalize value-laden cultural principles in the work community and then teach them to followers who then internalize them in their actions.

2. Identify and analyze the ideas contained in the above statement. List these key ideas.

3. Prepare a response to these ideas—either agreeing with all or some of them or disagreeing with them as important from a leadership point of view.

CHAPTER 23

Technique 20:
Creating Community

Most people live much of their productive lives in formal groups. Inner leaders need to know as much as they can about how to make successful work groups, for this is the place where they spend most of their productive time. The continuing task is to create a unified work group and then nurture its values and customs among all stakeholders. The objective is to make a unified community reflective of the leader's goals and to relate followers to the community's goals. In doing this, inner leaders build a unique work community culture, different in real ways from the overarching corporate culture, to help differentiate and set apart their core of coworkers from all other subgroups. Without this community-building, values-based relationships that recognize and honor the whole person of both leader and led do not happen.

DEFINING LEADERSHIP COMMUNITY

The word, *community* comes from the Latin root meaning "with unity." Work communities are a kind of social entity that operates out of shared values and beliefs, a common vision, and known patterns of behavior. The inner leader's task is to build workplace community. No work community—no society—can function well unless most members behave most of the time because they voluntarily heed the moral commitments and social responsibilities (Etzioni, 1993) laid out by the communities in which they hold membership. If member actions are not consistent with these cultural constraints, the work community may run into trouble. Giving people power—empowering them—is a good idea, but the power to do something without a unifying focus leads to chaos. Inner leaders must couple empowering followers with community building to make progress toward their personal goals.

Many of the most important choices people make—choices that make life happy or sad—are not individual choices, but group ones. Most of the important, meaningful outcomes in life cannot be attained alone. People need other people to help them become their best selves. Leadership focused on the whole person of all stakeholders—their values, aspirations, goals, and customs—is not an option in today's world (Pinchot and Pinchot, 1994), it is a requirement. Hence the need for community structures.

Most people relate more to their work or work-community relationships than they do to any other social grouping, with the possible exception of the family. They value their corporate citizenship sometimes more than they do their associations in any other community of interest. The work community influences how they act, what they value, how they measure themselves and their actions. It gives definition to their feelings about whom they care about and how they care about their coworkers, the level of personal growth they aspire to, their level of competency, and their happiness. Given the power of the work community, inner leaders shape, strengthen, and use the work-community culture; and they define new culturally appropriate ceremonies and rituals that bring people together to form unities around their vision. Controlling—leading—the corporate culture becomes the central inner leader's task. This is, at heart, a value-displacement activity.

Creating a Compatible Culture

The work community's culture is a powerful force guiding member behavior. It consists of the pattern of basic assumptions about which group members agree. It determines work practices and validates those practices. The community culture determines the basis for measuring individual member success. It includes both historical precedent and present experience and defines future behavioral expectations (Bjerke, 1999). Cultural features determine not only the ways workers solve problems, but also what is considered a problem in the first place. It defines the essential—spiritual—nature and character of the work community and, by extension, of its individual members. Absent broad agreement on legitimate behavior and the values used to measure interaction within the group, members are free to follow divergent paths. Taken to the extreme, the absence of a controlling culture spells chaos, and the community itself disappears.

Each work community has a culture of its own shaped by the inner leader or by chance. The values array inner leaders foster in the group is the single most critical factor in determining their success (Fiedler, 1974). Their set of values determines who leaders are, what they do, and how they do it. The inner leader's values set also conditions work-community member actions, beliefs, and behavior and is the nucleus of any work culture developed (Schein, 1985). It constitutes the core values held by the group, that is, it defines the group's and individual member's work essence, their collective spirit. These leader-set cultures provide meaning, direction, and necessary social energy to move the work community to productive action (or destruction). So important are the leader's values and the work culture that they delimit that unless the cultural context of the group is compatible (or is made compatible by the leader), inner leadership is impossible.

No coherent, cooperative action is possible where common agreement—at least implicitly—in a knowable culture is lacking. Creating and maintaining a culture conducive to attainment of the leader's core goals for him or her self and the group is the hallmark of inner leadership. Seen in this light, inner leaders lead from their core spiritual nature. They develop group cultures that incorporate their personal values and practices (Peters and Waterman, 1982).

Creating Community

The task for inner leadership in the twenty-first century is transforming (McMillen, 1993) the workplace into a viable, attractive work community capable of attracting workers with needed skills and talents. Building inviting workplace communities is critical. As inner leaders create work communities they effectively counter current tendencies toward worker disaffection. A sense of community invigorates member's lives with a sense of purpose (Carson, 2001) and a feeling of belonging to an integrated group doing something worthwhile.

Work communities operate out of a shared belief and values system that the inner leader creates. The present resurgence of interest in flexibility, cultural inclusiveness, and full acceptance of difference in individual group members is antithetical to community—and to leadership itself (Fairholm, 1994). While emotionally attractive, endorsement of all diverse values, customs, and behavior of followers is operationally toxic. Rather, successful inner leaders build group relationships, not just membership. They create corporate spirit, a force that honors high performance, compassion, empathy for others, and individual contributions while also building wholeness in both individuals and the community per se. Building community drives out factions and factionalism.

Community is a powerful force. It directs the life of members both as individuals and in their relationships with coworkers. The work community acts as an emotional filter that can block acceptance of alternative cultures—even the parent corporate culture. A work community's values can isolate the individual members from other cultural associations. It is critical that these values can also unite individuals into strong coalitions of mutually interdependent teams. The key to attaining this latter result is the nature and the strength of the community the inner leader builds. Some of the main factors in community building are discussed in the following sections.

Creating the Work Team

Inner leaders create teams and committees within their work community to consider process-improvement changes or other enhancements to help the community be more productive and a more unified, cohesive group. Teams are subordinate work groups characterized by members who are interdependent, similarly motivated, and have an attitude fostering continuous improvement. Teams have initiative, accept feelings and attitudes as legitimate, are able to diagnose relationships, are willing to risk trying new ways to work together, and can see tangible results of their effort. A team is a group of people in which individual members share a common purpose and the work done by each interdependent person contributes something needed to the whole. A team is a unified, cohesive group.

Team members function together in a culture of understanding of self and others and high communication and performance. Team relationships are another value-orientation often associated with work community cultures within which inner leadership can flourish. Team building conforms fully to the values inherent in the inner-leader model. Historically, team building can trace its origins to the special techniques of Organizational Development (OD), a training regimen popular in the 1950s, 1960s, and 1970s that uses concepts from sociology and psychology to sensitize people to the values and feelings dimensions of interpersonal relationships.

Creating a Sense of Ownership

Belonging to a work community brings a sense of belonging, and more. It connotes a sense of coownership. Inner leaders strive to make all work-community members feel that they share fully in the overall responsibility for the group—for its success, its purposes, its processes, its leadership. When followers feel ownership, they feel they are, in part at least, in control of their work situation. Ownership is another way to describe commitment, but it goes beyond commitment and adds a personal feeling of proprietorship. "Owners" typically perform at a higher level of quality than do workers, who see themselves as merely employees or, worse yet, subordinates.

Ownership implies involvement in the work community and its survival and growth. Owners make decisions that affect their lives and their work communities. Ownership implies autonomy. Owners become more than workers— they pledge themselves to the work community, its work, and its success. The effect of the inner leader's work of inducing followers to feel ownership is that followers come to think they are working for themselves. They will do better work, more work, and higher quality work because they see the task in personal ownership terms. They have to deliver because they are free to do the work their own way.

METHODS OF BUILDING COMMUNITY

Modern corporate and social life has isolated most people from their traditional communities of family, farm, and neighborhood—the source of personal, intimate spiritual regeneration. Now workers spend most of their waking day in work-related activity and, as a result, have lost or diminished the impact on their behavior of traditional sources of personal spiritual rejuvenation (Bolman and Deal, 1995). They are searching for alternatives to traditional—family or church—sources of strength. Some are beginning to ask the work community and its leader to supply this need. They are responding by creating cultures and work communities that support and honor the whole person of all workers, not merely their economically valuable skills and knowledge.

Shaping the Work-Community Culture

Cultural features shape life experiences, historical tradition, social class, position, and political circumstances. They are powerful forces that define the group and that resist change (Reynolds, 1987). Inner leadership is unique in specifying a specific culture centered around a few leader-set values that delimit both individuals and the group and that define group membership and delineate those values members will not compromise. The work-community culture they create is not so much the official system of announced values as it is the whole range of shared models of social action containing both real and ideal elements.

A variety of factors affects work-community culture, including the goal context and the channels of communication used. The ambient corporate culture is also reflected in the behavior of work-community members, as are official documents and the verbal expression of what ideal behavior should be. Even humorous renderings help determine a work-community's culture. Culture is importantly dependent on the actions of inner leaders. The inner leader's goals, vision, values, and behavior provide crucial clues about what the work community will expect and accept. Often they are more powerful in shaping group member action than official policies and procedures.

The inner leader's task in creating and maintaining a dynamic culture is essentially a values displacement activity (Bjerke, 1999). Leaders engage in action to alter members' values and behaviors that support their conception of what the work community is and can become. Obviously, each leader and each group develop uniquely. Analysis of American work groups, however, suggests that the following values define much of the essential nature of work-group life:

- Respect for all people evidenced by placing priority on fostering freedom of choice, justice, unity, and stakeholder satisfaction.
- Values that foster work community and personal creativity and innovation.

- Values of high-quality performance in all aspects of work done.
- Values that foster team approaches to task activity, that delegate more discretion over their work to the team and to individual team members.
- Values that encourage the formation of traditions that foster and inculcate core spiritual values.

Inner leaders practice values-based leadership in a work-community culture that also promotes clarity of vision. This culture encourages and rewards effective performance throughout the work community. It fosters program or task champions. A central feature of this kind of a work culture is close interaction between leaders, workers, and customers at all levels. These systems and values emphasize concern with process rather than product and with people over either product or process (Porter, Sargent, and Stupack, 1981). Such a culture focuses on one service or product system as opposed to multidifferentiated service systems.

Building Community Citizenship

Building community is a critical inner leadership task. This task needs to engage the people making up these communities in meaningful work, in work that ennobles them and their customers. As the workplace becomes a community in which members live much of their productive lives, the task increasingly becomes one of making the work community not only productive but personally inspiring and attractive to followers.

The resurgence of the idea of community in the workplace is a reaction against a controlled social process that robs people of their sense of self and substitutes a senseless conformity to a sterile, abstract, and spiritless system. As people come to recognize the power of their work in shaping not only their own lives but those of their children, they are forcing business to change—to be more accommodating to human moral, even spiritual, values.

No one can buy a worker's citizenship in the work community. It is voluntary. Freedom of action—autonomy—is a prime value implicit in work-community citizenship. If inner leaders use authority, that usage must fall within the followers' "zone of acceptability" or members will resist it (Barnard, 1968). Work-community citizenship is defined, in part, as acceptance of the inner leader's values. The association is either an ethical association or a contractual, economic, or social one. In any case, inner leaders define their workers' association in the work community not by mere membership but by acceptance of the community's values and commitment shown by action in accord with them.

Similarly, obligation, consent, and participation are also elements of community membership and characteristic of the work community the inner leader builds. Citizenship entails both rights the work community must honor and responsibility to the community to be involved, committed, and supportive.

Community citizenship is a mutual relationship with opportunities and duties on both sides. Whether the relationship is total or limited to task, this kind of work-community association asks both inner leader and follower to accept common values and act according to them. Values become the adhesive of citizenship in the work community. The inner leader becomes a custodian of the community values system.

Rather than looking to the family and the small social neighborhoods of the past to recognize and legitimize spiritual values and needs, many workers are looking to their work—its structures and leaders—to provide those needs. Changing a group of workers into a community of like-minded people involves inner leaders in new tasks and mind-sets. This activity focuses on developing interpersonal skills that increase cooperation and build better relationships and group functioning. Understanding the need and developing the skills to get along with others more efficiently and improve working relationships are critical to achieving work-community goals and increasing worker productivity.

Techniques of Community Building

Creating a work community involves leaders in several important creation and implementation techniques as they invent a unique culture for their own work community. These techniques do not constitute the full range of expertise needed by inner leaders. A review of present-day literature, however, points to the following kinds of skills and techniques inner leaders need to master to accomplish their culture-creation goals. Taken together, these functions begin to flesh out the inner leader techniques of community creation as they apply in this context.

Setting Values

Inner leaders rely on a strong values orientation as the basis of their work culture. They initiate action to adopt a formal set of basic beliefs to inculcate values they want their stakeholders to honor. This technique sometimes includes use of symbols to explain and reenforce desired values. It also embodies the declaration of and subsequent institutionalization of these values in relations leaders have with both workers and customers. Values setting also asks leaders to persuade stakeholders to accept these values as their own. The leader's job is to gain control over this cultural change process by facing problems and developing innovative solutions in terms of these values and the following situations.

- Responsiveness to customers, adjusting to satisfy small differences in demand.
- Supporting innovation wherever it is found in the group.
- Empowering stakeholders to make full use of their capacities and interests.

- Inspiring change through actions to replace traditional controls and substituting an inspired vision, leadership by example, and being an involved visible leader.
- Simplifying systems and structures, redirecting systems effort toward quality, innovation, and flexibility.

Critical Issues Planning

Inner leaders undertake formal programs of long-range strategic issues identification and planning for their implementation as a way to try to understand where the work community is in today's world and, more important, where it can be in the horizon future. Strategic plans operationalize the vision—a self-definition of the future of the work community—and guide subsequent implementation tasks.

Dealing with Change

Change is ever present in any work community given the ubiquity of technological improvements, system restructuring, and the rapid evolution of corporate policy and customer demands. Such change places pressures on inner leaders to change to stay competitive. They initiate such change and accept changes made by others and help their stakeholders feel comfortable with the adaptions they need to make to accommodate change.

Fostering a Service Mentality

Effective customer service is a result of well-trained people performing direct customer contact whether in person or on the telephone or Internet. Creating a service focus, therefore, involves inner leaders in both direct contact with stakeholders and indirect influence to more effectively and sincerely support and serve them. The need to efficiently deliver such service increases the need to use effective programs for managing job pressure and rapid change. Inner leaders serve their stakeholders as they develop their personal energy and cope with both the physical and human resources making up their work community. A service orientation asks inner leaders to institute change, improve their coping skills, and organize support networks to help their followers. It asks them to also differentiate useful job stress from dysfunctional job pressure and otherwise do what is necessary to let their followers increase their efficiency and improve overall individual and unit productivity.

Setting Patterns of Action

Inner leaders create and adopt patterns of action within the work community that facilitate desired levels of performance and interrelationships among members. In this way, they help create a work climate supportive of their own values. These patterns of action become criteria measuring performance against desired vision results. The leader's task is to generalize the action patterns so all concerned understand them and automatically act in conformity to them. To be useful in building community, these patterns of action should be clear, exacting, feasible, and desirable. They become visible symbols of the work community's self-definition. Inner leaders set these action patterns, teach them, live them, and inspire their followers to live them.

Mentoring

Ensuring that members understand, accept, and adapt to the parameters of the work community's culture inner leaders desire requires them to continually council and guide their followers. Building community, like most inner leadership tasks, is a mentoring task that includes inspiring members, encouraging teamwork, facilitating cooperative joint action, counseling, sitting in council with them, training, and in other ways shaping member behavior in desired ways. Inner leaders make use of an array of skills, including motivating others, delegating tasks, encouraging teams, managing time, solving problems, making decisions, setting performance norms, and improving morale and efficiency.

Maintaining the Community

Building community involves the leader in a variety of tasks the result of which is continual adaptation of the established work community as the ambient situation dictates change is needed. The requirement here is expertise in changing to team-based structures that underscore the need for developing the skills to help members get along with one another. It also asks inner leaders to develop effective working relationships critical to achieving community goals and increasing productivity. In doing this, inner leaders function in supportive relationships to enhance cooperation and teamwork in understanding and then implementing problem-solving processes. Inner leaders place priority on developing cooperation skills and applying these skills in operational problem-solving situations.

The Technique of Team Building

Team-building techniques embody the important concept of participation. Teams involve employees in the key decisions about what and how the team's work is to be done. Team building is about getting work done in concert with others. It concerns changing work-community members and focusing them toward a common purpose, excellence in performance, and people-oriented coleadership. Team relationships help the work community identify with and support the leader. They help the group identify and create positive action characterized by service, communications, and opportunity (Santovec, 2001). They also allow members to align with the community's culture and the purposes of the team. Team building increases member commitment. It leads to synergy in individual and the work community actions (Kelley, 1992). Teams are formed in groups where the following is present:

- Group interdependence.
- A commitment to improvement.
- A generalized motivation to change.
- Perceived power to make changes.
- A realistic expectation of tangible end results.
- Willingness to risk trying new ways to work together.
- Willingness and ability to diagnose relationships.
- Acceptance of feelings and attitudes as useful in working together.

Methods of Fostering Ownership

Ownership inspires followers. To foster it, leaders must allow followers some control in their work and let them know what the work community is about. Ownership is grounded in self-control; the perception that the individual can independently determine factors in his or her work environment or tasks. If we treat all employees as coleaders, they will become coleaders. Several implementation practices inner leaders use include these:

1. Create small problem-solving teams.
2. Insure that information goes to as wide an audience as possible.
3. Seek solutions as low in the work-community hierarchy as possible.
4. Don't overcontrol. Allow coworkers some resources to do their job their way.
5. Decentralize to the maximum extent possible.
6. Create leaders at several levels in the work community.
7. Create a climate of individual dignity, challenge, and opportunity to be successful.
8. Create a sense of individual and work-community worth.
9. Reward success, not conformance or mere energy use.

DISCUSSION ISSUES AND QUESTIONS

Issues

1. Each work community has a culture of its own, shaped by the inner leader or by chance.
2. The inner leadership techniques keyed to creating the work community revolve around the leader's values. The leader's values condition member

actions, beliefs, and behavior; become the nucleus of group culture; define the group's core values; and embody its spiritual essence.

3. The work community's culture acts as an emotional filter that can block acceptance of alternative cultures—even the parent corporate culture.

4. The leader's vision, values, and behavior are more powerful in shaping member action than are official policies and procedures.

5. Inner leadership flourishes in a culture that values both group member growth and high-quality performance.

6. The task of creating and maintaining culture is essentially a values-displacement activity.

7. Modern life has isolated most people from their traditional communities of family, farm, and neighborhood, the traditional sources of personal, intimate spiritual regeneration. Today, they are seeking this support from their work.

Questions

1. Have I established a culture that encourages new ideas and independent thought that enhances the work community's values?

2. Do I encourage teamwork, inspire cooperation, and otherwise encourage member behavior toward collegial action to accomplish the community's goals?

3. Do I understand the main elements of work-community structure and leadership and use them in helping my work community be successful?

4. What are some of the major forces affecting modern work communities? How may the inner leader use these forces to help his or her followers be more productive?

5. Describe the processes and techniques inner leaders use to serve their followers. How many of these do you use in your work as an inner leader?

6. Building community is a continual role inner leaders play. Which of the elements of this process are most important? Explain.

COMMUNITY BUILDING LEARNING ACTIVITIES

Activity 1: Ownership

Instructions. One intent of inner leadership is to get followers to accept a kind of feeling of coownership of the work community and its goals. The idea is that "owners" become more than workers, they commit to the work community, its work, and its success. In effect, they come to feel they are working for themselves. They will do better work, more work, higher-quality work because they see the tasks in personal, ownership terms. They have to deliver because they are free to do the work their own way.

1. Brainstorm a listing of specific actions you can take individually in your work community to help all members take ownership for their part of the group's work.

2. Include ideas that will work with coworkers, customers, suppliers, and other specific constituency groups relevant to your work community.

3. List actions you can take immediately—or almost immediately—and without significant new resources.

4. List actions you can take that may require some time or other resources.

5. Prioritize your lists in terms of the most feasible and efficacious.

6. Take all possible steps to implement these actions.

Activity 2: Questionnaire—Pressure Points

Instructions. This activity will help you identify and assess the strengths of pressure points in your work community as a way to begin to improve member performance.

1. Read each statement and circle the number that matches your response to how typical this situation is in your work community.

Does your work community or its leaders

	Never				Always
1. Hold periodic meetings to explain goals and targets?	1	2	3	4	5
2. Appoint followers to task forces or teams to recommend action or policies affecting them?	1	2	3	4	5
3. Provide followers with the time and resources to pursue their own developmental goals?	1	2	3	4	5
4. Create awareness of the need for change?	1	2	3	4	5
5. Recognize followers' achievements with encouragement and support?	1	2	3	4	5
6. Disseminate information in a manner that takes into account the culture of the system?	1	2	3	4	5
7. Encourage followers to improve?	1	2	3	4	5
8. Explain the benefits of achieving system goals and targets to followers?	1	2	3	4	5
9. Communicate changes honestly and explain the rationale for changes?	1	2	3	4	5
10. Feed back information to followers that tells them how their individual performances contribute to the system's performance?	1	2	3	4	5
11. Walk the talk? (Behave consistently with their words.)	1	2	3	4	5

12. Allow front-line personnel to "bend the rules" to satisfy
    customers within defined parameters?   1 2 3 4 5

13. Ask followers to translate system goals into department
    goals?   1 2 3 4 5

14. Deal openly with people's concerns?   1 2 3 4 5

15. Use a performance management or appraisal system for
    all followers that includes internal customer feedback? 1 2 3 4 5

16. Regularly meet with followers to discuss their needs?   1 2 3 4 5

17. Encourage followers to set up or join to work on process
    improvements?   1 2 3 4 5

18. Ensure that individual follower goals and work group or
    department goals relate to the achievement or system goals? 1 2 3 4 5

19. Give people a role in introducing change?   1 2 3 4 5

20. Set up some form of variable compensation, such as
    bonuses, tied to system goals?   1 2 3 4 5

2. Transfer the number that you recorded for each question to the corre-
   sponding space in the second column of the chart on the next page.

3. Add the scores in each section for each pressure point. Place these totals
   in the third column. (Note: The larger the number, the more effective you
   are in each category.)

Pressure Points	Individual Question Score		Total Score
Vision focus and alignment	Q 3 _____	Q13 _____	
	Q 8 _____	Q18 _____	_____
Communication flow	Q 1 _____	Q11 _____	
	Q 6 _____	Q16 _____	_____
Member involvement	Q 2 _____	Q12 _____	
	Q 7 _____	Q17 _____	_____
Leading change	Q 4 _____	Q14 _____	
	Q 9 _____	Q19 _____	_____
Clear links between performance	Q 5 _____	Q15 _____	
and consequences	Q10 _____	Q20 _____	_____

4. What is getting in the way of your effective use of the pressure points you
   scored low on?

5. How could you effectively leverage pressure in your system?

6. Are these pressure points (areas of potential change or destruction) in
   your work community?

7. How would your coworkers view these pressure points?

Activity 3: Are You a Team Leader?

Instructions. Leading teams is an important inner leader task. Skill in this technique can help inner leaders accomplish both their personal and the corporation's goals. Completing the following questions may help provide insight into your present capacity to lead teams and point to areas for further development.

1. Rate yourself on each of the following items using the scale provided here:

1	2	3	4	5
Strongly disagree	Somewhat disagree	Neither agree nor disagree	Somewhat agree	Strongly agree

_____ 1. I enjoy helping others get their jobs done.

_____ 2. Managing others is a full-time job in and of itself.

_____ 3. I am good at negotiating for resources.

_____ 4. People often come to me to help them with interpersonal conflicts.

_____ 5. I tend to be uncomfortable when I am not fully involved in the task that my group is doing.

_____ 6. It is hard for me to provide people with positive feedback.

_____ 7. I understand organizational politics well.

_____ 8. I get nervous when I do not have expertise at a task my group is performing.

_____ 9. An effective leader needs to have full involvement with his or her team.

_____ 10. I am skilled at goal setting.

_____ Total

Scoring key: Reverse score items 2, 5, 6, 8, and 9 (1 = 5, 5 = 1). Add your score on all items. Maximum possible score is 50. The higher the score, the more team leadership skills you have.

CHAPTER 24

Technique 21: Developing Stewardship Structures

As inner leaders bring their personal sense of self—their spiritual identify—to the workplace, a new idea of the individual-in-the-work community emerges. This newly revived (but always a part of true leadership) idea was classically called stewardship, and recently nominated ownership (Stern and Borcia, 2000). The contemporary behavior theory idea of ownership is shifting to classical stewardship (McMillen, 1994). Ownership connotes possession, control, and proprietorship. Experts recommend that leaders nurture feelings of ownership in coworkers as a way to foster more complete follower commitment to work-community goal attainment. And it works—sometimes.

A more dependable leadership technique—one used by inner leaders—to secure follower commitment and compliance is to form the work community along stewardship structural lines. Seeing the work community as a steward-ship asks both leaders and led to hold work assets in trust for all stakehold-ers—coworkers, clients, customers, suppliers, the larger community. In a stewardship orientation, the focus is on viewing membership in the commu-nity, the work, the workers, and the community itself as an almost "sacred office," one held temporarily and about which the leader—and followers—owe deference.

DEFINING STEWARDSHIP

In a stewardship work community, the inner leader's power is shared with each steward to help accomplish the work-community members'—not just the steward-leader's own—ends. Stewardship is a collective idea suggesting that leadership is most successfully demonstrated by sharing (holding) power with others in the work community. In this way, the workplace becomes one, united, a true community.

A stewardship is, in one of its dimensions, a structural form of corporate community. Elements of a stewardship structure are seen today in the self-managed team or worker councils. These teams are one of the basic building blocks of stewardship work communities—along with the leader, a common purpose, and unifying values. In its authentic form, a stewardship community may be composed of several such teams. Self-managed teams are based on the assumption that a successful work community links individual workers in ways that elicit a high level of group commitment (or creativity, or loyalty, or integrity) that is greater than the sum of each individual's contribution. The self-managing stewardship community encompasses systems that enable their effective operation. They include structures for productive work, individual and team accountability, and recognition (Spencer, 1995). Through these teams, inner leaders can tap follower capacities to enhance the quality of service provided to each other and to their customers.

Features of Stewardship Work Communities

Stewardship is based on free moral choice. The steward has the freedom of self-governance. Every steward has the same rights and is subject to identical limitations in the exercise of self-direction. This sharing of power preserves harmony and good will. The leader is also a steward subject to the same limitations and advantages as other stewards. The stewardship structure ensures that every steward has a single voice when sitting in council with other stewards and a full vote in the process of generating unit consensus. Stewardships preserve oneness by procedures that enhance common consent. In this way each steward is protected against unjust or dominating leaders.

A steward role asks inner leader and those led to risk losing hierarchal distinctions and privilege in the pursuit of mutual growth and work-community improvement. Being a steward means living fully a set of values and creating a work community where members personally reclaim the institution as their own. Stewardship operates at the whole-person—spiritual—level of existence and interrelationship. It combines seemingly antithetical ideas of teamwork and individual free choice.

The stewardship unit, the community, is critical. As members come to identify with their stewardship community, they are participating at a level beyond consensus and compromise. At this level, a member does not merely accept another member's position. Rather, the position becomes an integral part of the community that all members accept, support, and foster. Stewardship asks inner leaders to facilitate relationships using shared values, habits, and practices that assure respect for others' rights.

METHODS OF PRACTICING
STEWARDSHIP LEADERSHIP

Stewardship Principles

The raison d'être of some businesses and top leaders appears to be capital generation and accumulation—a constantly improving bottom line. However, for most inner leaders and their stakeholders, profitability is not enough. Like any tool, the bottom line is only as effective as the person who uses it (Douglas and Wykowksi, 1992). Making money per se doesn't capture their spirit, motivate them to excel, or sustain them in troublesome times. Stakeholders need something more to spur them on to provoke the best of themselves. By identifying and articulating shared values and principles indigenous to stewardship structures, inner leaders drive a work community beyond the bottom line, positively affecting both work and life—short- and long-term—satisfaction. In doing this through stewardship work communities, inner leaders capture the spirit, values, and principles of their stakeholder work community in the formal structure, as well as in its values construct.

Summarizing the idea and practice of stewardship work communities existing in the literature, one can identify several elements of the task of the inner leader as steward. The following principles of inner leadership match closely other elements of this model discussed throughout his book.

Ethics

A core principle of stewardship is ethics. Profit and ethics often clash in contemporary corporate culture, but they do not have to and shouldn't. When improving the bottom line is successfully done, it is always ethical. When inner leaders do the right thing, all stakeholders benefit—profit—from the experience. Mid-level leaders make decisions not only because they are profitable to stakeholder and the work community but because they are also the right things to do.

Values

Part of the ethical stewardship community is a set of common values, standards, policies, and actions that function as guidelines. They help define corporate identity (Deal and Kennedy, 1988) and the character of the joint enterprise. Inner leaders establish core values like integrity, fairness, unity, satisfaction, and respect for the individual (Fairholm, 1991) as the basis of their relationships with their volunteer stakeholders. They endeavor to embrace and live these values at every level—from the formation of the work community itself to standards-setting and policy-formulation to the practical aspects of their relationships both internally and corporationwide. If problems occur, they can usually be traced to a deviation from these shared values (Beckett, 1999).

Vision

Stewardship concepts are reflected in the corporate vision statement. A strong sense of stewardship relationships and practices comes from developing a common vision and value system and then using it as the criterion for group actions, from making judgments (Covey, 1997) to assessing results.

Commitment

A stewardship orientation unites the inner leader and stakeholders in the common enterprise in otherwise not possible ways. In a stewardship community, inner leaders can commit members to a common set of relationships so that each has a role in helping to meet preset goals using agreed-upon principles and the shared vision. Each is accountable to all other members (Covey, 1997).

Decision Making

Stewardships preserve member independence via procedures that maximize the exercise of shared decision making. In this way each steward is protected against unjust or dominating leaders. And inner leaders gain committed colleagues in what becomes, by their decisions, the common enterprise. The strength of the work community is derived from the choice-making built into the culture.

Ownership

Like all others, inner leaders struggle in today's workplace to create and maintain a strong sense of shared ownership in the corporation and its work. The solution is stewardship. As the business world forges ahead with mergers, acquisitions, and alliances, the connections between ownership and stewardship overlap. Ownership is an expression of independence—each steward taking personal responsibility for the whole. On the other hand, stewardship is a clear expression of interdependence, which is the nature of the new psychological contract about work now emerging in the workplace. Inner leaders have always known what many top leaders are just learning—that leader and led are interdependent; neither can succeed without the other. Stewards go beyond ownership to equitable, interdependent stewardship (Ramsey, 1994).

Free Choice

Emile Durkheim wrote "When mores are sufficient, laws are unnecessary; when mores are insufficient, laws are un-enforceable" (Quoted by Covey, 1997). The capacity to make free-will choices is integral to the idea of stewardship. The expectation that stewards can be free to make most of their own choices in the work community is fully American. Many of the most important choices people make—that make life happy or sad—are not individual choices but work-community choices. Inner leaders build a stewardship community as they let members make choices about whom to partner with, what products or services to buy from internal or external suppliers, how to spend discretionary funds and time, and how to serve their customers.

Interdependence

Stewardship assumes that work-community members represent or are part of someone or something else—that their freedom of choice is bounded by respect for coworkers and the demands of the common enterprise. The in-the-middle leader's task is to ensure that stakeholder choices are constrained by shared visions and values and common standards of behavior and conduct (Bjerke, 1999). The more stewardship values reign, the less dependent the work community is on the strengths and weaknesses of individual members. Stewardship is an expectation of production in proportion to what is given. It involves accounting, but essentially postulates unrestrained support of the steward until the time of accounting.

Equivalence

The stewardship team is based on decentralization. How inner leaders lead is as important as what they do. Stewardship communities eliminate status distinctions. All community members—stewards—are equal. All have equal opportunity for administering their part of the stewardship. All have equal access to available rewards for a smoothly functioning stewardship. They are equal in social status. The steward–leader is also a steward and subject to the same limitations and advantages as other stewards. The tasks of leadership do not lessen the sense of equality. Every steward has a single voice in stewardship councils and a single vote in the power of consent.

Accountability

The age-old concept of stewardship is very consistent with the new psychological contract emerging in the workplace, since everyone becomes accountable for everybody else. Inner leaders represent the stakeholders who are most relevant in their particular area of responsibility. They are not representing just themselves; they are representing the shared vision, mission, and value systems that everyone has participated in developing (Covey, 1997).

The stewardship character of inner leadership is not a simple, easy approach. At its core, inner leadership is a long-term, transformational approach to life and to work. It is a way of behaving that has the potential for creating fundamental and positive change (Spears, 1998). Stewardship emphasizes the trust between the inner leader and stakeholders in order to blend long-term socio-economic, human, and environmental growth (Petrick, Scherer, Brodzinski, Quinn, and Ainina, 1999).

Measuring Stewardship Success

Building self-managed stewardship communities asks inner leaders to pay attention to benchmarking, learning, balancing of uneven team performance, and costs. Success can be measured by the following criteria:

- *Fiscal health*—a primary measure of survivability.
- *Customer satisfaction*—the measure of the relevance and quality of services offered by the work community to meet client needs and standards.
- *Empowered community*—the measure of the group's operational capacity to perform.
- *Transformation*—the capacity for the work community and its members to change on an ongoing basis. (Spencer, 1995)

Each of these is accelerated in a stewardship work community

Applying Stewardship Ideas

Stewardship principles have always been part of the underlying skeleton of leadership in the middle of the corporation. Inner leaders can accomplish more of their personal agendas when they have a well-trained, competent, and sophisticated community of workers who see themselves as connected in important—structural and psychic—ways (Crosby, 1996). Inner leaders with a team of almost-leaders, who can make independent choices to move forward the common work, can accomplish more than top leaders, who often rely on coercive authority mechanisms.

However, few researchers have done more than identify the concept of stewardship or recommend its application. They have done little to instruct the fledgling inner leader in the mechanics of leading stewards in a stewardship community. Successful inner leaders rely on a set of competencies useful in selecting, developing, and guiding them and all stakeholders as they form a stewardship structure from their work community (Dunn, 2000). According to Dunn, the following are among those most obvious in this connection:

Agree on key expectations. Stewardship is based on common assumptions and practices that inner leaders set in the initial stages of community creation.

Identifying needed competencies. Inner leaders then translate their expectations into a framework of task competencies and skill-sets necessary to accomplish their part of overall corporate goals.

Articulating the task competencies. Generalizing needed competencies and approaches broadly in the work community asks inner leaders to inform, train, and commit followers in work tasks, as well as stewardship attitudes that they also model in their routine behavior.

Setting performance expectations. Inner leaders establish standards for steward performance, including behavioral descriptions of acceptable and proficient performance.

Integrating performance expectations into an accountability measurement system. Inner leaders incorporate a kind of performance sanctions and appraisal system as part of the stewardship.

Act in terms of the work community's best long-term interests. Inner leaders know that instant gratification often promotes poor stewardship health (Levinson, 1997). Thus, they focus stewards on long-term rather than short-term goals.

Individual development. Inner leaders must also ensure that stakeholder competencies are incorporated into individual development planning for the work community.

Reinforcing the behaviors. Inner leaders reinforce desired behaviors and encourage sharing of successes as stewards learn and then implement these actions.

Rewarding excellent performance. Awards, bonuses, and other rewards recognize proficiency in and commitment to stewardship competencies and skills.

DISCUSSION ISSUES AND QUESTIONS

Issues

1. The contemporary work community idea of "ownership" is shifting to classical stewardship.

2. In a stewardship, the focus is on viewing membership in the community, the work, the workers, and the community itself almost as a "sacred office," one held temporarily and about which the leader—and followers—owe deference.

3. Stewardship is an idea suggesting that leadership is most successfully demonstrated by collectively sharing power with others in the workplace which becomes one, united, true community.

4. In a stewardship, every steward has the same rights and is subject to identical limitations in the exercise of self-direction. This sharing of power preserves harmony and good will.

5. Leaders in a stewardship lose the hierarchal distinction and privileges of being "in charge."

6. A stewardship community lets members make free choices about whom to partner with, what products or services to produce, whom to buy from (internal or external suppliers), how to spend discretionary funds and time, and how to best serve their customers.

7. Stewardship ideas incorporate principles such as ethics, vision, shared decision making, ownership, values, standards, policies, freedom of choice, production in proportion to what is given, decentralization, and accountability.

8. Stewardship is based on common assumptions and practices that inner leaders set initially and then translate into a framework of task competencies and skill sets necessary to accomplish overall corporate goals.

9. Stewardship techniques include efforts by inner leaders to inform, train, and commit followers in work tasks, as well as in their stewardship roles.

10. Awards, bonuses, and other rewards recognize proficiency in and commitment to stewardship competencies and skills.

Questions

1. Do I structure the office to control what is happening or to allow what needs to happen to happen?

2. Do I include the chance for others to lead the work community as I structure work?

3. Do the hierarchies I create focus on maintaining and keeping power or broadly sharing and distributing power?

4. Do coworkers share a stewardship perspective and work within stewardship structures?

STEWARDSHIP LEARNING ACTIVITIES

Activity 1: Coalition Building

Instructions. Building a collaborative work culture is all-important in forming a stewardship community. Stewardship is based on the success inner leaders have in persuading diverse, often conflicting, stakeholders to agree on a common agenda and a common pattern of behavioral interaction.

Dynamic stewardship organizations use closely knit coalitions to achieve desired results. These coalitions are, by definition, made up of people from different functions, levels, backgrounds, and biases; and the members may have agendas and commitments that, initially at least, are at odds with one another. While these differences make such stewardship structures one of the best sources of innovation and breakthrough, they can also be, and often are, the source of dysfunction and failure. The challenge in building a stewardship coalition is to insure the former result (Bennis, 1999).

The first step in building a coalition is to decide who should participate. The individuals and groups that get involved should, potentially, support what you are trying to do. They should also represent the range of characteristics and attributes you need to ensure that you achieve your goal.

1. Think about your present work community—team, unit, division. Evaluate each member individually against the following characteristics needed in any stewardship work community.

Characteristics of Key People in Coalitions

Styles	Power	Information	Competencies	Representation
Thinking	Authority	Needs	Technical	Functions
Communication	Charisma	Capabilities	Interpersonal	Business Units
Work	Relationships	Benchmarks	Special Experience	Customers
Leadership	Credibility	Data	Management	Suppliers

2. What attributes does each individual coworker possess that would qualify him or her to be immediately effective in helping to form a stewardship structure in your work community? (*Note*: It is not essential that each person possess all of these characteristics, only that the work community collectively possess these capacities for success.)

3. Evaluate your present status:
   - Who among your followers will be most helpful in initial stages of development?
   - Who will be least helpful?
   - Where are the most significant gaps in needed capacities in your work community?
   - What steps might you take to fill these gaps? Training? New hires? Other?

4. What is your assessment for the current readiness of your work community for stewardship?

5. Prepare an outline plan to implement a stewardship structure in your work community considering this evaluation and other information you have about the details of your present work situation.

6. Consider sharing this plan with your colleagues and your boss.

Bibliography

Abramis, David J. "Humor in Healthy Organizations." *HR Magazine*, August 1992, pp. 72–74.

Abshire, David, "The Character of George Washington: The Challenges of the Modern Presidency." *Vital Speeches of the Day*, February 15, 1999, pp. 263–267.

Adair, John. *Effective Teambuilding*. Brookfield, VT: Gower, 1986.

And, Dale E. "Trust and Managerial Problem Solving." *Administrative Science Quarterly*, Vol. 17, 1972, pp. 229–239.

Antonioni, David. "Leading, Managing, and Coaching." *Industrial Management*, September/October 2000, pp. 27–33.

Avolio, Bruce J., Jane M. Howell, and John J. Sosik. "A Funny Thing Happened on the Way to the Bottom Line: Humor as a Moderator of Leadership Style Effects." *Academy of Management Journal*, Vol. 42, No. 2, April 1999, pp. 219–228.

Badaracco, Joseph L., and Richard R. Ellsworth. *Leadership and the Quest for Integrity*. Boston: Harvard Business School Press, 1989.

Barbour, G. P., and G. A. Sipel. "Excellence in Leadership: Public Sector Model." *Public Management*, August 1986, pp. 151–154.

Barnard, Chester. *The Functioning of the Executive*. Cambridge: Harvard University Press, 1968.

Barnett, E. M. "The Dynamics of Role Interaction." *Hospital Materiel Management Quarterly*, Vol. 17, No. 3, February 1996, p. 9.

Barns, Louis B. "Managing the Paradox of Organizational Trust." *Harvard Business Review*, March–April 1981.

Barsoux, Jean-Louis. "Why Organisations Need Humour." *European Management Journal*, Vol. 14, No. 5, October 1996, pp. 5–8.

Bass, B. M. *Stogdill's Handbook of Leadership*. New York: The Free Press, 1981.

―――. "Transformational Leadership and the Falling Domino Effect." *Group and Organizational Studies*, Vol. 12, No. 1, March 1987, pp. 73–78.

Beckett, John D. "NOBLE Ideas for Businesses." *Management Review*, March 1999, p. 62.

Bedell, Gene. "Gentle Persuasion." *Executive Excellence*, April 2001, p. 6.

Bender, Peter Urs. *Leadership from Within*. Toronto: Stoddart, 1997.

Bennis, Warren. "The Artform of Leadership." *International Management*, May 1982, p. 21.

―――. *Organizational Genius: The Secrets of Creative Collaboration*. Reading, MA: Addison-Wesley, 1997.

―――. "Lead with Character." *Executive Excellence,* April 1999, p. 4.

―――. "Leading in the New Millennium." *Executive Excellence*, March, 2001, pp. 3–5.

―――, and Burt Nanus. *Leaders: The Strategies for Taking Charge*. New York: Harper and Row, 1985.

―――, and R. Townsend. *Reinventing Leadership*. New York: William Morrow, 1995.

Bilchik, Gloria Shur. "Leaders Who Inspire." *Health Forum Journal*, March/April 2001, pp. 10–15.

Bjerke, Bjorn. *Business Leadership and Culture: National Management Styles in the Global Economy*. Cheltenham, UK: Edward Elgar, 1999.

Blanchard, Kenneth H. "Maintain High Ethical Standards." In *New Traditions in Business: Spirit and Leadership in the 21st Century*, ed. John Renesh. San Francisco: Berrett-Koehler, 1992.

Bleskan, Michele. *Rediscovering the Soul of Business: Soul Transformation, Learning from Our Dreams*. San Francisco: Sterling and Stone, 1995.

Block, Peter. *Stewardship: Choosing Service over Self-Interest*. San Francisco: Berrett-Koehler, 1993.

Bolman, Lee G., and Terrence E. Deal. *Leading with Soul*. San Francisco: Jossey-Bass, 1995.

Bowman, James S. *Ethical Frontiers in Public Management*. San Francisco: Jossey-Bass, 1991.

Bradford, D. L., and A. R. Cohen. *Managing for Excellence*. New York: John Wiley and Sons, 1984.

Braham, Jim. "The Spiritual Side." *Industry Week*, February 1, 1999, pp. 48–56.

Brandt, John R. "Questions of Character." *Industry Week*, March 6, 2000, p. 4.

Britton, Paul, and John Stallings. *Leadership Is Empowering People*. Lanham, MD: University Press of America, 1986.

Brown, David S. "Reforming the Bureaucracy: Some Suggestions for the New President.*" Public Administration Review*, March–April 1977, pp. 59–60.

Brumback, Gary B. "The Power of Servant Leadership." *Personnel Psychology*, Autumn 1999, pp. 807–810.

Burns, James M. *Leadership*. New York: Harper and Row, 1978.

Caill, Peter. "Introduction to Spirituality for Business Leadership." *Journal of Management Inquiry*, June 2000, pp. 115–116.

Cappelli, Peter. "Can This Relationship Be Saved?" *Wharton Alumni Magazine*, Spring 1995, pp. 5–6.

Carson, Scott E. "Three Joys You Can Count On." *Executive Speeches*, August/September 2001, pp. 4–7.

Cashman, Kevin, and Cecile Burzynski. "Value-Creating Communication." *Executive Excellence*, November 2000, p. 9.

Catron, Bayard L., and Kathryn G. Denhart. "Ethics Education in Public Administration and Affairs: Research Report and Recommendations." Unpublished report of the American Society of Public Administration, October 1988.

Chambers, Harry E. "The Agencies of Leadership." *Executive Excellence*, August 1999, p. 12.

Chrislip, David D., and Carl E. Larson. *Collaborative Leadership: How Citizens and Civic Leaders Can Make a Difference*. San Francisco: Jossey-Bass, 1994.

Clement, Linda M., and Scott T. Rickard. *Effective Leadership in Student Services: Voices from the Field*. San Francisco: Jossey-Bass, 1992.

Conger, Jay A. *Spirit at Work: Discovering the Spirituality in Leadership*. San Francisco: Jossey-Bass, 1994.

———, and Rabindra N. Kanungo. *Charismatic Leadership: The Elusive Factor in Organizational Effectiveness*. San Francisco: Jossey-Bass, 1988.

Covey, Stephen. "The Seven Habits of Highly Effective People." *I/S Analyzer*, February 1991, pp. 15–16.

———. "Sense of Stewardship." *Executive Excellence*, July 1997, pp. 3–4.

———. "Natural Instincts." *Incentive*, September 2001, p. 39.

Crocker, H. W., III. "Robert E. Lee on Leadership: Executive Lessons in Character, Courage, and Wisdom." *Prima*, July 1999, p. 108.

Crosby, P. *The Absolutes of Leadership*. San Diego: Pfeiffer and Company, 1996.

Crozan, Thomas E. "Thinking and Learning about Leadership." In *Contemporary Issues in Leadership*, 2d ed., ed. W. E. Rosenbach and R. L. Taylor. Boulder, CO: Westview Press, 1989.

Daley, Dennis M. "The Decline and Fall of the Roman Empire: Lessons on Management." *International Journal of Public Administration*, Vol. 21, No. 1, 1998, pp. 127–143.

Danforth, Douglas D. "The Quality Imperative." *Quality Progress*, February 1987, pp. 17–19.

Deal, T., and A. Kennedy. *Corporate Cultures*. London: Penguin Books, 1988.

Dean, Alan L. "Re-establishing Confidence in Government." *Public Administration Review*, January–February 1977, pp. 156–159.

Deane, Russell. "Coaching—A Winning Strategy." *British Journal of Administrative Management*, May/June 2001, pp. 22–23.

Deming, W. Edwards. *Out of the Crisis*. Cambridge: Massachusetts Institute of Technology, Center for Advanced Engineering Study. 1986.

Denison, Daniel R. *Corporate Culture and Organizational Effectiveness*. Toronto: John Wiley and Sons, 1990.

DePree, Max. *Leadership Is an Art*. New York: Doubleday, 1989.

Dering, Nancy Z. "Leadership in Quality Organizations." *Journal for Quality and Participation*, January/February 1998, pp. 32–35.

Douglas, Neil, and Terry Wykowksi. "Beyond the Bottom Line." *Executive Excellence*, August 1992, p. 8.

"Do You Consider Yourself a Leader or a Follower?" *Adweek*, Eastern ed., November 14, 1994, p. 1.

Drehmer, D. E., and J. H. Grossman. "Scaling Managerial Respect: A Developmental Perspective." *Educational and Psychological Measurement*, Vol. 44, 1984, pp. 763–767.

Drennan, David. *Transforming Company Culture: Getting Your Company from Where You Are Now to Where You Want to Be*. Berkshire, England: McGraw-Hill International, 1992.

Drucker, Peter. "The Coming of the New Age of Man." *Harvard Business Review*, January–February 1988, pp. 45–53.

Dunn, Richard L. "A Special Trust." *Plant Engineering*, January 2000, p. 10.

Eadie, Douglas C. "Putting a Powerful Tool to Practical Use: The Application of Strategic Planning to the Public Sector." *Public Administration Review*, September–October 1983, pp. 447–452.

Erteszek, Jan J. "The Common Venture Enterprise: A Western Answer to the Japanese Art of Management?" *New Management*, Vol. 1, No. 2, 1983, pp. 4–10.

Etzioni, A. *The Spirit of Community*. New York: Crown, 1993.

Fairholm, Gilbert W. *Values Leadership: Toward a New Philosophy of Leadership*. Westport, CT: Praeger, 1991.

———. *Organizational Power Politics: The Tactics of Leadership Power*. Westport, CT: Praeger. 1993.

———. *Leadership in a Culture of Trust*. Westport, CT: Praeger, 1994.

———. *Capturing the Heart of Leadership: Spirituality and Community in the New American Workplace*. Westport, CT: Praeger, 2000a.

———. *Perspective on Leadership: From the Science of Management to Its Spiritual Heart*. Westport, CT: Praeger. 2000b.

———. *Mastering Inner Leadership*. Westport, CT: Quorum Books, 2001.

Fairholm, Matthew R., and Gilbert W. Fairholm. "Leadership amid the Constraints of Trust." *Leadership and Organization Development Journal*, Vol. 21, No. 2, 2000, 102–109.

Fiedler, Fred E., and Martin M. Chamers. *Leadership and Effective Management*. Glenview, IL: Scott Foresman, 1974.

Finer, Herman. "Administrative Responsibility and Democratic Government." *Public Administration Review*, Vol. 1, Summer 1941, pp. 335–350.

"Forecasting Techniques for Managers." *The Futurist,* September/October 2001, pp. 64–65.

French, John R. P., and Bertram Raven. *Studies in Social Power*, ed. Dorwin Cartwright. Ann Arbor: University of Michigan Institute for Social Research, 1959, pp. 150–165.

Gaertner, Karan M., and Gregory H. Gaertner. "Proactive Roles of Federal Managers." *The Bureaucrat*, Fall 1985, pp. 19–22.

Gambetta, Diego. "Can We Trust Trust?" In *Trust: Making and Breaking Cooperative Relations*, ed. Diego Gambetta. Cambridge, MA: Basil Blackwell, 1988.

Gardner, John. W. "Leadership and the Future." *The Futurist*, Vol. 24, No. 3, 1990, pp. 8–12.

Gareau, Bernhard H. "Driving Change: Up the Organization." *Hospital Materiel Management Quarterly*, Vol. 21, No. 1, August 1999, pp. 59–65.

Garton, Richard D. "The Business of Being Ethical." *Vital Speeches*, May 1, 1989, pp. 435–437.

Gibb, Jack R. "Defense Level and Influence Potential in Small Groups. In *Leadership and Interpersonal Behavior*, ed. L. Petrillo and B. M. Bass. New York: Holt, Rinehart and Winston, 1961.

———. *A New View of Reason and Organizations Development*. New York: The Guild of Tutors' Press, 1978.

Goldstein, William. Quoted in *Modern Theory and Method in Group Training*, ed. William Dyer. New York: Van Nostrand Reinhold, 1961.

Gortner, Harold F. *Ethics for Public Managers*. Westport, CT: Praeger, 1991.

"The Greatest Motivators of the Century." *Incentive*, September 1999, pp. 38–66.

Graham, John, "Prescription for Success Overlooks Today's Harsh Realities." *Business Realities*, January 1994, pp. 27–29.

Greenleaf, Robert T. *The Servant Leader*. New York: Paulist Press, 1977.

Gross, William H. "Row, Row, Row Your Boat." *The New Leaders*, March/April 1995, p. 1.

Gunn, Bob. "A Leader's Path." *Strategic Finance,* Vol. 83, No. 3, September 2001, pp. 13–16.

Handy, Charles B. *Understanding Organizations*. Middlesex, England: Penguin Books, 1976.

Hart, David K. "Life, Liberty, and the Pursuit of Happiness: Organizational Ethics and the Founding Values." *Exchange*, Spring 1988, pp. 1–5.

Hart, Vivian. *Distrust and Democracy: Political Distrust in Britain and America*. New York: Cambridge University Press, 1978.

Hawley, Jack. *Reawakening the Spirit in Work: The Power of Dharmic Management*. San Francisco: Berrett-Koehler, 1993.

Heenan, David A., and Warren Bennis. "How to Be a Great No. 2." *Across the Board*, July/August 1999, pp. 38–42.

Heerman, Barry. "Spiritual Core Is Essential to High Performing Teams." In *The New Leaders*. San Francisco: Sterling and Stone, March/April 1995, p. 1.

Hersey, Paul, and K. H. Blanchard. *Management of Organizational Behavior*. Englewood Cliffs, NJ: Prentice-Hall, 1978.

Hertzberg, Frederick. *Work and the Nature of Man*. Cleveland: World, 1966.

Hinckley, Gordon B., ed. *Conference Report*, October 1967, p. 89.

Hodgkinson, C. *The Philosophy of Leadership*. Oxford: Basil Blackwell, 1983.

Hodgkinson, Christopher. *Toward a Philosophy of Administration*. New York: St. Martin's Press, 1978.

Hollander, E. P. *Leadership Dynamics: A Practical Guide to Effective Relationships*. New York: The Free Press, 1978.

Hughes, R. L., R. C. Ginnett, and G. L. Curphy. *Leadership: Enhancing the Lessons of Experience*. New York: Irwin, McGraw-Hill, 1999.

"Interview with Warren Bennis: Leading in the New Millennium." *Executive Excellence*, March 2001, pp. 5–6.

Jacobson, Stephen. *Spirituality and Transformational Leadership in Secular Settings: A Delphi Study*. (An abridgment of an unpublished dissertation completed in 1994 and available through University Microfilms.) Goleta, GA, 1995.

Johnson, Theodore A. "Partnerships: Should You or Shouldn't You?" *LIMRA's MarketFacts*, May/June 1999, pp. 44–46.

Kalafut, Pamela Cohen. "The Value Creation Index: Quantifying Intangible." *Strategy & Leadership*, September/October 2001, pp. 9–15.

Kelley, Robert E. *The Power of Fellowship*. New York: Doubleday, 1992.

Kidder, Rushworth M. "Whose Values Will You Teach?" In *The Years Ahead*, ed. H. F. Didsbury. Bethesda, MD: World Future Society, 1993.

Kiechel, Walter, III. "Sniping at Strategic Planning." *Planning Review*, May 1984, p. 1.

———. "The Leader as Servant." *Fortune*, May 4, 1992, pp. 121–122.

Klenke, Karin. *Women and Leadership*. New York. Springer, 1996.

Klimoski, Richard J., and Barbara L. Karol. "The Impact of Trust on Creative Problem solving Groups." *Journal of Applied Psychology*, Vol. 61, No. 5, 1976, pp. 630–633.

Kouzes, James, and Barry Posner. *The Leadership Challenge*. San Francisco: Jossey-Bass, 1987.

Kulwiec, Ray. "Self-Managed Work Teams—Reality or Fad?" *Material Handling Management,* April 2001, pp. 15–22.

Leavenson, Henry. *The Exceptional Executive: A Psychological Conception*. Cambridge: Harvard University Press, 1968.

Lee, Chris, and Ron Zemke. "The Search for Spirit in the Workplace." *Training*, June 1993, pp. 26–41.

Leigh, Pamela. "The New Spirit at Work." *Training and Development*, Vol. 51, No. 3, March 1997, pp. 26–34.

Levinson, William A. "Stewardship and Service." *Executive Excellence*, July 1997, p. 4.

Lewin, Kirt. Quoted in *The New Leaders*. San Francisco: Stirling and Stone, March/April, 1994, p. 4.

Likert, Rensis. *New Patterns in Management*. New York: McGraw-Hill, 1961.

Locke, Edwin A. *The Essence of Leadership: The Four Keys to Leading Successfully*. New York: Lexington Books, 1991.

Lombardi, Vincent H. "Coaching for Teamwork." *Financial Services Advisor*, July/August 2000, pp. 40–41.

Maccoby, Michael. *The Leader*. New York: Simon and Schuster, 1981.

Maslow, Abraham H. *Toward a Psychology of Being*, 2d ed. New York: Van Nostrand, 1962.

———. *The Further Reaches of Human Nature*. Middlesex, England: Penguin Books, 1971.

McClelland, D. C., and R. Burnham. "Power Is the Great Motivator." *Harvard Business Review*, March–April 1976, pp. 121–129.

McGregor, Douglas. *The Human Side of Enterprise*. New York: McGraw-Hill, 1960.

McLaughlin, Kathleen. "The Lighter Side of Learning." *Training*, February 2001, pp. 48–52.

McMillen, Kim. "The Workplace as a Spiritual Haven." In *When the Canary Stops Singing*, ed. John Renesh. San Francisco: Berrett-Koehler, 1993.

———. *The New Leaders*. San Francisco: Stirling and Stone, September/October 1994, pp. 8–9.

Meadow, A., S. J. Parnes, and H. Reese. "Influence of Brainstorming Instructions and Problem Sequence on a Creative Problem-Solving Test." *Journal of Applied Psychology*, Vol. 43, 1959, pp. 413–416.

Metzger, Norman. "Beyond Survival to Excellence." *The Health Care Supervisor,* January, 1987.

Michlitsch, J. F., "High-Performing, Loyal Employees: The Real Way to Implement Strategy." *Strategy & Leadership*, November/December 2000, p. 28.

Miller, William, C. "Put Spiritual Values to Work." In *New Traditions in Business: Spirit and Leadership in the 21st Century*, ed. John Renesh. San Francisco: Berrett-Koehler, 1992.

Moxley, Russell S. *Leadership and Spirit: Breathing New Vitality and Energy into Individuals and Organizations*. San Francisco: Jossey-Bass, 2000.

Nair, Keshavan. *A Higher Standard of Leadership: Lessons from the Life of Gandhi.* San Francisco: Berrett-Koehler, 1994.

Naisbitt, John, and Patricia Aburdene. *Reinventing the Corporation.* New York: Warner Books, 1985.

Nalbandian, John. "Professionalism in City Management." In *Ideal and Practice in Council-Manager Government*, ed. ICMA. Washington, DC: International City Management Association, 1989.

Nelson, Bob. "The Ironies of Motivation." *Strategy and Leadership*, January/February 1999, pp. 26–32.

Ott, J. Stephen. *The Organizational Culture Perspective.* Belmont, CA: The Dorsey Press,1989.

Palmer, Parker. "Leadership and the Inner Journey." *Leader to Leader*, Fall 2001, p. 61.

Pascale, R. T., and Anthony G. Athos. *The Art of Japanese Management: Applications for American Executives.* New York: Simon and Schuster, 1981.

Peters, Tom, and Nancy Austin. *A Passion for Excellence: The Leadership Difference.* New York: Random House, 1985.

Peters, T. J., and R. H. Waterman, Jr. *In Search of Excellence: Lessons from America's Best-Run Companies.* New York: Harper and Row, 1982.

Petrick, Joseph A., Robert F. Scherer, James D. Brodzinski, John F. Quinn, and M. Fall Ainina. "Global Leadership Skills and Reputational Capital: Intangible Resources for Sustainable Competitive Advantage." *The Academy of Management Executive*, February 1999, pp. 58–69.

Pfeffer, Jeffery. "The Ambiguity of Leadership." *Academy of Management Review*, Vol. 2, 1977, pp. 104–112.

Pinchot, Gifford, and Elizabeth Pinchot. *The End of Bureaucracy and the Rise of the Intelligent Organization.* San Francisco: Berrett-Koehler, 1994.

Plas, J. M. *Person-Centered Leadership: An American Approach to Participatory Management.* London: Sage, 1996.

Porter, Lyman W., Robert W. Allen, and Harold L. Angle. "The Politics of Upward Influence in Organizations." In *Research in Organizational Behavior*, ed. L. L. Cummings and Barry M. Staw, Vol. 3, 1981, pp. 408–422.

Ramsey, Sajeela Moskowitz, "Leading with Art and Soul." *Executive Excellence*, December 1994, p. 18.

Rapoport, Rhona, Lotte Bailyn, Joyce Fletcher, and Bettye Pruitt. *Beyond Work–Family Balance: Advancing Gender Equity and Workplace Performance.* San Francisco: Jossey-Bass, 2001.

Reuss, L. E. "Catalysts of Genius, Dealers in Hope." *Vital Speeches of the Day*, January 1, 1987, pp. 173–176.

Reynolds, Peter C. "Imposing a Corporate Culture." *Psychology Today*, March 1987, pp. 33–38.

Roberts, B. H. "Revelation and Inspiration." In *Defense of the Faith and the Saints*, ed. B. H. Roberts. Salt Lake City: Deseret News Press, 1907.

Rogers, Carl B. *On Becoming a Person.* Boston: Houghton Mifflin, 1964.

Rokeach, M. *Understanding Human Values.* New York: The Free Press, 1979.

Rosenback, W. E., T. S. Pittman, and E. H. Potter. "The Performance and Relationship Questionnaire." Gettysburg, PA, 1997.

Rosner, Bob. "Is There Room for the Soul at Work?" (Interview with Martin Rutte). *Workforce*, February 2001, pp. 80–82.

Rossiter, Charles M., Jr., and Barnett W. Pearch. *Communicating Personally.* New York: Bobbs-Merrill, 1975.

Rotter, Julian B. "Generalized Expectancies for Interpersonal Trust." *American Psychology*, Vol. 26, 1971, pp. 651–665.

Rowan, Roy. *The Intuitive Manager.* Boston: Little, Brown, 1986.

Ruppert, Paul, "Compelling Strategies for a Competitive Workplace." *Equifax Pub.*, 1991, p. 15.

Samuelson, R. J. "In Search of Simplicity." *Newsweek*, April 30, 1984, p. 70.

Santovec, Mary Lou. "Yeeaa-Haw!" *Credit Union Management*, March 2001, pp. 26–28.

Sashkin, Marshall. "True Vision in Leadership." *Training and Development Journal*, May 1986, p. 58.

Schein, Edgar H. *Organizational Culture and Leadership.* San Francisco: Jossey-Bass, 1985.

Scott, William G., and David K. Hart. *Organizational America.* New York: Houghton Mifflin, 1979.

Segil, Larraine. "Great Leadership." *Executive Excellence*, June 1999, p. 5.

Selznick, P. *Leadership in Administration.* Evanston, IL: Row, Peterson, 1957.

Senge, Peter. "The Leaders' New Work: Building Learning Organizations." *Sloan Management Review*, Fall 1990, pp. 133–136.

———, Charlotte Roberts, Richard Ross, Bryan Smith, and Art Kleiner. *The Fifth Discipline Fieldbook: Strategies and Tools for Building a Learning Organization.* New York: Currency/Doubleday, 1994.

Serven, Lawrence MacGregor. *The End of Office Politics as Usual: A Complete Strategy for Creating a More Productive and Profitable Organization.* New York: Amacom, 2002.

Sims, Ronald R. "The Challenge of Ethical Behavior in Organizations." *Journal of Business Ethics*, Vol. 11, 1992, pp. 939–948.

Sinatar, Marsha. "Building Trust into Corporate Relations." *Organizational Dynamics*, Winter 1988, p. 73.

Slywotzky, Adrian J., and David J. Morrison. "Pattern Thinking: A Strategic Shortcut." *Strategy and Leadership*, January/February 2000, pp. 12–17.

Spears, Larry C. "Servant Leadership." *Executive Excellence*, Vol. 15, No. 7, July 1998, p. 11.

Spencer, Raymond J. "Success with Self-Managed Teams and Partnering." *Journal for Quality and Participation*, July/August 1995, p. 48.

Spitzer, Robert J. *The Spirit of Leadership: Optimizing Creativity and Change in Organizations.* Provo: Executive Excellence Publishing, 2000.

Spreitzer, Gretchen M., Suzanne C. De Janasz, and Robert E. Quinn. "Empowered to Lead: The Role of Psychological Empowerment in Leadership." *Journal of Organizational Behavior*, July 1999, pp. 511–526.

Stern, Gerry, and Yvette Borcia. "Motivation Strategy." *Executive Excellence*, June 2000, p. 18.

Stogdill, R. M. *Leadership and Structures of Personal Interaction.* Columbus, OH: State University, Bureau of Business Research, 1957.

Suzaki, Kiyoshi. *Results from the Heart: How Mini-Company Management Captures Everyone's Talents and Helps Them Find Meaning and Purpose at Work.* New York: The Free Press, 2002.

Terry, Larry D. *Leadership of Public Bureaucracies: The Administrator as Conservator*. Thousand Oaks, CA: Sage, 1995.

Tesolin, Arupa L. "How to Develop the Habit of Intuition." *Training and Development*, March 2000, p. 76.

Throgmorton, J. A., Seymour J. Mandelbaum, and Margot W. Garcia. "On the Virtues of Skillful Meandering: Acting as a Skilled-Voice-in-the-Flow of Persuasive Argumentation." *Journal of the American Planning Association*, Autumn 2000, pp. 367–383.

Townsend, P. L., and J. E. Gebhardt. *Commit to Quality*. New York: John Wiley, 1990.

Truskie, Stanley D. *Leadership in High Performance Organizational Cultures*. Westport, CT: Quorum, 1999.

Vaill, Peter. *Managing as a Performing Art*. San Francisco: Jossey-Bass, 1989.

———. "Introduction to Spirituality for Business Leadership." *Journal of Management Inquiry,* June 2000, pp. 115–116.

———. *Spirited Leading and Learning*. San Francisco: Jossey-Bass, 1998.

Vanfleet, David D., and Gary A. Yukl. "A Century of Leadership Research." In *Contemporary Issues in Leadership*, ed W. E. Rosenbach and R. L. Taylor. Boulder, CO: Westview Press, 1989.

Wheatley, Margaret J. *Leadership and the New Science: Learning about Team from an Orderly Universe*. San Francisco: Berrett-Koehler, 1992.

Wildavsky, Aaron. *The Nursing Father: Moses as a Political Leader*. Birmingham: University of Alabama Press, 1984.

Witham, Donald C., and John D. Glover. "Recapturing Commitment." *Training and Development Journal*, Vol. 4, No. 4, April 1987, pp. 42–45.

Yearout, Steve, Gerry Miles, and Richard H Koonce. "Multi-Level Visioning." *Training and Development*, March 2001, pp. 31–39.

Zaleznick, Abraham. "Managers and Leaders: Are They Different?" *Harvard Business Review*, May-June 1977, p. 67.

Index

ABOUT THE AUTHOR

Gilbert W. Fairholm is Adjunct Professor of Management Systems at the University of Richmond and Adjunct Professor of Leadership at Averett University. He is an emeritus member of the faculty of the Department of Political Science and Public Administration at Virginia Commonwealth University and a Senior Fellow of The George Washington University Center for Excellence in Municipal Management. A frequent consultant to business and government, he focuses on leadership training and development, strategic visioning, and community development.